Leveson Francis Vernon-Harcourt

Achievements in engineering

During the last half Century

Leveson Francis Vernon-Harcourt

Achievements in engineering
During the last half Century

ISBN/EAN: 9783337106201

Printed in Europe, USA, Canada, Australia, Japan

Cover: Foto ©ninafisch / pixelio.de

More available books at **www.hansebooks.com**

Robert Stephenson.

ACHIEVEMENTS IN ENGINEERING

DURING THE LAST HALF CENTURY

BY

L. F. VERNON-HARCOURT
M.A., M. Inst. C. E.,
AUTHOR OF 'RIVERS AND CANALS,' AND 'HARBOURS AND DOCKS.'

With Illustrations and Diagrams

LONDON
SEELEY AND CO., LIMITED
ESSEX STREET, STRAND
1891

PREFACE

My endeavour in this book has been to describe briefly some of the principal engineering works carried out, at home and abroad, within the last fifty years, avoiding technical phraseology as far as possible, so that the descriptions may be perfectly intelligible to the general reader, and, at the same time, introducing various details and comparisons which may interest engineers as well. As the chief engineering triumphs have been accomplished in the last half century, there has been no lack of materials; and some branches of engineering have necessarily been passed over, as indicated in the concluding remarks at the end of the book. I trust, however, that an adequate variety of engineering works of great magnitude, difficulty, and importance have been described, to justify the view that engineers, in directing the forces of nature to the use and convenience of man, are amongst the greatest benefactors of mankind.

Various details about several of the works described have been gleaned from papers in the *Minutes of Proceedings of the Institution of Civil Engineers;* some particulars relating to the Hudson Tunne works have been obtained from 'Tunnelling under the Hudson

River,' by S. D. V. Barr; about the Severn Tunnel from the late Mr T. A. Walker's book; and about the Forth Bridge from *Engineering;* and information about American bridges and works has been gathered from the *Transactions of the American Society of Engineers*.

I am indebted to Mr G. F. Deacon, the Liverpool engineer of the Vyrnwy works, for particulars about those works, for affording me an opportunity of inspecting them, and also for a photograph of the dam and lake from which the illustration in the book has been produced. The view of the Manchester Ship Canal works, at Eastham, is from a photograph given me by Mr Leader Williams, the engineer-in-chief of the canal; the Tower Bridge illustration is from an engraving furnished me by Mr J. W. Barry, the engineer of the bridge; and the Louvière Lift is from a photograph by Mr Lyonel Clark, of Messrs Clark & Standfield who carried out the work. The view of the Eddystone Lighthouse is reproduced, by permission, from an illustration accompanying Mr W. T. Douglass's paper on 'The New Eddystone Lighthouse,' in the *Minutes of Proceedings of the Institution of Civil Engineers;* and the engraving on page 164, illustrating the blasting operations at Hell Gate, New York, is taken from the plate accompanying my paper on that subject in the same *Minutes of Proceedings*. Three of the sections of American railways in the diagram on page 30, and the diagram of the switchbacks on the Oroya Railway, were obtained from 'The Economic Theory of the Location of Railways' by A. M. Wellington, a book containing a considerable amount of information on American railway practice.

The name of Robert Stephenson, whose portrait appears on the frontispiece, will ever be associated with the development of railways; and though his labours were terminated by his untimely death in 1859, before attaining the age of fifty-six, and thus are only identified with the earlier portion of the period covered by the book, he was the pioneer, in the Britannia Bridge, of the system of long span girder bridges, which has since received such a marvellous extension. In a book describing engineering works, I have deemed it preferable to devote the limited illustrations to the works of engineers of recent times, rather than to portraits of living engineers, otherwise many honoured names should have found a place amongst its pages. Amongst the eminent engineers whose works have been recorded in the following pages may be mentioned Sir John Hawkshaw, the engineer-in-chief of the Severn Tunnel and of the Amsterdam Ship Canal; Sir John Fowler and Sir Benjamin Baker, the engineers of the Forth Bridge, and the former the engineer of the Metropolitan Railway; Sir James Brunlees and Sir Douglas Fox, the engineers-in-chief of the Mersey Railway; the late Captain Eads, engineer of the St Louis Bridge and of the Mississippi Delta works; General Newton, engineer of the Hell Gate Improvement works; Mr G. F. Lyster, the engineer-in-chief to the Mersey Docks and Harbour Board; Sir John Coode, the engineer of Table Bay and Colombo harbours; Sir Charles Hartley, engineer of the Danube Delta works; Voisin Bey, the engineer-in-chief of the Suez Canal works; the late Mr J. F. Bateman, the engineer of the Manchester Waterworks; Mr Thomas Hawksley, the engineer-in-chief formerly of the Vyrnwy Reservoir works; and Sir James Douglass, the engineer-in-chief of the new Eddystone Lighthouse.

If this book should succeed in stimulating, and also to some extent in satisfying, the interest felt by most persons in large engineering works, and should lead to a due appreciation of the principles on which such works are designed, the methods by which they are carried out, and the difficulties experienced in their construction, and, moreover, if the book should establish the claim of these works to be classed amongst the 'events of our own time,' the objects aimed at will be accomplished.

L. F. VERNON-HARCOURT.

6 QUEEN ANNE'S GATE,
   WESTMINSTER,
      10th March 1891.

CONTENTS

		PAGE
I.	THE LONDON METROPOLITAN RAILWAYS, AND THE NEW YORK ELEVATED RAILWAY,	1
II.	RAILWAYS ACROSS THE ALPS, THE ROCKY MOUNTAINS, AND THE ANDES,	25
III.	NARROW GAUGE, FELL, RIGI, PILATUS, AND ABT MOUNTAIN RAILWAYS,	54
IV.	PIERCING THE ALPS,	70
V.	THE DETROIT, HUDSON, MERSEY, AND SEVERN TUNNELS, THE THAMES SUBWAYS, AND THE SARNIA TUNNEL,	85
VI.	THE PROGRESS AND PRINCIPLES OF MODERN BRIDGE CONSTRUCTION,	112
VII.	THE HAWKESBURY, ST LOUIS, GARABIT, HOOGHLY, BROOKLYN, FORTH, AND TOWER BRIDGES,	132
VIII.	SUBMARINE MINING AND BLASTING,	159
IX.	THE PORTS OF LONDON, LIVERPOOL, ANTWERP, MARSEILLES, AND NEW YORK,	172
X.	THE BREAKWATERS OF TABLE BAY, ALEXANDRIA, BOULOGNE, COLOMBO, DOVER, AND NEWHAVEN HARBOURS,	189
XI.	IMPROVEMENT WORKS ON THE TYNE, THE SEINE, THE MAAS, THE DANUBE, AND THE MISSISSIPPI,	206
XII.	THE WEIRS OF POSES ON THE SEINE, AND OF CHARLOTTENBURG ON THE SPREE; AND THE HYDRAULIC CANAL LIFT OF LA LOUVIÈRE,	224
XIII.	THE AMSTERDAM SHIP CANAL, AND THE MANCHESTER SHIP CANAL,	238
XIV.	THE SUEZ, PANAMA, NICARAGUA, AND CORINTH CANALS,	253
XV.	THE MANCHESTER WATERWORKS, AND THE VYRNWY DAM AND LAKE,	270
XVI.	THE EDDYSTONE LIGHTHOUSE, AND THE EIFFEL TOWER,	286

LIST OF ILLUSTRATIONS AND DIAGRAMS.

	PAGE
PORTRAIT OF ROBERT STEPHENSON,	*Front.*
NEW YORK ELEVATED RAILWAYS,	18
RAILWAYS ACROSS THE ALPS, ROCKY MOUNTAINS, AND ANDES,	30
ST GOTHARD RAILWAY, LOOPS AND SPIRALS,	35
OROYA RAILWAY, PERU, SWITCHBACKS AND LOOPS,	48
RIGI MOUNTAIN RAILWAY,	64
MERSEY AND SEVERN TUNNELS,	96
BRIDGES WITH LONG SPANS,	134
BROOKLYN BRIDGE,	144
THE FORTH BRIDGE,	148
THE TOWER BRIDGE,	154
BLASTING OPERATIONS AT HELL GATE, NEW YORK,	164
EXPLOSION OF MIDDLE REEF, NEW YORK,	170
SECTIONS OF BREAKWATERS,	192
RIVER IMPROVEMENTS,	208
DRUM WEIR ON THE SPREE,	232
HYDRAULIC CANAL LIFT AT LA LOUVIÈRE,	236
SHIP CANALS,	242
THE MANCHESTER SHIP CANAL WORKS,	246
THE SUEZ CANAL,	256
VYRNWY DAM AND LAKE,	280
THE EDDYSTONE LIGHTHOUSE, 1882,	290
THE EIFFEL TOWER,	298

*** *The Portrait of Mr Robert Stephenson is engraved by permission of Messrs Henry Graves & Co.*

Achievements in Engineering

CHAPTER I.

THE LONDON METROPOLITAN RAILWAYS, AND THE NEW YORK ELEVATED RAILWAYS.

PROBABLY no better concise description of the most marked features of the present time could be given than the passage which occurs in the Book of Daniel, relating to the latter days, namely, 'many shall run to and fro, and knowledge shall be increased.' The development of railways, and the facilities thus afforded for locomotion, together with the extension of education and trade, have given a great impulse to traffic in large cities, and especially in London. With a rapid growth of population in the metropolis, and constantly increasing requirements, the traffic in the most important thoroughfares necessarily largely augments; whilst little can be done to relieve the excessive traffic along the main streets, beyond a few new roads, constructed at enormous expense. Accordingly, schemes were naturally started, about the middle of this century, for enlarging and facilitating the means of communication, without encountering the delays and increasing the congestion of traffic in the principal thoroughfares.

The growth of the metropolitan traffic, moreover, is not merely measured by the increase of population in the ever-extending area of London itself; but the very large number of persons who now reside in the suburbs and neighbouring country districts, and come regularly into London for their day's work, have to be considered. It is of importance for this suburban population, and for travellers from a distance, that they should be able readily to get from the railway stations to their places of business, and from one terminus to another. Increased facilities of access have been provided by doubling the lines of way of all the principal railways running into London, and by extending the lines in some instances further into the heart of the metropolis; such as the extension of the railways, terminating at Battersea, to Victoria Station in 1860; the extension of the South-Eastern Railway from London Bridge to Charing Cross and Cannon Street, constructed between 1860 and 1866; the London, Chatham, and Dover Railway extension, from Ludgate Hill to the Holborn Viaduct, about 1873; and the Great Eastern Railway extension, from Shoreditch to Liverpool Street, opened in 1875. Some idea of the great development of railways within the metropolis in the last thirty-five years may be gathered from the consideration that, whereas no railway bridge crossed the river Thames within the metropolitan area before 1860, there are now four railway bridges over the river below Chelsea, namely, at Pimlico, Charing Cross, Blackfriars, and Cannon Street, which have been all doubled in width since their erection. Moreover, trains now pass unseen through the world-famed Thames Tunnel, opposite the London Docks, completed in 1843, and purchased about twenty-five years later by the East London Railway Company to enable them to cross the river.

UNDERGROUND METROPOLITAN RAILWAYS.

As early as 1834, steam carriages were run along the Marylebone Road for conveying passengers between Paddington and Moorgate Street; and in 1837 the question of the improvement of railway communication in the metropolis was brought forward. The steam carriages could only carry a few persons; and the tramways, laid down subsequently in various parts of London, whilst affording a comfortable means of locomotion, can only be placed along the less frequented wide thoroughfares, and, like ordinary omnibuses, tend more or less to impede the general traffic in the streets. In 1845, nineteen Bills were presented to Parliament for constructing railways in the metropolis, one of them consisting of a scheme for a general central station, an idea which has since been successfully carried out in some towns of more moderate size. At last, in 1854, an Act was obtained for constructing an underground railway from Paddington to Farringdon Street; but, owing to difficulties in raising the necessary capital, the works were not begun till 1860. This first section of the Metropolitan Railway was opened early in 1863: the first portion of the District Railway between Kensington and Westminster was opened at the end of 1868, and extended to Mansion House Station in 1871; and, finally, the completion of the 'Inner Circle,' from Mansion House to Aldgate, was effected in 1884. The Underground Railway is termed the 'Inner Circle,' to distinguish it from the outer circle of railways with which it is in connection, going round by Addison

Road, Willesden, Chalk Farm, Broad Street, the Thames Tunnel, New Cross, and Clapham Junction, which latter railways both connect the outlying portions of the various lines converging to the metropolis and serve the suburbs encircling London. The Inner Circle, however, is not really circular in form, for it is an irregular oval, 5 miles long from east to west and 1¾ miles wide from north to south; and its shape suggests the idea that a railway cutting across the narrow central portion of the oval, say from Victoria, or Charing Cross stations, to Baker Street, Portland Road, or Gower Street stations, would be a distinct gain to the public, though probably not to the shareholders of the metropolitan railways. This shorter diameter, however, of the oval is traversed by omnibuses in connection with the railways.

The advantages of an underground railway in a city are that it does not occupy any of the surface area; that it is hidden from view, and therefore presents no unsightliness or cause of discomfort in the neighbourhood of important buildings and main thoroughfares;[1] that the purchase of land is avoided when it passes along under the line of a road, or in tunnel; and that it does not cause any interference with the roads and railways which it traverses in its underground course. On the other hand, such a railway necessitates the construction of an almost continuous covered way, resembling a succession of tunnels, through which trains have to run in the dark, and the ventilation of which is more or less imperfect. Buildings, also, have to be underpinned or pulled

---

[1] Authority could certainly not have been obtained for the construction of a railway on a viaduct in front of Westminster Abbey, or along the Thames Embankment, in the line followed by the District Railway.

down along the line of the railway; the diversion of the gas and water mains, intersected by the excavations, has to be effected; and pumping has to be resorted to for keeping the low-lying works free from water during construction, and for draining the line after completion.

Persons travelling in the Underground Railway might very naturally imagine that the greater part of the railway had been made by tunnelling, just as high ridges are pierced by railways in tunnels, such as the Box, Merstham, Sydenham, and other well-known tunnels. The depth, however, selected for the railway, below the surface of the ground, was not sufficient for the adoption of this method of construction, except in two places, namely, between King's Cross and Farringdon Street, where a tunnel, 728 yards in length, was driven under Clerkenwell, and between High Street, Kensington, and Notting Hill Gate, where a tunnel was made under Campden Hill for a length of 421 yards. The rest of the covered way was constructed on what is termed the 'cut and cover' principle; for the ground was excavated from the top to the requisite depth, and the side walls, inverted arch at the bottom, and arch overhead were then built, and covered over at the top with earth again, thus forming a sort of continuous arched bridge under ground. Where the line runs along under the streets, the roadway had to be kept open for traffic, which was accomplished by forming a temporary road over the excavations, with planking laid upon cross beams of timber spanning the opening. In some cases, houses along the line of the railway were pulled down, and subsequently rebuilt over the arch of the covered way; in other cases, the houses were left standing, and were supported on a framework of main and cross iron girders inserted under the walls, the main girders resting upon the side walls of the railway. In some of these houses a timber floor alone intervenes between the railway and the kitchen; whilst in others, small brick arches have been built between the girders, and support the floor. Considering the distinctly perceptible vibration which is felt even at some distance from the Underground Railway, houses standing directly over the covered way can hardly be regarded as very quiet and desirable residences, especially where a timber floor is supposed to afford an adequate safeguard against the rattle of the constantly passing trains. Nevertheless, habit has a marvellous influence in rendering people unconscious of frequently recurring sounds, so that noises which jar upon the nerves of a casual visitor pass unnoticed by the regular inmate, who is more than compensated for apparent discomfort by a reduced rent.

The excavations were in every instance carried out in very short lengths, of about 4 to 6 feet, strongly strutted across with timber, and rapidly followed by the permanent brickwork of the retaining walls, so as to avoid the inevitable movement of the ground, and consequent damage to adjacent property by settlement, which results when any large excavation is made in the neighbourhood of buildings. Underpinning, which consists in carrying foundations down to a lower level by building underneath them into firm ground not liable to be disturbed by the excavations, has also to be effected with the greatest care, and in short pieces, so that the first portion may be rendered quite secure before the adjacent portions are dealt with; and the operation necessarily involves excavating underneath a short length of foundation, and supporting it temporarily by beams and props. This, and the avoidance of settlement, constitute some of the main difficulties in carrying out underground work through towns. A brick arch has been adopted for the top of the covered way, wherever the depth below the surface was sufficient, as being cheaper and more durable than iron girders; but in places where the headway was inadequate, girders have been employed. The covered way supports a great many buildings erected since the construction of the line; and extreme instances of the weights thus imposed are noticeable at Westminster and Blackfriars stations, where buildings 80 feet high are borne on girders spanning these stations. It is to be hoped that these girders may be successfully protected from corrosion; for such a massive weight, resting on a girder, imperceptibly but gradually weakened by the oxidising influences to which it is exposed, would be liable in course of time to a serious catastrophe.

The importance of placing the numerous stations within easy access of the surface has led to the line being laid out, for the most part, in conformity with the surface slopes of the ground, just as in an ordinary railway, with ascending and descending gradients, but so as to keep always at a suitable depth below the surface. Owing to the greater elevation of the ground in the northern district, the level of the railway varies considerably at different parts, reaching about 80 feet above mean sea level at Edgware Road, on the Inner Circle; rising to 167 feet at the Swiss Cottage, on the St John's Wood branch; and falling, near Victoria Station, to 9 feet below mean sea level. The steepest gradient, of 1 in 70, occurs in rising from beyond

Gloucester Road, through the Campden Hill tunnel, to Notting Hill Gate; and the next steepest, of 1 in 75, in rising from the valley of the old Westbourne stream to Paddington. The sharpest curves, of 10 chains (220 yards) radius on the Inner Circle, and $6\frac{2}{3}$ chains (147 yards) radius on the King's Cross branch, are of smaller radius than commonly employed, and in the latter case the smallest curve that has been adopted on a line of ordinary gauge; but these curves were required to keep the railway within certain boundaries of property, and to form connections with existing lines, and the trains are never run at high speed over them. In consequence of the proximity to the surface at which the railway was formed, the excavations were mainly carried through the alluvial deposits of the Thames valley, and made ground, overlying the London clay which was reached towards the bottom of some of the excavations, and through which the Clerkenwell tunnel was driven.

One of the most interesting portions of the Inner Circle is where the Great Northern branch from King's Cross dips under the main line, in order to branch off on the opposite side to Snow Hill, so that the Underground Railway is actually burrowed under by another line; and at one place passengers by the main line can see the crossing train almost vertically below them through the open girder work supporting the line on which they are travelling. Advantage was taken of the Thames Embankment Works to construct simultaneously the Underground Railway from Westminster to Blackfriars, through the land reclaimed by the Embankment; and a much-needed street improvement was effected, in conjunction with the construction of the last link of the Inner Circle between the Monument and the Tower. The railway, on passing from under Cannon Street across King William Street, had to be carried directly under the granite statue of William IV., weighing 160 tons, which had to be most carefully underpinned previous to the carrying out of the excavations, and now rests on the top of the brick arch of the covered way, so that the trains run exactly underneath the statue. The intersected sewers were lowered for some distance on each side of the line, where practicable, and carried under the railway. In some instances, however, the sewers had to be taken over the railway, an example of which arrangement may be observed at Sloane Square Station, where the Ranelagh sewer is carried in a cast-iron tube, 9 feet in diameter, across the upper part of the station, being supported by girders on each side. The Fleet sewer and the Middle Level sewer have been similarly carried over the railway. The sewer running down the middle of Cannon Street, Eastcheap, and Great Tower Street had to be removed, and two new sewers had to be constructed, running outside the covered way on each side; and the increased width consequently occupied by the works necessitated the underpinning of most of the houses along these streets. The provisions requisite for the temporary diversion of the sewers, and other pipes, during the progress of the works, naturally added considerably to the difficulties experienced in pushing forward the operations in the very limited space available.

When the Metropolitan Railway was first designed, it was intended that the traffic should be worked by smokeless, hot-water locomotives, not burning fuel, as it was supposed that the trains would be small, and that locomotives from other lines would not travel over it to any important extent. Accordingly, no attention was paid to the subject of ventilation in the first section of the Metropolitan Railway; and the Baker Street, Portland Road, and Gower Street stations were built entirely underground. When, however, on the opening of the line, heavy locomotives of the ordinary type were adopted, the glass had to be removed from the side openings at these stations, and openings made in portions of the covered way, to afford an outlet for the smoke from the engines; and even now at times the relief thereby afforded is very imperfect at the stations above mentioned. These defects in ventilation have been avoided in the more recently constructed portions of the line, by placing the stations in uncovered places where possible, with access to the open air at each end, and with occasional openings between the stations. Where, as at Cannon Street and Mark Lane stations, access to the open air above the stations was impracticable, large openings for ventilation have been provided at the side; and fans for producing artificial ventilation have been set up along this section of the line. In spite of all the precautions taken and improvements adopted, the atmosphere at some of the stations is still considerably vitiated on damp, oppressive days by the offensive smoke from the locomotives; and the removal of this nuisance, by the adoption of some other form of motive power not open to this objection, such as electricity, would unquestionably add to the popularity of the Underground Railway. If the Inner Circle formed a separate system, without suburban branches, and without connections with other lines, there ought to be no difficulty in introducing a smokeless motive power; but the matter is complicated by the variety of the connections, and the distances to which some of the branches extend. Some trains merely traverse a portion of the Inner Circle on their way from one place to another, as for instance from Richmond to New Cross, and from Woolwich to Finsbury Park; whilst trains run from the metropolitan railways to Edgeware, Enfield, Hatfield, Hendon, Brentford, Ealing, Hounslow, Wimbledon, Willesden, the Crystal Palace, and Chesham. Any special system of traction could not therefore be easily applied to such varied routes, on some of which the trains are drawn by locomotives belonging to different companies. Even, however, if a smokeless system was only adopted for the Inner Circle trains, and those passing also over the loop round by Addison Road, the line would be relieved from the smoke of over eighteen trains per hour throughout the day, or about one in every three minutes, which would greatly reduce the vitiation of the air throughout the covered portions of the line.

The extensions of the Metropolitan Railway have far exceeded the anticipations of its early promoters, who contemplated merely a sort of improved and accelerated underground omnibus, or tramcar service; whereas the railway is now in communication with most of the metropolitan lines, and luggage trains may be seen passing over it late in the evening. The public mind, also, is occasionally somewhat startled by hearing of the proposed extension of the 'Underground Railway' to Aylesbury, and even to Oxford, which is considered an unwarranted departure from its mole-like character. The Inner Circle alone, which constitutes the real underground railway, has a length of only $13\frac{1}{10}$ miles; whereas the Metropolitan

Railway has nearly 20 miles of line open, and the Metropolitan District Railway, owned by a separate company, has 13 miles open, making a total, with the city link jointly owned by the two companies, of $34\frac{1}{2}$ miles. The extensions of the Metropolitan to Chesham, and of the Metropolitan District to Hounslow, Richmond, and Wimbledon, have indeed made these lines cease to be exclusively metropolitan, whilst extending their capabilities and advantages. The Inner Circle, however, will always remain the special feature of these railways, on account both of the novelty of the design, and the special difficulties involved in its construction. It has also satisfactorily achieved one of the main objects kept in view by the legislature during its development, namely, the connection of the termini of the various lines entering London; for it is in direct communication with the Great Western, the Great Northern, the Midland, and the Chatham and Dover railways near their termini; with the East London Railway, through Whitechapel, and thence with the Great Eastern, Brighton, and South-Eastern railways. The Inner Circle is also in fairly direct communication with Cannon Street Station, on the South-Eastern, through Snow Hill, Holborn Viaduct, and Blackfriars Bridge, and is connected somewhat circuitously with the North-Western and North London railways through Willesden; with Victoria, by Battersea; and with the South-Western by a similar route. Moreover, Praed Street Station adjoins Paddington, Gower Street Station is near Euston, King's Cross Station is close to both St Pancras and the Great Northern terminus, and Bishopgate Station adjoins Broad Street and Liverpool Street stations; whilst Cannon Street, Charing Cross, and Victoria stations, on the Inner Circle, are very near to the respective termini of the same names. Waterloo Station alone is at a little distance from the Inner Circle, owing to its situation on the opposite side of the Thames; but even in this case, Westminster Bridge and Charing Cross stations are as close to Waterloo as circumstances permit.

Considering the scattered positions of the various termini of the railways entering London, and the difficulties inseparable from the construction of a railway right across London, it must be acknowledged that the Inner Circle, though the result of several successive extensions, has been remarkably well laid out, as a whole, for accommodating the various lines ; while, at the same time, it gives quick and easy communication between distant parts of the metropolis, and even between one suburb and another on opposite sides of London. The Great Western, Midland, and Great Northern railways have specially profited by the Underground Railway, for they are indebted to it for their access to the city, and the consequent development of the suburban traffic along their lines. Moreover, though the final link in the city, which completed the circuit of the Inner Circle, has not hitherto brought the traffic anticipated from the trains being able to run round continuously in both directions, owing probably to the considerable elongation of the narrow end of the oval eastwards, this link, with the Whitechapel extension, has placed the populous East End and the eastern suburbs in direct communication with the Inner Circle and its numerous branches.

The rapid succession of trains on the Inner Circle required for serving the Addison Road loop, and the numerous branches, in addition to the Circle trains running at intervals of ten minutes each way throughout the day, has been only rendered possible of accomplishment by the introduction of the block system and the employment of continuous brakes. The block system insures, by a carefully arranged system of signalling, that, if the engine-driver pays proper attention to the signals exhibited, no two trains on the same line shall be in the same block, or interval between two adjacent signal cabins, at the same time. Each signalman is instructed not to lower his signal, and by the most recent electrical contrivance he is prevented from lowering his signal, for the passage of a train, till the signalman in the next cabin in advance informs him, by telegraph, of the passage of the train in front past that cabin, and consequently that the interval between the two cabins is empty. The occurrence of accidents is accordingly prevented, if the signals are obeyed, by interposing an interval of space between each train and the next. There are signal boxes at every station; and intermediate cabins are sometimes placed between the stations where the interval is rather greater, or the traffic very large, notwithstanding the small distance between the stations along the Inner Circle. The number of blocks, indeed, into which a railway can be divided is only limited by the necessity of making the shortest block longer than the longest train; but whilst a greater number of blocks within a certain distance increases the number of trains which can be admitted to that section of a railway at the same time, it reduces the speed of the trains, owing to the frequency of the signal boxes at which the engine-driver must be prepared to pull up if necessary. The accommodation, however, of a number of trains is of more importance on the metropolitan railways than great speed; and the continuous brake enables the train to be pulled up within a very short distance, on approaching a signal set at danger. The continuous brake puts a brake on the wheels of every carriage of a train simultaneously, instead of the brake being only applied to the engine and the guard's van, as in former days; and thus, by increasing the frictional area and applied weight, a train entering a station at a good speed can be brought to rest by the time the engine has reached the further end of the station. This rapid stoppage of the train, combined with the quick starting again of the engines, reduces the time occupied at stations to a minimum; so that the average period of transit between the stations, including stoppages, on the Inner Circle is only about $2\frac{2}{3}$ minutes. Accordingly, the continuous brake, besides ensuring a greater immunity from accidents, facilitates rapidity of transit. Iron rails wore rapidly under the much increased friction, due to the augmented brake power, entailing frequent repairs and costly renewals. The introduction, however, of heavy steel rails, at a moderate cost, has greatly increased the durability of the rails, and reduced the expenses of maintenance. The success, therefore, and safe working of the numerous trains running on the Inner Circle are due to a combination of a variety of improvements; and the only important amelioration which appears needful is an improved ventilation of the covered way.

Metropolitan Railway proposed for Paris.—The great advantages derived from the London metropolitan railways have led to various schemes for obtaining similar accommodation in the centre of Paris. The outskirts of Paris are served, and the several lines converging on

Paris are connected, by the 'chemin de fer de ceinture,' or Outer Circle, which completely encircles Paris on the outside. The growing density, however, of the population in Paris renders additional and more rapid means of communication within the city very desirable. Schemes for overhead railways, on masonry viaducts, connecting the most important parts of the town, have been proposed, as well as underground lines resembling in principle the Inner Circle. No scheme has, hitherto, been finally adopted, though the circular underground or partly underground lines seem to be preferred, the hesitation about providing the necessary capital being apparently partly due to the poor returns on part of the capital invested in the London Underground Railway.

Berlin Metropolitan Railway.—Berlin, like Paris, possesses an outer circle railway connecting the various Berlin railways, and serving the suburbs. It was considered impracticable to make a circular underground line in Berlin, owing to the level of the River Spree, which runs through the city. A metropolitan railway has, consequently, been constructed on a viaduct, forming a diameter to the Outer Circle Railway. It connects the Charlottenburg Station, at the west end, with the Silesia Station, at the east end, having a total length of $7\frac{1}{2}$ miles, with four lines of way to keep the through and local traffic distinct. This line has nine stations; it was commenced in 1875, and completed in 1882.

THE NEW YORK ELEVATED RAILWAYS.

Manhattan Island, on which the city of New York is situated, has an average width of 2 miles, with a length of 13 miles. The business part of the city is concentrated at the southern end of the island; and, owing to the narrowness of the island in proportion to its length, easy and rapid means of communication was required from the southern end northwards, that a development of the city to the north, for residences, might accommodate the increasing population, which, for want of convenient access, tended to crowd up towards the southern part. In 1867, the engineers of New York set to work at the development of the needed railway facilities across the city in a characteristic manner. Burrowing underground involves costly works and unforeseen contingencies, especially on an island where the neighbourhood of two deep rivers rendered probable the presence of alluvial deposits in places, and consequently treacherous foundations. An ordinary railway, on an arched viaduct, necessitates a heavy expenditure in the purchase of valuable land, as well as the cost of the works themselves, including spanning by bridges the streets traversed. The method of construction commenced in 1867, and subsequently extended, has enabled the New York Elevated Railway Companies to avoid underground operations, and at the same time to escape from any purchase of land. The railways have been carried along the streets; they are raised above the street traffic on girders resting upon wrought-iron lattice columns, standing at convenient places on the line of the curb of the pavements, or in the roadway itself where the traffic is not too heavy or the streets too narrow. (*See illustration.*) No payment has been made for placing these columns along the streets; and no compensation has been paid for damages to residential property fronting the avenues and streets which the railways traverse, though the trains are constantly running a very short distance off, and on the level of the first-floor windows. The depreciation, due to the continual noise and loss of privacy, has reached in some cases as much as fifty per cent.

The columns, which support the girders over which the trains run, are placed at intervals of from 37 to 44 feet along the curb, on each side of the roadway, where the street is too narrow or too crowded with traffic to allow of the columns being placed in the roadway. In these cases, if the proximity of the railway to the houses is of no consequence, the columns are widened out at the top to carry the two longitudinal girders, placed 5 feet apart, directly under each rail; and, under these circumstances, the up and down trains run exactly over the line of columns placed along the curb on each side of the roadway. If, on the contrary, it is important to keep the railway as far as possible from the houses on each side, girders are fastened on each pair of columns across the street, from 28 to 45 feet long, according to the width of the street; and these girders carry the longitudinal girders placed under the rails, which can thus be brought nearer to the centre of the street than the lines of columns, the centres of the up and down lines being not more than 20 feet apart. Where the roadway is wide, and not so frequented as to render the erection of columns in it inadmissible, the rows of columns are placed along the roadway, at a clear distance apart of 22 feet, so that two tramway lines can pass between them. The columns are widened out at the top, as in the first example described, so as to receive the longitudinal girders placed under each rail; and the whole structure is further

NEW YORK ELEVATED RAILWAYS.

strengthened by bracing together the pairs of columns across the street, at the level of the girders. A minimum clear height of 14½ feet is provided under the girders, so that the traffic along the roadways may not be interfered with. The gradients of the railway follow approximately the inclination of the roadway, except where frequent changes of inclination, or a steep inclination, render a modification of the gradient for the railway expedient. The columns, accordingly, vary in height according to circumstances, the variation generally being between 18 and 21 feet; but in one part columns 65 feet high have been adopted, which have been specially braced together in groups to ensure stability. The steepest gradient of these railways is 1 in 50. Owing to the avenues and streets in New York being at right angles, and the necessity for the railway to keep to the line of the roadway, the curves on the railway for changing its course are necessarily very sharp; and the sharpest curve on the main line has a radius of a little under 1½ chains (33 yards), though the gauge of the railway is the same as the ordinary gauge of Great Britain. Such a small curve is more in conformity with the practice of tramway lines on roads; and, compared with this, the minimum curve on the London Metropolitan Railway, of 6¾ chains (147 yards), appears ample; but, on the New York Elevated Railway, special bogie locomotives are exclusively employed,[1] whilst any locomotive may have to pass over the Metropolitan.

The first portion of the Elevated Railway, constructed in 1867, was worked by a wire rope, moved

---

[1] The term bogie is applied to the two pairs of small wheels and framework pivoted centrally under the frame of the front of a locomotive, or towards each end of a long car, which, by turning independently, enables the locomotive and car to pass easily round sharp curves.

by a stationary engine; and owing to the want of success of this system, no further progress was made till 1875, when a commission reported in favour of the elevated system of railways in preference to the underground plan, which resulted in the construction of the xisting lines of railways in New York. The Elevated Railway has been carried along the Second, Third, Sixth, and Ninth Avenues; and it also has branches, one of which connects it with the New York Central Railway, and another with the New York City and Northern Railway. The elevated railways are owned by two separate companies, and worked by a third company, to whom the lines are leased for 199 years, by means of locomotives, with coupled driving wheels $3\frac{1}{2}$ feet in diameter, and bogie wheels 2 feet in diameter. The total length of the lines is about $32\frac{1}{2}$ miles.

The stations on the Elevated Railway are about one-third of a mile apart, which is somewhat closer than on the London Inner Circle, where the average distance between the stations is half-a-mile. The trains are necessarily provided with continuous brakes, to allow the frequent stoppages to be rapidly effected. In the busiest part of the day, the trains run at intervals of two minutes, and at other times at intervals of four or five minutes. There are no parapets or railings along the line, and the width of the cars is equal to the length of the cross sleepers. Gates are placed, therefore, across the platforms at the ends of the cars, which are only opened at the stations; for any passenger leaving the train, except alongside the station platform, would be precipitated into the street. Guard timbers are laid on both sides of each rail to secure the trains from leaving the road, for such an accident would not merely involve injury to the passengers, but serious casualties to the persons in the street below. Open spaces of one foot in width are left between the cross sleepers along the line, so that anything dropping from the engine, except at the stations, where protection is afforded, is liable to fall on the people underneath. This, together with the frequent noise of the passing trains, must be a nuisance to the people traversing the streets.

The cost per mile of the Elevated Railway was only £81,000, which appears a very small amount when compared with the cost per mile of the London metropolitan railways, amounting to about £575,000, which indicates the great financial advantages of the permission to construct overhead railways along the main thoroughfares, and of being exempted from the purchase of land, and from the payment of compensation.

The Elevated Railway is a marvel to the English visitor in New York, not on account of any special skill exhibited in the design, which is quite simple, but owing to the contrast it presents to the system of railways in London, the boldness of the conception of carrying an overhead railway along crowded thoroughfares, and the impossibility of obtaining powers for any similar construction in England. A comparison of the Metropolitan Railway with the Elevated Railway forcibly manifests the different views entertained in the two countries, with regard to the rights of railway companies in relation to the streets, and as to the claims of owners of house property for compensation for injuries inflicted. The boldest part of the design consists in placing a railway on the top of a narrow superstructure, resting upon a single row of isolated columns, only $1\frac{1}{4}$ feet by $1\frac{1}{2}$ feet wide, placed 44 feet apart, along the curb on each side of a crowded roadway, and then allowing trains to run constantly, at a speed of 18 miles an hour, along this open, unprotected track, which has a maximum width of 8 feet at the top. The work has proved an engineering success; it has attracted a very large and increasing traffic, and has effected the desired development of the northern part of the island of Manhattan; whereas previously the want of means of access forced the increasing population to migrate in large numbers to Jersey City and Brooklyn. Imperative necessity, however, could alone justify such a method of construction, which, though doubtless very convenient to the passengers, must be a source of discomfort to the people passing along the streets below, and still more to those living alongside, and a very serious loss to the householders in the streets traversed by the railway. The number of passengers conveyed by the railway increased from 61 millions in 1880 to $171\frac{1}{2}$ millions in 1888.

The London metropolitan and New York elevated railways have been selected for description, as illustrating two novel systems of railway construction in the latter half of the nineteenth century, under circumstances of peculiar difficulty; but they constitute only a very small part of the general development of railway construction and traffic which has occurred during this period. It is sufficient to turn to the Returns, issued yearly by the Board of Trade, to see how great the railway development has been, since the middle of the century, in the United Kingdom alone. In 1849, the number of miles of railway open in the United Kingdom was 6031; it is now 19,943, so that the total length of railways has been trebled within the l... forty years. The capital invested was £230,000,0... in round numbers in 1849, and £876,600,000 in 1889, showing that the capital invested in railways in the United Kingdom has been nearly quadrupled in the last forty years. The number of passengers carried, exclusive of season ticket holders, was 64,000,000 in 1849, and 775,000,000 in 1889, indicating that the railway passengers now are more than twelve times the number forty years ago, without allowing for the great increase in the season ticket holders. These figures show that the capital has increased in a greater ratio than the length of lines opened, owing doubtless, in great measure, to the doubling of the lines near London, which is not taken account of in the Returns, improved station accommodation, and costly extensions. The passengers, however, have increased in a far greater proportion than the capital, showing the advantages of improved accommodation, and the growing propensity of the population to travel. The growth of the passenger traffic is, indeed, very steady, for there has been an increase every year in the numbers for the last forty years, with the sole exception of 1879, when there was a slight decrease as compared with 1878, which was, however, much more than recovered in the following year. These figures, relating to the United Kingdom alone, give some faint idea of the marvellous development of railways since the middle of the century, not merely throughout Europe, but in almost every civilised country, with the exception of China This enormous extension of railways, and the greatly increased facilities thereby afforded for travelling to the constantly growing population of the world, are the combined results of the skill of the engineer, the energy of the contractor, the labour of his men, and the confidence of the capitalists in the success of the undertakings. A very satisfactory feature in the great increase of traffic is that the improvements in safety appliances have more than kept pace with the growth of traffic, so that railway travelling, in spite of the much greater frequency of trains, is safer than formerly; and it is certain that a person is more secure from accident in a railway carriage than when walking through the crowded parts of London.

CHAPTER II.

RAILWAYS ACROSS THE ALPS, THE ROCKY MOUNTAINS, AND THE ANDES.

THE gradients and curves adopted for a railway, through a hilly district, exercise a very important influence on the cost of construction; for with steep gradients and sharp curves, it may be possible to follow approximately the general levels of the ground, and the contours of the valleys; whereas flat gradients and easy curves would necessitate deep cuttings and high embankments, in order to pierce the ridges and cross the valleys. In the early days of railway enterprise, when the main lines of this and other countries were laid out along the most suitable routes, it was considered expedient, and generally found practicable, to adopt in most places gradients rising not more than 1 foot in 300 or 400 feet of length, and curves having radii of little less than one mile. This course has enabled heavy trains to run with safety at the high speeds now so common on many main lines. On the contrary, steep gradients and sharp curves, whilst reducing the first cost of construction in rough country, diminish also the available speed and tractive power of the locomotives, and increase the wear and tear on the lines. Accordingly, economy in construction, under such conditions, involves increased cost in working and maintenance; and therefore it was wise in the earlier principal main lines, with a large traffic, to secure rapid, easy travelling with comparatively moderate working expenses, at the cost of a larger capital outlay in the heavier portions of the lines. When, however, the development of railways, and the public demands for increased facilities of communication, necessitated the extension of railways across mountainous districts, the conditions became altered; and the steep gradients and sharp curves, which would have been considered quite inadmissible in early days, became absolutely essential for carrying railways, at any reasonable expense, across the Alps and the Rocky Mountains. Moreover, railway extensions into undeveloped districts, like the western parts of North America, are the pioneers of civilisation, and require to be carried out as rapidly and cheaply as possible, leaving improvements in the lines to be effected when the development of the countries traversed affords sufficient increase of traffic to warrant the outlay.

ALPINE RAILWAYS.

Semmering Railway.—The first railway carried across the Alps was constructed by the Austrian Government, in 1848-54, to connect Vienna with its seaport Trieste. It crosses the Styrian Alps at the Semmering Pass, from which it takes its name of the Semmering Railway. The lowest point of the ridge, at the pass, is 3248 feet above sea level; but the railway pierces the top of the ridge by a tunnel of nearly a mile in length, so that its summit level is only 2892 feet above sea level. Before reaching the tunnel, however, at the summit, the railway has to rise 1297 feet in a little less than 13 miles, going through fourteen tunnels and over sixteen viaducts in its course, and having gradients of 1 in 45 to 1 in 40 along the greater part of this distance. On the opposite side of the ridge, descending towards Trieste, the slope is less rugged; so that the descent to Murzzuschlag, of 402 feet in 7 miles, has been effected without tunnels or viaducts, and with gradients rarely steeper than 1 in 45. Accordingly, this railway, which cost £98,000 per mile, or more per mile than the New York Elevated Railway, was not able to be constructed, even at this outlay, without gradients which in old days would have been considered excessive, amounting to from eight to ten times the steepness at first deemed advisable on main lines. Moreover, in addition to the steep gradients and heavy works on the Vienna side of the ridge, the railway had to be carried up this slope in a circuitous line, with sharp curves of as little as $9\frac{1}{2}$ chains (209 yards) radius, so as to wind round the projecting spurs, and also to gain an easier gradient by an increase in length. This is the only instance of quite such sharp curves being adopted, even upon Alpine railways; and they occupy altogether $4\frac{1}{2}$ miles of the line. Such a combination of steep gradients and sharp curves on a main line was unprecedented in 1854, when the line was opened for traffic; and special locomotives had to be designed for traversing this section of the line. The passenger locomotives proved capable of drawing passenger trains up the inclines, at a speed of $11\frac{3}{4}$ miles an hour; and eventually two goods locomotives, one in front and one behind, were able to take up goods trains, of 350 tons, at a rate of 9½ miles an hour. The cost of traction on the Semmering inclines is about two and a half times the cost on the other portions of the line, so that, in this respect, the inclines are equivalent to an addition of one and a half times the length of this section. The speed, under the most favourable conditions, could never be much increased with safety over such sharp curves on a line of ordinary gauge. The Semmering Railway was the precursor of other Alpine railways, of greater length and higher elevation, across the main chains of the Alps; but though the gradients have in some cases been made even somewhat steeper than on the Semmering, the very small radius of the sharpest curves has not been equalled on any other Alpine line, or even approached, except in one instance. Notwithstanding the moderate elevation of the summit of the line, trains on the Semmering are occasionally impeded by snow.

Brenner Railway.—To the Austrian Government belongs the honour of constructing the second railway across the Alps, as well as the first, and in this second case across the main Alpine chain, over the Brenner Pass. The object of the Brenner Railway was to connect Austria by railway with its possessions in the Tyrol and Venetia; but as a result of the war with Italy, in 1866, the latter possessions were ceded by Austria to Italy before the completion of the railway. Though the Brenner Railway was a much greater and more formidable undertaking than the Semmering, the route is the most favourable one for crossing the main chain of the Alps, as the Brenner is the lowest of the main

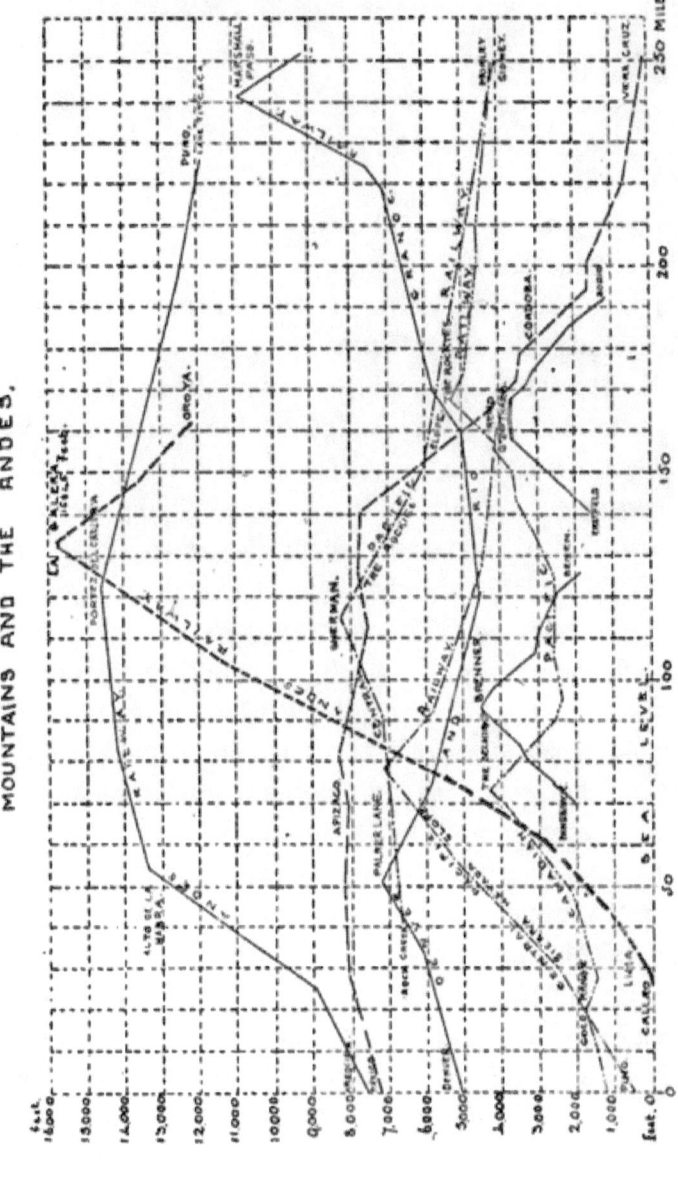

Alpine passes, and is less encumbered by snow, owing to its distance from the highest peaks. The total length of the mountain line between Innsbruck and Botzen is $78\frac{1}{2}$ miles; and the summit of the ridge is crossed without any tunnel, at a height of 4497 feet above sea level. (*See page* 30.) The rise on the northern slope, in the 23 miles between Innsbruck and the summit, is 2586 feet, making an average ascent of 1 in 47, which is mainly accomplished by gradients of 1 in 40 along $17\frac{1}{2}$ miles of the way. The fall on the southern slope is 3624 feet in the $55\frac{1}{2}$ miles between the summit and Botzen, giving an average descent of 1 in 81, in which the steepest gradient is 1 in 44, which extends along $10\frac{1}{2}$ miles of the upper part of the slope. The railway passes through fourteen tunnels on the northern slope, and through only three tunnels on the southern slope, which is less steep and rugged than the other. The line winds along the valleys in ascending the slopes; and it forms a long narrow loop about half way between Sterzing, on the southern slope, and the summit, and a shorter loop on the northern slope. This winding course has necessitated making the line curved for nearly half its length, and the introduction of curves of the minimum radius of about 14 chains (308 yards), over a total distance of $9\frac{3}{8}$ miles. The express trains ascend the slopes at a speed of $15\frac{1}{2}$ miles an hour, and descend at $23\frac{1}{2}$ miles an hour.

The Brenner Pass possesses the interest of having been the first main Alpine pass traversed by carriages, and also the route by which Attila's forces and other barbarian armies descended on Italy. The Brenner Railway was the first which surmounted one of the principal chains of the Alps, and the only one which has done so without a summit tunnel; but it rises to a greater elevation than any of the others, its summit level being 104 feet higher than the highest level of the Mont Cenis Railway. The railway passes on from Botzen to Verona, and thus first afforded Austria and Germany direct communication with Northern Italy and the port of Brindisi. It was commenced in 1864, and completed in 1867.

Mont Cenis Railway.—Though the Semmering and Brenner railways, with their tortuous course, sharp curves, and exceptionally long and steep gradients, were remarkable examples of engineering skill and progress in surmounting most formidable obstacles, they did not attract the world-wide notice which another mountain line, commenced seven years before the Brenner, and only completed about four years after it, has done. This railway, known as the Mont Cenis, from the pass of that name on the road between France and Italy, owes its renown to the tunnel of unparalleled length required for piercing an insurmountable ridge at its summit level, of which a description will be given in a following chapter. The other features of the line are very similar to the Semmering and the Brenner. There is, however, only one loop of importance, situated near the French end of the long tunnel; and the sharpest curve has a radius of 17 chains (374 yards). On the other hand, the gradients are steeper generally than those on either of the earlier lines, the maximum gradient on both slopes being 1 in $33\frac{1}{3}$. The rise on the French slope is 2037 feet in the 21 miles from St Jean de Maurienne to the entrance of the tunnel, and 2683 feet in the $24\frac{1}{2}$ miles on the

Italian slope, between Bussoleno and the tunnel. The line passes through fourteen tunnels on the northern slope, and through twenty-six tunnels and over eight viaducts on the southern slope. The open portion of the railway reaches an altitude of 3793 feet above sea level on the French side, and 4270 feet on the Italian warmer southern side; but these elevations, though inferior to the summit level of the Brenner, are exposed to the chilling influence of the proximity of the highest peaks of the Alps. The Mont Cenis Railway gives direct communication between Paris and Turin; it was commenced in 1857, and opened for traffic in 1871; and the effect of its opening was to change the port for the transmission of the Indian mails from Marseilles to Brindisi, as this latter route caused a saving of distance of 103 miles between London and Alexandria. There was, moreover, a saving of time by the new route, owing to a journey by land being substituted for a portion of the sea route, as trains travel faster than steamers. Altogether, the saving of time effected by the change of route amounted to forty-two hours in the transit between London and Alexandria. The Mont Cenis and the Brenner railways traverse the Alps near the extremities of the principal range, passing outside Switzerland on each side, and afford railway access to Italy from Western and Central Europe.

St Gothard Railway.—During the construction of the Mont Cenis Railway, four schemes were brought forward for another Alpine railway, intermediate between the Brenner and the Mont Cenis. The four routes proposed followed approximately the line of the passes of the Simplon, the St Gothard, the Lukmanier, and the

Splugen. The Germans were naturally anxious to have a more direct route to Italy, and to avoid having to traverse a considerable distance in French territory on the one hand, or in Austrian territory on the other; and Switzerland was desirous to secure the accommodation of an Alpine railway. All the routes involved the construction of a long tunnel at the summit; but the St Gothard was the most central between the Mont Cenis and the Brenner, and was consequently given the preference, both by Switzerland, which it traverses centrally in its widest part, and by Germany, which thereby has direct access to Italy, without passing through any other foreign country than Switzerland.

On approaching the south-eastern end of the Lake of Lucerne, by Fluelen and Altorf, the traditional scenes of the legendary exploits of William Tell, the scenery becomes grander, and the country more rugged. The wild gorges of the valley of the Reuss torrent, encircled as they are with a halo of romance, formed a suitable commencement for the first Swiss trans-alpine railway, which, from the novel method by which the difficulties of the steep slopes of the St Gothard Pass have been surmounted, is the most interesting of the group. The St Gothard Railway does not rise to the same elevation as the Mont Cenis; and, unlike the Mont Cenis, the levels of the open portions at the entrances to the summit tunnel on each side are not very different. The railway, however, commences its ascent at a lower level than the Mont Cenis, on both sides. It rises 2077 feet on the northern slope, in the $17\frac{3}{4}$ miles between Erstfield and Goeschenen, at the northern extremity of the summit tunnel, and 2785 feet, in the $28\frac{1}{3}$ miles between Biasca and Airolo, on the southern slope.

(*See page* 30.) Owing to the steepness of the northern slope, in the 14⅔ miles between Amstag and Goeschenen, the heavy average gradient of 1 in 42⅖ could not be obtained without lengthening the line, and thus easing the gradient, by a spiral and two long parallel loops near Wasen. (*See diagram.*) This spiral was accomplished by making the rising line enter a curved tunnel, and, by a continuous curve and ascent, eventually pass over the spot again which it had traversed in tunnel at a lower level. The double open loop added still

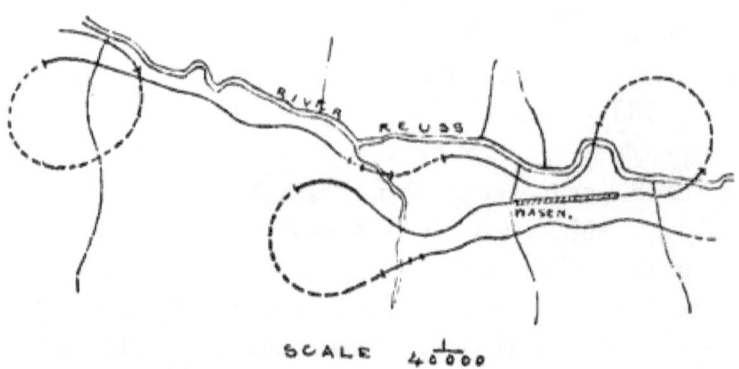

ST GOTHARD RAILWAY.
LOOPS AND SPIRALS NEAR WASEN.

SCALE 1/40000

more to the length than the spiral, and was effected by gradually rising along one side of the valley till a projecting ridge was reached on which the line could wind round in tunnel, and crossing the valley, rise on the opposite side in a reverse direction till another ridge afforded an opportunity for curving back and retracing its steps, at a higher level, up the slope. The length of the loops is nearly 2 miles, so that an additional length of about 4 miles was gained by this process of doubling back. Though the average slope on the southern side was not so steep as on the northern side, four spirals were adopted for easing the gradient at steep places. These loops and spirals, combined with the general rugged nature of the valleys, involved the construction of twenty-one tunnels on the northern slope, and twelve tunnels on the southern slope, with a total length of $9\frac{1}{2}$ miles. Accordingly, with the long tunnel at the summit, one-third of the whole length of 56 miles between Erstfield and Biasca is in tunnel. The maximum gradient on the St Gothard, of 1 in 37, is slightly easier than the worst on the Mont Cenis; but, owing to the spirals and loops, the curves are sharper and more continuous, curves of 14 chains (308 yards) radius occupying a length of nearly 3 miles, and curves of less than 20 chains (440 yards) extending over $15\frac{3}{4}$ miles. Curves, indeed, of 30 chains (660 yards) radius and less occupy altogether 24 miles out of the $46\frac{3}{4}$ miles of railway, exclusive of the summit tunnel, showing what tortuous windings railways in mountainous districts require to keep down the gradients within practicable limits. The works were commenced in 1872, and the line was opened for traffic in 1882; but in this case, as with the Mont Cenis, the duration of the works mainly depended on the period required for executing the summit tunnel. The opening of the St Gothard route drew a good deal of the traffic to Belgium and Germany which previously passed through France, and by the Mont Cenis route, thus somewhat seriously affecting French traffic and trade. Consequently, fresh schemes have been proposed for another Alpine railway calculated to bring back some of this traffic into France. The route which has found most favour is across the Simplon, which would both shorten the distance between Calais and Brindisi, and also, by keeping to a level even lower than the Semmering Railway, would reduce the cost of traction and improve the rate of transit. The Simplon route would approach the St Gothard Railway towards the south, as it would run direct to Milan, like the St Gothard; but this would not be an objection to a line competing with the St Gothard for traffic. The traffic on the existing lines would not justify the heavy expenditure required for a fourth line across the Alps to Italy, on commercial grounds alone; but the French might support the scheme on account of its national importance, for bringing back to France some of its lost traffic and trade; and it would improve the communications of Italy and Switzerland with Northern Europe. The Simplon approach railways, however, to the summit tunnel would be simpler and shorter than those of the St Gothard; and in order to find a parallel to the loops and spirals of the St Gothard Railway, it is necessary to turn to the railways of another hemisphere.

Arlberg Railway.—One more Alpine railway deserves a brief notice before leaving the Alps for the Rocky Mountains, as, though less known than the others, it involved works little inferior to those of the Mont Cenis, and it attains an elevation surpassed only in that region by the Brenner and the Mont Cenis. The Austrian Government, for the third time, undertook the construction of an Alpine railway, passing through the Arl mountain, for the purpose of connecting France with Austria, across Switzerland alone. The railway runs from Innsbruck to Bludenz; but the mountain portion only commences at Landeck, $44\frac{1}{2}$ miles from Innsbruck, ascending 1721 feet in $17\frac{1}{2}$ miles on the east slope, and 2158 feet in $16\frac{3}{4}$ miles on the west slope before entering the summit tunnel. The ascent on the west side is steeper than on any of the other Alpine lines, and it also has the steepest gradient, of 1 in $32\frac{1}{2}$. The sharpest curves on this line, of 10 chains (220 yards) radius, are but slightly exceeded by the Semmering; and the length of over 9 miles of curves not exceeding 14 chains (308 yards) in radius, places the Arlberg Railway in a worse position in this respect than the other lines. The greatest height in the open, of 4270 feet above sea level, is attained at the western entrance to the summit tunnel, so that fortunately, as in the other cases, the greatest elevation occurs on the warmer side of the ridge. This elevation is 514 feet higher than the St Gothard, and only 227 feet lower than the summit of the Brenner Railway.

RAILWAYS ACROSS THE ROCKY MOUNTAINS.

The mountain railways of America have been constructed under different conditions to those across the Alps. The Alpine railways of the Brenner, the Mont Cenis, and St Gothard, were made in order to obtain a quicker and more direct route from Northern Europe to Italy and the port of Brindisi; and they had to be so laid out as to be always open except in quite exceptionally severe weather, and to be run over at a fair speed. Moreover, the choice of route was restricted to three or four passes; and the St Gothard Railway had to be designed so as to compete for traffic with the previous lines. When, however, railway connection with the far west of the United States became expedient, for the development of that very extensive district, necessitating the passage of the Rocky Mountains, it was important that the railways should be made as economically as possible in the first instance, leaving improvements to be effected as soon as the amount of traffic permitted. The choice of route was quite unrestricted in an unsettled country; and a reduction in first cost was of much greater consequence, on a line with little traffic at first, than low working expenses and high speeds. Moreover, in America, the blocking of trains by snow in winter is a more common event; a regular system of clearing the lines by snow ploughs is in use; and a temporary stoppage of the traffic in winter between the east and west is of less importance than along through routes in Europe to distant parts of the world. Consequently, high elevations, more subject to snow than the highest limits of the Alpine railways, may be traversed in America. This is, in fact, the only method of carrying railways across the Rocky Mountains; for, besides the prohibitive cost of constructing long tunnels for pioneer railways, these ranges, though not higher than the Alps, have a very much greater width, and could not therefore be similarly pierced at a moderate elevation.

United States Western Railways.—There are three main lines traversing the western portion of the United States, and extending to the Pacific Ocean, namely, the Union or Central Pacific, which was the first line constructed across the Rocky Mountains, and was opened in 1869; the Northern Pacific, further north, commenced in 1870, and completed in 1883; and the Southern Pacific, to the south, constructed during the same period. New York is in direct connection with these three lines; and the route from New York to Pittsburg is common to them all. At Pittsburg two main lines branch off, one going westwards to Chicago, and the other south-west to St Louis. The Northern Pacific and the Union Pacific branch off from Chicago, the one going north-west to Portland, and the other to the west, past Omaha, Ogden, and the Salt Lake, and then turning southwards to San Francisco. The Southern Pacific is reached from St Louis, and passing through Indian Territory, part of Texas, and New Mexico near the Mexican boundary, it proceeds by Mojave to Los Angelos, and towns on the Pacific coast, with a northern branch from Mojave to San Francisco. There is a fourth line, the Atlantic and Pacific, which appears to have been intended to run nearly parallel to, but a good deal north of the Southern Pacific, from St Louis to Mojave Junction, by Vinita and Albuquerque. Though, however, the line is constructed from Albuquerque to Mojave, there is a gap left between Sapulpa, a little beyond Vinita, and Albuquerque, so that passengers by the Atlantic and Pacific Railway have to make a détour from St Louis, by Kansas, Dodge City, and Santa Fé, to Albuquerque. The fragment of a through line from St Louis, which terminates at Sapulpa, has the grand, but misleading, title of the St Louis and San Francisco Railway; whereas travellers by it would be landed on the Arkansas River, in the middle of the Indian Territory, with part of Texas and more than half of New

Mexico between them and Albuquerque, the point of commencement of the Atlantic and Pacific Railway.

The Union or Central Pacific Railway reaches its highest elevation, of 8248 feet above sea level, in traversing the Rocky Mountains, at Sherman's Pass, on the eastern edge of the ridge; and after passing across a high table land, with a minimum elevation of 6112 feet, it rises over the Aspen Pass, on the western edge, to a height of 7546 feet. (*See page* 30.) It then traverses the table land between the Rocky Mountains and the Sierra Nevada, having an elevation of 3897 feet at its lowest point; and after crossing the ridge of the Sierra, at a height of 7021 feet, it descends rapidly towards the western coast to Sacramento, about 140 miles from San Francisco. For a distance of 440 miles across the Rocky Mountains, the railway never descends within 1600 feet of the highest altitude of the Brenner Railway, which attains the highest elevation of all the Alpine railways; and from the eastern slope of the Rocky Mountains to the western slope of the Sierra Nevada, a distance along the line of 1300 miles, the railway is never lower than 110 feet above the summit level of the St Gothard Railway. This immense stretch of high land, across a mountain range whose peaks do not reach the elevation of the higher Alpine peaks, shows how totally different the conditions are for the construction of a railway across the Rocky Mountains to those of the Alpine lines. Though the maximum elevation reached is about the level of perpetual snow in the Alps, and within 750 feet of double the elevation attained by the Brenner Railway, there is a very long, gradual ascent on the eastern side for 500 miles from Omaha; and the steep gradients are mainly confined to the passage of the ridges at each edge of the Rocky Mountains, and the Sierra Nevada, the longest and steepest gradient being the descent from this latter ridge to the low land near the Pacific coast. This descent, from the summit to a place 25 miles short of Sacramento, is 6545 feet in a distance of 80 miles, with a maximum gradient of 1 in $45\frac{1}{2}$, and an average gradient of 1 in 64. The steepest part of the ascent, from the east to the highest point at Sherman's Pass, is only a rise of 2204 feet in 33 miles, with a maximum gradient of 1 in 66; whilst a steeper though shorter ascent leads to the summit on the eastern side of the Sierra Nevada, where the rise is 1005 feet in $13\frac{2}{3}$ miles, with a maximum gradient of 1 in 50. The line is necessarily very much curved in threading its way through this vast mountainous region, so as to obtain satisfactory gradients, the curved portion of this section of the line attaining a total length of 870 miles, whilst the sharpest curves have a radius of $8\frac{3}{4}$ chains (193 yards).

The Northern Pacific and Southern Pacific railways cross the Rocky Mountains where this range is less broad and less high than along the line of the Central Pacific Railway; and they also escape having to cross a second ridge near the Pacific Ocean, and therefore avoid steep gradients on the west slope as well as the east. The Northern Pacific Railway reaches its maximum altitude, of about 5800 feet above sea level, in crossing the western ridge of the Rocky Mountains at Deerlodge Pass, and the Southern Pacific in crossing the eastern ridge, at a height of about 5720 feet. The steepest ascents on these lines are a rise of 1668 feet in about $14\frac{1}{2}$ miles, with a gradient of 1 in $45\frac{1}{2}$, on the Northern Pacific, and a rise of 2674 feet in 25½ miles, with a similar maximum gradient, on the Southern Pacific. This latter railway has a spiral tunnel, about three-quarters of a mile long, similar to the St Gothard tunnels; and its sharpest curves have a radius of 8¾ chains (193 yards), like the Central Pacific. The tunnels on all these western lines nowhere attain a mile in length.

The Central Pacific Railway is pre-eminent amongst the Pacific main lines, both in the elevation reached, and in the altitude it has to maintain for such a great distance, together with the long and rapid descent it has to make towards the western coast, owing to the configuration of the mountain ranges at the latitude which it follows. All the three lines attain heights considerably in excess of those reached by any Alpine railway; and whereas their gradients are better than those found necessary in the Alps, their curves are sharper. The system of pivoting each car on two bogies, with a small wheel-base, employed in the United States, enables the trains to run easily and safely round sharp curves, especially at the moderate speed adopted on the western lines; and the use of sharp curves reduces the cost of construction, and also the maxima gradients, which is of considerable importance where the ascending gradients are continuous for very long distances.

Some of the branch 3-foot gauge lines near Denver present even more remarkable features than the main western lines, though on a smaller scale. Thus a branch of the Denver and Rio Grande line rises 3675 feet in 25 miles, with a maximum gradient of 1 in 25, and with curves having a minimum radius of 3⅝ chains (80 yards); and it reaches an elevation at the Marshall Pass of 10,850 feet. (*See page* 30.) The Calumet Mine branch rises about 2700 feet in 7 miles, with a gradient of 1 in $12\frac{1}{2}$, and curves having a minimum radius of $3\frac{1}{2}$ chains (77 yards), and is the steepest line worked by ordinary locomotives. On the Georgetown branch there is a spiral where the railway curves round and crosses over its own track, on a viaduct, at an elevation of 75 feet above its former level. It is also on one of these lines that the railway, in crossing a deep cañon, emerges directly from a tunnel on to a bridge, without any parapet, spanning the perpendicular chasm, so that passengers, on emerging, straight from the darkness on to an unseen bridge, feel as if the train had suddenly leapt into a fathomless abyss.

Canadian Pacific Railway.—A fourth railway traverses North America, along the southern portion of Canada, connecting Montreal, on the St Lawrence, with Vancouver, on the Pacific, opposite Vancouver Island. This railway, accordingly, which passes by Winnipeg, affords direct communication by rail and steamer between the east of Canada and China and Australia. The Canadian Pacific Railway, which was completed in 1885, and opened in 1886, ascends gradually, on the eastern side, to Stephen's Pass on the Rocky Mountains, 5296 feet above the sea, the highest point of the railway, rising 1921 feet in 123 miles. (*See page* 30.) It then descends rapidly on the western slope of the range, where the maximum gradient, of 1 in $22\frac{1}{2}$, occurs, 4 miles long, along a temporary portion of line, for which another route, with the authorised maximum gradient, of 1 in $45\frac{1}{2}$, is to be eventually substituted. From the summit to the western base of the Rocky Mountains, the railway descends 2742 feet in 43 miles, and then traverses the fairly level table land between the Rocky Mountains and the Selkirk range, having an average elevation of about 2500 feet. The railway then rises 1920 feet in 18 miles, to surmount the Selkirk range at an elevation of 4300 feet above sea level, and descends 2830 feet, on the western slope, in 47 miles. The curves have a minimum radius of $8\frac{2}{3}$ chains (190 yards). The Canadian Pacific Railway, accordingly, resembles the Central Pacific Railway in having to surmount two distinct ranges; but the elevation and width of the ranges are considerably less on the Canadian Pacific. Owing, however, to the high latitude of over 50° of this northern line, the summit of the line is only about 1000 feet below the line of perpetual snow. Nevertheless, no protection has been required for the line, in the passage of the Rocky Mountains, against snow drifts and avalanches; but at the crossing of the Selkirks, in consequence of the much greater falls of snow on the Pacific side, it has been found necessary to erect a number of snow sheds at places along the upper part of the eastern slope and more than half way down the western slope. The tunnels on the Rocky Mountain section of the line are quite short.

One feature about all these western lines is the large employment of wood for bridge construction, and trestles for viaducts, owing to timber being so often found on the spot; and these erections, in the older lines, have frequently been replaced in time by more durable and lighter structures in iron, with greater spans. Timber viaducts are also sometimes substituted for embankments, in order to save time in construction, cheapness and rapidity of construction being the main objects sought in these lines which open up undeveloped countries.

Mexican Railway.—The railway from Vera Cruz to the City of Mexico, commenced in 1864 and opened in 1872, rises from the sea level, on the Atlantic coast, to a height of over 8000 feet, in order to reach the high, wide plateau on which the City of Mexico is situated; and this ascent has to be accomplished in the first 107 miles, out of a total length of line of 263 miles. (*See page* 30.) The principal portion of the ascent, amounting to 6400 feet, is effected in the 54 miles between Atoyac and the edge of the plateau, with an average rise of 1 in $44\frac{1}{2}$, and a maximum gradient of 1 in 25. Even to obtain these gradients, the line has to wind about, forming three or four open loops, with curves having a minimum radius of 5 chains (110 yards). As soon as the edge of the plateau is reached, at Boca del Monte, the railway follows a circuitous but tolerably level course, descending a little to Mexico. The steep part of the line is worked by Fairlie engines (*page* 56), which type was first used on the Festiniog Railway, with a 2-foot gauge. This line ascends to about the same elevation as the Central Pacific Railway; but though the mountainous portion of the line is a good deal shorter, it has both steeper gradients and sharper curves than the Central Pacific.

RAILWAYS ACROSS THE ANDES.

Peruvian Railways.—Though railway enterprise might appear to have reached its limit in traversing the Rocky Mountains, and in reaching an altitude of 10,852 feet at the Marshall Pass, still more formidable obstacles have been surmounted and greater elevations attained in ascending the Peruvian Andes. The Andes form a continuous mountain chain along the western side of South America, as the Rocky Mountains do in North America; but they rise higher, and approach in places nearer to the coast. One railway connects Mollendo, a port on the Pacific, with Arequipa, situated 7560 feet above sea level; it is 107 miles in length, and was completed in 1870. This railway has been prolonged from Arequipa, up the Andes, to Puno, on the shore of Lake Titicaca, on the other side of a ridge which it crosses, in a shallow cutting, at an elevation of 14,660 feet above the sea. (*See page* 30.) The line was completed as far as Puno in 1874, situated at an altitude of about 12,000 feet above sea level, and is to be prolonged to Cuzco, to the north-west of Puno. For a portion of the ascent, the gradient is 1 in 25, by means of which the line rises about 4500 feet. Since the construction of the railway steamers have been placed on Lake Titicaca, and thus place Bolivia in communication with this line and with the Pacific Ocean.

Another still bolder railway was commenced, in 1870, by an American engineer, for connecting Lima, the capital, with Oroya, situated on the eastern slope of the Andes, at an elevation of 12,178 feet. It starts from Callao, the port of Lima; and for the first $33\frac{1}{2}$ miles, up to Chosica, it rises with comparatively moderate gradients, not exceeding 1 in 40, to a height of 2800 feet. (*See page* 30.) After passing Chosica, the country becomes more rugged, and the line rises with gradients of 1 in 25, following the winding course of the gorge through which the Rimac river flows, which is crossed by the Capiche bridge. The increasing rise of the valley of the Rimac, on reaching San Bartolomé, 46¾ miles from the coast, at an altitude of 4900 feet, has necessitated the introduction of switchbacks in places between this point and the summit, together with long loops, making the railway retrace its steps at a higher level, combined with curves having a minimum radius of 6 chains (132 yards), in order not to exceed the maximum gradient of 1 in 25. A switchback is a sort of siding, up to which

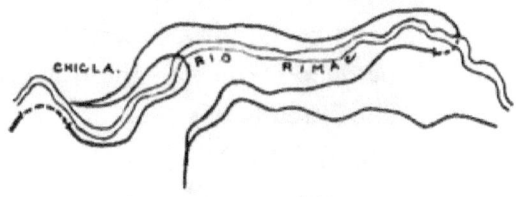

OROYA RAILWAY, PERU.
SWITCHBACKS AND LOOPS

SCALE 40000

the train is drawn; and the train is then shunted in the reverse direction, and pushed by the engine, which is now at the back of the train, up a line following a higher slope; and thus, by a series of zigzags, the train rises up the steep mountain sides to a higher elevation. (*See diagram.*) After passing San Bartolomé the switchbacks begin, and the line crosses and recrosses the river Seco; and after passing through two tunnels, it crosses a deep gorge on the Verrugas Viaduct, a light-looking structure, 573 feet long, supported on three piers, at a maximum height of over 250 feet above the bottom of the ravine. The railway then winds about, with gradients of 1 in 25, passing through tunnels whose entrances may be descried at different altitudes up the steep slope; and it then passes across the Challapa gorge, on a bridge raised 160 feet above the bottom of the gorge. Matucana, which is reached at $62\frac{1}{4}$ miles from the coast, is only 27 miles from the summit of the railway in a direct line; but a devious course of $42\frac{1}{4}$ miles has to be traversed to overcome the difficulties of the ascent, without exceeding the gradient of 1 in 25. At this part of the line, about half way up the ascent, the cliffs encountered on the route are so precipitous that workmen had to be lowered by ropes from ledge to ledge, cut out of the side of the cliff, till the railway level was reached. The engineers, also, had to be conveyed from one side of the deep ravines to the other, in slings hung to a wire cable stretched across at the top. In a distance of 15 miles, between Tambo de Viso and Anchi, the railway passes through twenty-two tunnels; and, between Anchi and San Mateo, the Los Infernillos cañon has to be crossed where the river Rimac passes between cliffs of red porphyry rising perpendicularly to a height of 1500 feet. The railway, on emerging from a tunnel through one of the cliffs, traverses a bridge spanning the chasm at a height of 165 feet above the bed of the river, and then enters a tunnel, through the opposite cliff, resembling the crossing of a cañon on the Denver and Rio Grande Railway previously alluded to. The loops and zigzags are sometimes so frequent that, at Chicla, five parallel lines, three on one side and two on the other side of the gorge, are visible (*see diagram, page* 48), rising one above the other to a considerable height; whilst the greatest horizontal distance between them does not exceed 500 feet. The head of the Rimac gorge is surrounded by such precipitous cliffs that the railway has to traverse them by means of seven tunnels, and then proceeds, through a desolate snow-clad region, to the summit tunnel, 3847 feet in length, which pierces a a narrow ridge. The summit level of the railway is 15,645 feet above the sea, higher than Monte Rosa or the Matterhorn, and only 136 feet lower than the top of Mont Blanc, and about three and a half times the height of the Brenner Railway. Moreover, this elevation has been attained in $104\frac{1}{2}$ miles from the coast, an ascent of 12,845 feet having been accomplished in a distance of 71 miles, giving an average rise of 1 in 29. The descent to Oroya, on the other side of the ridge, is only 3467 feet in a distance of $31\frac{1}{2}$ miles; and the total length of the line is 136 miles. As Oroya is situated in the valley of the Huallaga, a tributary of the Amazon, on which steamers run from the Peruvian ports on its banks to the Brazilian port of Tabatinga on the Amazon, this railway opens up a means of communication between the Pacific and Brazil. This railway is quite unique in the rugged character of the district traversed, the difficulties encountered, the length of steep gradients, and the great elevation attained; and it furnishes the most remarkable example of railway construction in the world. (*See page* 54 *for cost.*)

Gradients, in proportion to their steepness, limit the weight of the train that a locomotive can draw up them; and as sharp curves have a similar influence, the steepest gradient and sharpest curve on a line should not be combined if possible. Steep gradients, however, involve less cost in working when they are concentrated in one part of a line than when they are scattered, for an auxiliary engine can be employed at that part. When two or three heavy gradients occur at different places on a line, the cost of working the whole line may have to be increased to provide for these proportionately short pieces of line, and in such cases it is more economical to make a détour in substitution for the shorter and steeper line. Moreover, on mountain lines, it is preferable to reduce the cost of the works by sharpening the curves, rather than by increasing the gradient beyond the limit adopted on other portions of the line.

The western part of South America offers the greatest difficulties in construction of any country hitherto penetrated by railways; whilst the central Pampas adjoining it, with immense flat plains, affords remarkable facilities for railway extension.

Railway Progress.—Though the extension of railways in Great Britain, the birthplace of the railway system, has become smaller in the last few years, railways are rapidly progressing in other parts of the world. Thus, in Europe, the length of railways has increased from 96,170 miles in 1877 to 129,126 miles in 1887, of which increase only 2501 miles belonged to the United Kingdom. In Asia, the increase was from 7910 miles in 1877 to 16,714 miles in 1887, of which 6757 miles were due to the development of railways in British India. In Africa, the railways increased in length from 1868 miles in 1877 to 4794 miles in 1887, the greater portion of the increase having occurred in the Cape Colony, and Algeria and Tunis, which nearly quadrupled their mileage in this period. In America, the railway mileage increased from 91,910 miles in 1877 to 180,398 miles in 1887, in which, of course, the United States are far ahead of all the other countries put together, though Canada, Mexico, Brazil, and the Argentine Republic show a larger proportionate increase in this period. The railways in Australasia, during the same period, increased from 3471 miles to 9505 miles. The total railway mileage in the world, during these ten years, increased from 201,329 miles to 340,539 miles, or an increase of about sixty-nine per cent. The greatest development of railways has occurred in the United States, where the number of miles open for traffic rose from 79,088 miles in 1877 to 149,281 miles in 1887, the greatest increase in any one year, amounting to 12,872 miles, having taken place in 1887. The increase in 1888 was 6801 miles, raising the total mileage of railways in the United States, at the end of 1888, to 156,082 miles, nearly half of the entire mileage of railways in the world; and it was doubled in the twelve years from 1876 to 1888. The number of passengers carried by railway in the United States has risen from 289,000,000 in 1882 to 451,000,000 in 1888, these numbers being exclusive of the very numerous passengers on the New York Elevated Railway. (*See page* 22.)

The great lines crossing North America from east to west have a very considerable unbroken length; for the Canadian Pacific Railway, from Montreal to Vancouver, traverses 2500 miles, eight times the distance by rail between London and Penzance; and the Union Pacific Railway, from New York to San Francisco, runs across about 3200 miles of country, or more than four times the distance from London to Thurso, the most northern station in Scotland. The average speed of travelling from New York to San Francisco is about 22 miles an hour, including stoppages; and the time occupied in the transit across America is six days and nights. A large number of miles, also, of railway, including their own system and other lines, are worked over by some of the large railway companies in the United States, for 6288 miles are worked by the Union Pacific Railway Company, and 5932 miles by the Southern Pacific.

Since 1850 the growth of the railway system has been enormous, though at that period a quarter of a century had elapsed since its inauguration by the opening of the Manchester and Liverpool Railway. The total number of miles of railway opened for traffic throughout the world was only 24,015 miles in 1850, or about double the mileage which the United States alone added to their railway system in 1887. This mileage had risen in 1860 to 67,002 miles; in 1870 to 129,874 miles, only slightly in excess of the mileage reached by Europe about seventeen years later; and in 1880 to 229,635 miles. Assuming the average rate of yearly increase between 1880 and 1887 to have been maintained, the total length of railways in the world will have reached about 388,000 miles at the close of 1890, making a total extension of 364,000 miles of railways in the last forty years. Statistics, however, show what vast areas are still devoid of railway accommodation in Asia, Africa, South America, and Australasia; and of all the countries in the world, China, with its vast extent and teeming population, and with only 28 miles of railway open in 1887, should, as soon as the prejudices of its rulers have been removed, take the lead in the future development of railways.

CHAPTER III.

NARROW GAUGE, FELL, RIGI, PILATUS AND ABT MOUNTAIN RAILWAYS.

RAILWAYS in mountainous districts are very costly in construction, even when they do not involve the making of the long tunnels at the summit, for which the Alpine railways are celebrated. Taking, for instance, the Peruvian railways described in the last chapter, where there are no long tunnels, and the expenditure has been kept down, as far as practicable in such rugged country, by very steep gradients and sharp curves, the line from Arequipa to Puno cost £18,730 per mile, and the line from Callao to Oroya cost £31,960 per mile. Accordingly, engineers have endeavoured to devise expedients for reducing the cost of construction, so as to extend railways to places out of the through lines of communication, or to parts where the prospects of traffic do not warrant a large expenditure.

Narrow Gauge Railways.—A smaller distance between the rails than the standard gauge of 4 feet 8½ inches has been adopted in several cases, with the object of reducing the first cost; and this system has received perhaps its largest development in the Denver and Rio Grande Railway and its branches, which wind through the gorges of the Rocky Mountains in Colorado. This railway system was laid to a gauge of 3 feet between the rails, and it extends over a length of 1467 miles. This arrangement, however, has not been followed on more recent lines in the United States. The Peruvian railways are laid to the standard gauge; and already 403 miles of the Denver and Rio Grande lines have been provided with a third rail outside, to adapt them to the standard gauge, thus widening the gauge to 4 feet 8½ inches, just as the Great Western Railway 7-foot gauge has been narrowed by a third rail, with the same object. The promoters of the earlier narrow gauge lines in India, Australia, and elsewhere, aimed at reducing the cost of construction by diminishing the width of the line, and thus reducing the quantity of land required, and the amount of earthwork in the cuttings and embankments, and also by enabling sharper curves to be adopted, owing to the smaller difference in curvature of the two rails when placed closer together.

A tramway, having a width of only 2 feet between the rails, was constructed as early as 1832, for the purpose of conveying slates from the quarries at Festiniog to Portmadoc for shipment. The line has a length of 13¼ miles, with a difference in level between the termini of 700 feet; and for 12¼ miles of this distance the average gradient descending to Portmadoc is 1 in 92, the steepest gradient on the line being 1 in 60¾. The line is very much curved, winding round the hills, and the radii of the curves are generally 8 to 7 chains (176 to 154 yards); but they descend in places to 6, 5, 4, and 3 chains, and occasionally even to 1¾ chains (27½ yards). Till 1863, the line was only used as a tram road; and the little trucks, specially designed for carrying slates, went loaded down the continuous incline by their own weight, and the empty trucks were hauled up the ascending gradients by horses. Locomotives were introduced for the first time in 1863; and in 1865 the railway was opened as a passenger line. The trains are drawn up to Festiniog by locomotives, and descend to Portmadoc by gravity. The traction up the long incline is satisfactorily effected by duplex bogie locomotives, introduced in 1869, having two engines, united by a tender common to the two, and hinged at the centre. These bogie engines, having two pairs of coupled driving-wheels each, called Fairlie engines after the name of their designer, can draw up a load of 150 tons, and pass easily round the sharp curves of the line. This miniature railway has worked very satisfactorily since the introduction of locomotives on it; and, in addition to goods, it conveyed 139,810 passengers in 1889. Though the gradients of the Festiniog Railway were considered steep at the period of its inauguration as a passenger line, steeper gradients are often adopted on main lines in the present day; and its ascending gradient, $12\frac{1}{4}$ miles long, has been far surpassed in America, both in the steepness of the maximum gradient and in the length of the incline, on lines of the ordinary gauge, as described in the last chapter. The curves on this line are unprecedentedly sharp, but their employment enabled the cost of construction to be considerably reduced in the hilly country traversed.

The powers of the locomotive have to be considered in settling the maximum gradient and sharpest curve that may be adopted. The tractive force of a locomotive depends on the adherence of the driving-wheels to the rails, which is governed by the weight on the driving-wheels. This adherence may be augmented by increasing the weight of the engine, and by throwing as much of this weight as practicable on to the driving-wheels. The whole of the weight of the locomotive may be utilised by coupling all its wheels together by means of a connecting rod on each side, and thus converting them all into driving-wheels; but this, by rigidly connecting all the wheels together, and, when there are three or more pairs of wheels, placing a longer distance between the front and hind wheels, which is termed the wheel-base, renders the locomotive less able to travel round curves. When, therefore, steep gradients are combined with sharp curves, a large rigid wheel-base, resulting from coupling three or more pairs of wheels together, to increase the adherence on the rails, is inadmissible, especially where the gauge is not narrow, for a long rigid rectangular frame cannot travel easily round a sharp curve. This result is obviated in some cases by only coupling two pairs of large wheels close together, so placed as to carry the main weight of the engine, and putting a bogie frame on two pairs of small wheels at the extreme front, so as to give stability and freedom of movement without taking off any large proportion of weight from the driving-wheels. The total weight, however, of the engines is utilised in the Fairlie system, by coupling the two pairs of wheels under each engine; whilst the central pivot, making the two engines bogies, enables the locomotive to run easily round very sharp curves, though retaining the stability of a long wheel-base. Thus the wheel-base of the coupled wheels of each half of the Fairlie duplex locomotive, introduced on the Festiniog Railway, was only 5 feet; whereas the actual wheel-base of the combined locomotive, or between the extreme wheels of the two halves, was 19 feet. The utilisation of the whole of the comparatively small weight of $19\frac{1}{2}$ tons was very important; whilst the duplex system of bogie engines afforded great stability, and yet allowed the locomotive to travel round experimental curves of only 50 feet radius. The same type of locomotive has been employed in Sweden; and a Fairlie locomotive was constructed for the Central Pacific Railway, at the time of its opening, to draw trains up the long and steep inclines of the Sierra Nevada. As, however, the gradients are steeper and much longer on this line than on the Festiniog line, whilst the curves are much easier, each half of the duplex locomotive was provided with three pairs of wheels coupled, $3\frac{1}{2}$ feet in diameter; and the total weight of the locomotive was 54 tons. As already mentioned in the last chapter, Fairlie engines are employed on the steep portion of the line from Vera Cruz to Mexico, where the gradients reach 1 in 25, and the curves 5 chains (110 yards) radius, for which they are specially well suited; and the same type of locomotive is used on the Iquique Railway in Southern Peru, which rises to 3067 feet above sea level in the first 19 miles, on its way to the nitrate of soda mines, with a maximum gradient of 1 in 25, and curves of from 15 to 5 chains (330 to 110 yards) radius.

Several pioneer lines in Canada, the Cape Colony, Australia, New Zealand, Tasmania, and Japan have been laid to a $3\frac{1}{2}$-foot gauge, and some branch lines in India, Brazil, and the Argentine Republic to a metre ($3\frac{1}{4}$ feet) gauge, with the object of reducing the cost of construction. The general opinion, however, amongst engineers is that, in most cases, the saving in expense of construction is more than counterbalanced by the inconveniences and cost of a break of gauge, involving the transhipment of passengers and goods, and two classes of rolling stock; and in the United States uniformity of gauge is being gradually attained. Some narrow gauge railways, indeed, in Mexico have been constructed so as to be easily converted into lines of ordinary gauge as soon as the traffic shall have adequately developed. Moreover, the superiority of the narrow gauge over the standard gauge, in suitability for sharp curves, has been to a great extent eliminated by the adoption of the bogie system, which, by introducing a pair of pivoted bogie trucks under each carriage, enables the whole train to run without danger or jar round most curves. Although no engineer has ventured to introduce, on railways of the ordinary 4 feet $8\frac{1}{2}$ inches gauge, as sharp curves as those successfully employed in the Festiniog line, with its 2-foot gauge, the most formidable obstacles have been surmounted on the Oroya line with curves of 5 chains (110 yards) radius. The admissibility of curves of 5 chains (110 yards) radius on lines of the standard gauge has been amply proved by their insertion in places on the Ceylon Government railways, of which the gauge is $5\frac{1}{2}$ feet, like the main lines of India. Accordingly, though narrow gauges have been advantageously used for some mountain railways and pioneer lines, with the object of diminishing the cost of construction, they do not appear likely to be extensively adopted in the future, except in places removed from contact with railways of the ordinary gauge, or under special conditions.

Fell Railways.—The steepest gradient hitherto considered surmountable by ordinary locomotives, drawing a regular train, is 1 in 25, which has only been employed in the exceptional instances of the Mexican and Peruvian railways. When, however, the slow progress of the Mont Cenis tunnel, by hand labour, for the first three or four years, seemed likely to postpone for several years the opening of the Mont Cenis Railway, Mr Fell proposed to complete the gap in the railway communication, of 48 miles, between St Michel and Susa, by constructing a line suitable for a special form of locomotive along the Mont Cenis road. The system consisted of an ordinary double-headed rail laid horizontally between the two rails, in the centre of the line of way, and at a higher level, gripped by horizontal wheels on each side, introduced underneath the locomotive. By gripping this central rail, the locomotive obtained additional adherence for ascending the steep gradients of the highroad over the Mont Cenis Pass, and brake power for the descent, and also security against running off the line in going round the sharp curves of the road. The railway was commenced in 1866, and opened for traffic in 1868; it followed the outer side of the Mont Cenis road, except where diversions became necessary to secure a more uniform gradient, or to avoid villages. The railway was laid to a gauge of 3 feet $7\frac{3}{8}$ inches, with a maximum gradient of 1 in 12, and curves having a minimum radius of 2 chains (44 yards). The rise from St Michel, on the French side, to the summit is about 4600 feet; the summit of the pass is 6772 feet above sea level; and the descent to Susa, on the Italian side, is about 5300 feet. The slope on the Italian side is considerably steeper than on the French side. The central rail was laid on all gradients steeper than 1 in 25, and was raised $7\frac{1}{2}$ inches above the surface of the ordinary rails. Though following the steep inclines and sharp turns of an Alpine mountain road, the trains ran with remarkable ease and safety. The trains performed the journey in six hours shorter time than the diligences, which enabled an accelerated mail service to India, *via* Brindisi, to be started. Trains weighing 36 tons were drawn up the line; and 28,000 passengers travelled by it in the course of a year. Difficulties were naturally experienced in keeping the line free from snow, though nine miles of covered way were constructed where the line was most exposed to snow-drifts, or liable to avalanches; but the trains were run with very few interruptions, till the line had to be closed on the opening of the tunnel line in September 1871.

A more permanent line, on the same system, has been constructed on an extension of the Cantagallo Railway in Brazil, which rises 3000 feet in about 10 miles, for crossing the Serra, with gradients of 1 in 20 to 1 in 12; and it winds round the projecting spurs, with curves of from 2 to 5 chains (44 to 110 yards) radius. After surmounting the ridge, it descends with easier gradients to Nova Friburgo. The gauge of this line is 3 feet $7\frac{3}{8}$ inches, like the temporary Mont Cenis mountain line. Fell locomotives carried on the traffic up the incline satisfactorily for some years, since about 1872; but, in the last two or three years, Baldwin locomotives, from Philadelphia, have been introduced, which, weighing 40 tons, and having eight wheels coupled, can draw a load of 38 tons up the incline of 1 in 12 at the rate of 8 miles an hour. The Fell system is undoubtedly better than the ordinary locomotive for drawing trains up steep inclines with sharp curves; but when the steep incline forms only a small part of the whole line, the employment of ordinary heavy locomotives capable of making the ascent enables other types of engines to be dispensed with. The Fairlie locomotive, however, has proved superior to the Baldwin locomotive for drawing trains up the long gradients of 1 in 25 of the Mexican Railway.

Fell locomotives have been running for over ten years on the Wellington and Featherstone Railway in New Zealand, where there is a gradient of 1 in 15 for a length of about $2\frac{1}{2}$ miles. The Rimutaka range stretches across the route of the railway, and the lowest point for crossing it is over the Rochfort saddle, 1448 feet above sea level. The ascent of the range from the Wellington side has been effected with a maximum gradient of 1 in 35; but the descent, on the opposite slope, is so steep that a continuous gradient, of 1 in 15, was resorted to in order to keep the works within reasonable limits; and the central rail system was adopted for conducting the traffic over it, with one, two, or three engines, according to the load. A tunnel of less than half-a-mile, piercing the highest part of the ridge, reduced the summit level of the railway to 1141 feet above sea level, 307 feet below the top of the ridge. The gauge of the line is $3\frac{1}{2}$ feet, and the sharpest curves have a radius of 5 chains (110 yards).

The Rigi Railways.—It has been seen that the central rail system has enabled gradients of 1 in 12 to be surmounted without difficulty, by special locomotives, even when combined with sharp curves. When, however, mountain sides had to be scaled, a different system was needed. The first idea of carrying tourists up a mountain by rail, instead of by road, appears to have been conceived by Mr S. Marsh, in the United States, in 1857, who proposed to make a rack railway for conveying persons to the top of Mount Washington, the highest of the White Mountains, in New Hampshire. Though treated at first as the dream of a madman, the work was eventually carried out between 1867 and 1869. The gradients were limited to a maximum of 1 in 3, and the curves to a minimum radius of about $7\frac{1}{2}$ chains (165 yards); and timber was largely employed in carrying the line across hollows. A similar system, on an improved plan, has been adopted for the construction of railways to the top of the Rigi. This mountain is well known to all travellers in Switzerland visiting Lucerne from the beautiful view obtained from its summit, which is 5906 feet above sea level. The railway was commenced from Vitznau, on the Lake of Lucerne, in 1869; it was opened up to about a mile from the summit in 1871, and completed in 1873. It has a total length of about $4\frac{1}{2}$ miles; and the rise from the Lake of Lucerne is 4472 feet. The engine and carriage run on rails laid to the ordinary gauge; but, unlike the systems previously described, the tractive force is not obtained by adherence to the rails, or by gripping a central rail, but by means of a cog-wheel working in a central rack laid on the incline between the rails. (*See illustration.*) In ascending, the cog-wheel, in revolving, mounts the sort of inclined ladder formed by the rack, and thus draws the engine and vehicle up with it. The line has a gradient of 1 in 4 for about one-third of its length; and the gradient of the remaining portion is never less than 1 in 6, except where nearly level pieces are introduced at the stations. The curves employed have a radius of $8\frac{1}{2}$ chains (187 yards). The rails and rack are laid on a strong framing of cross sleepers, fastened to longitudinal timbers, so as to insure the maintenance of the position of the rack; and the framing is prevented from sliding down hill by being secured at intervals to masonry foundations built into the solid rock. The engine and carriage are controlled, in descending the steep incline, by a powerful brake acting upon the axle of the driving cog-wheel, which, when stopped from revolving, keeps a cog engaged in the rack, and thus arrests the descent; another cog-wheel, also, is placed on the front axle of the engine, which can be prevented from revolving in the same manner as the driving axle; and a sort of air brake can also be supplied to the piston. Accordingly, the carriage, containing accommodation for fifty-four persons, can be pushed up, or led down the mountain sides in perfect safety, at an average rate of about $4\frac{3}{8}$ miles per hour.

Another similar line has since been constructed, starting from Arth, on the Lake of Zug, and rising up the opposite side of the mountain. The maximum gradient on the Arth line is 1 in 5. There are two carriages in each train on this line, capable of holding forty persons each. The view in ascending this slope is not so fine as on the Vitznau line, but the grand panorama bursts with more effect on the traveller on approaching the summit.

A third railway has also been constructed on the Rigi, worked in the ordinary manner, by locomotives suited for steep gradients; it traverses the upper part of the mountain from the Kaltbad Hotel, which is at an elevation of 4700 feet, and a little over a mile from the Rigi Kulm, or principal summit, to the Rigi Scheidegg, another summit, 5407 feet above sea level. The line winds about a good deal in contouring the slopes, and has a length of $4\frac{1}{4}$ miles, which is traversed in 25 minutes. This railway is at a higher level than the summit level of the Brenner, the highest of the main Alpine railways, and the Rigi Kulm is 1400 feet higher than the Brenner Railway summit; but

RIGI MOUNTAIN RAILWAY

this does not signify materially in respect of obstruction by snow, as these railways only run during the summer months of the year.

The Pilatus Railway.—A rack railway, with steeper slopes, and attaining a higher level than the Rigi Railway, for the purpose of ascending to the summit of Mont Pilatus, was opened in 1889. The railway starts from Alpnach, on the Lake of Lucerne, and ascends 5363 feet to the summit, 6812 feet above sea level. The total length of the line in which this ascent is accomplished is only $2\frac{3}{4}$ miles, half of which is straight, and half has curves of 4 to 5 chains (88 to 110 yards) in radius. The inclines of the railway are consequently very steep, the rise averaging rather less than 1 in 3, which is equivalent to a rise of 1 foot for each 3 feet traversed, or nearly the slope of a staircase; and the steepest portions have a rise of 1 in 2. The road, therefore, had to be made very solid, to prevent a chance of its sliding down gradually, and the engine and carriage as light as possible on so steep an incline. The line is laid on iron sleepers, bolted to solid longitudinal masonry walls founded in the solid rock. The two ordinary iron rails on which the carriage runs are laid to a gauge of 2 feet $7\frac{1}{2}$ inches; and the rack rail, with teeth on each side, composed of steel, is placed in the centre between the rails. Masonry bridges carry the line over streams and gorges, and the line traverses seven short tunnels. The engine and carriage have been placed on the same frame, for the sake of lightness, and run on two pairs of wheels; whilst two pairs of horizontal cog-wheels work on each side of the rack. The vehicle has necessarily to be provided with very powerful brakes, to ensure its not breaking away down the steep incline. There are two hand brakes, one of which alone could stop the vehicle in its descent; there is also an atmospheric brake, acting on the piston, as on the Rigi Railway; and there is also an automatic brake, in reserve, which comes into action directly the downward speed exceeds about 3 miles an hour, so that the safety of the vehicle is secured as far as possible. Seats are provided for thirty-two persons, which are jointed so as to adjust themselves to changes of incline. The line was carried out in sections, commencing at the base, whereby the security of the line could be tested, and materials conveyed by the completed line for the construction of the next length higher up. The vehicle is provided with two clips, encircling the head of each rail, so as to prevent its being blown off the road by the vehement storms which occasionally burst upon the mountain. The surmounting of inclines of 1 in 2 by a self-propelling carriage is a very remarkable feat, and has not been surpassed elsewhere, though the load carried is very small compared to ordinary trains.

A similar rack railway has recently been constructed from Capo di Lago, on the St Gothard Railway, at the Italian end of Lake Lugano, to the summit of Monte Generoso, 5561 feet above sea level. The rise of 4620 feet is accomplished by a length of line of about 5 miles, with gradients, in this case, of only 1 in $4\frac{1}{2}$ to 1 in 5. The sharpest curves have a radius of 3 chains (66 yards), and the gauge of the railway is 2 feet $7\frac{1}{2}$ inches. The ascent is accomplished in about an hour; and magnificent views of the Alps, the Italian lakes, and the plains of Lombardy are obtained from the summit.

Abt Rack System for Mountain Railways.—The rack system has not been confined to tourist lines, but has also been employed for ascending specially steep inclines on ordinary railways, or for affording railway accommodation to towns occupying elevated positions. Thus the Abt system, combining traction by adhesion with traction by a rack and pinion, has been employed for working the traffic on the Hartz Mountain Railway, where the steepest gradients are 1 in 16; and the rack system has been adopted for taking trains up a gradient of 1 in 12, about a mile and a half in length, on the Puerto Cabello and Valencia Railway of Venezuela. The railway, also, from Visp to Zermatt, about $22\frac{1}{2}$ miles long, having a $3\frac{1}{4}$ feet gauge, gradients of 1 in $8\frac{1}{3}$, and curves of 5 chains (110 yards), and the railway from Eisenerz to Vordenberg in Styria, $12\frac{1}{2}$ miles long, of ordinary gauge, with gradients of 1 in 14, and curves of 9 chains (198 yards) radius, are constructed with the addition of a rack to aid the tractive force of adhesion at the steep inclines. The rack principle is specially advantageous for enabling trains to ascend short steep inclines, situated at various places on a railway, which could not be surmounted with considerable loads by adhesion alone; and such inclines, being scattered about the railway, would not be well adapted for the employment of the older system of rope traction for steep inclines, by means of a stationary engine, so much used in mines, and adopted with advantage for the haulage of tramcars up steep ascents, notably at San Francisco. There would be the same advantage in the use of the central rail system, except that the machinery of the locomotive for gripping the central rail is more complicated than the arrangements for working in a rack; and locomotives of this type have not hitherto been made equally serviceable for ordinary work.

An interesting example of the application of the rack system to occasional steep inclines is furnished by the Transandine Railway, in course of construction, for connecting Buenos Ayres on the Atlantic with Valparaiso on the Pacific, which has to traverse the Chilian Andes at an elevation of 10,466 feet above sea level, in a summit tunnel $3\frac{1}{4}$ miles long. The lowest ridge of the Andes in these parts rises 12,467 feet above the sea; and though 2000 feet of this rise are saved by the summit tunnel, it has been found necessary, for saving expense and avoiding avalanches, to introduce several inclines of 1 in $12\frac{1}{2}$ on the mountain section of the railway between Mendoza in the Argentine Republic and Santa Rosa in Chili, a distance of 149 miles. Abt locomotives will work in a rack on these steep inclines which will extend over 17 miles of the line, there being one continuous steep incline 10 miles long on the Chilian slope, and the other 7 miles of inclines distributed. The length of the completed railway from Buenos Ayres to Mendoza is 648 miles, laid to a gauge of $5\frac{1}{2}$ feet; and of the railway from Valparaiso to Santa Rosa, on the Pacific side, 53 miles, having a gauge of 4 feet $8\frac{1}{2}$ inches. The mountain section of the railway is to have a gauge of $3\frac{1}{4}$ feet; the first 84 miles from Mendoza has gradients not exceeding 1 in 40, and only the western 65 miles will require Abt locomotives. The line, accordingly, from ocean to ocean, will be 850 miles long, very much shorter than the Pacific lines of North America, but it will have three different gauges.

The problem of cheaply and efficiently working ordinary railway traffic up steep inclines is of great importance for the future development of railways. If an economical method of hauling trains up occasional steep inclines can be attained by the Abt system, or any other, more especially with the same engine employed along the flatter parts of the line, steep inclines could be introduced without hesitation wherever abrupt changes of level in a country render them expedient, and a great reduction in the cost of construction of a railway through mountainous districts would be thereby secured.

CHAPTER IV.

PIERCING THE ALPS.

THE construction of tunnels is generally a slow and somewhat uncertain kind of work. The exact nature of the material to be traversed at some distance from the surface is imperfectly known; faults may be encountered, slips may occur, and springs may burst forth. One of the earliest tunnels on record is said to have been made in 1608, for draining the plateau on which the City of Mexico stands. It passed under the ridge of Nochistengo, for a distance of 6 miles, through a peculiar kind of earthy stratum called tepetate; and it is stated to have been executed in the remarkably short period of eleven months. The conditions must, however, have been exceptionally favourable, if the period given is correct; but the tunnel was destroyed during a flood, and an open cutting, with a maximum depth of 200 feet, was substituted for it, after great labour and the loss of many lives. The first tunnel made in England was the Harecastle Tunnel, for the Trent and Mersey Canal; and eleven years, 1766 to 1777, were employed in its construction, though its length is only 1 mile 5 furlongs. On the introduction, however, of railways, tunnelling became more common and more expeditious; and several railway tunnels have been constructed in England of more than a mile in length. Amongst some of the longest of these are the Box Tunnel, on the Great Western, near Bath, 1 mile

6⅔ furlongs long; the Sevenoaks Tunnel, on the South-Eastern main line, a little over 2 miles long; the Bramhope Tunnel, on the North-Eastern Railway, near Leeds, 2 miles 1 furlong in length; the Woodhead Tunnel, between Manchester and Sheffield, 3 miles long; and the Standege Tunnel, on the London and North-Western Railway, between Manchester and Huddersfield, a little more than 3 miles long. All these tunnels, however, besides being excavated from each extremity, were also approached by vertical shafts sunk from the surface, on the line of the tunnel, down to the level adopted for the railway; and thus it was possible to attack two more faces of the tunnel from each shaft, and thereby greatly expedite the work. On the contrary, when the construction of the Alpine tunnels had to be undertaken, for piercing the steep ridges intervening between the summit levels of the Alpine railways, no shafts were practicable on the high ridges. The tunnels could, therefore, be only driven from each end; and in every case the material to be excavated for the tunnel was composed of the hardest primitive rocks, which had resisted for ages the disintegrating influences of snow, ice, and atmospheric changes.

In designing railways through mountainous regions, it is expedient if possible, with a main line subject to competition, to restrict the open portion of the railway to an altitude where it is not liable to be frequently blocked by snow drifts. This has not been practicable on the North American lines leading to the Pacific Ocean, owing to the great width of the ranges traversed; and the great cost of long tunnels would have prohibited their adoption on the Peruvian railways. On the Alps, however, though the ridges to be traversed were not quite insurmountable, as proved by the temporary working of the Fell system of railway over the Mont Cenis, the heights to be attained would have approached the line of perpetual snow, and therefore it would have been very difficult to keep the railway open in the winter. The increasing steepness, also, of the upper parts of the valleys, would have rendered a very circuitous line and steeper gradients indispensable, together with increasingly heavy works. The ridges, also, separating the valleys on each side, were in places sufficiently reduced in width to suggest the possibility of a tunnel, though exceeding in magnitude any previous works of the kind. Moreover, even a large outlay on a tunnel might not be unwisely undertaken in providing a railway with fair gradients, of sufficiently moderate altitude to be kept open generally in winter without great difficulty, and thus securing the main traffic between Northern Europe and Italy and the East. These are the principles which were kept in view in laying out the Mont Cenis and St Gothard railways; and it is certain that if one of these had been made a circuitous, steep, open line, and the other made in its existing form, the more direct and easier tunnel line, less exposed to delays in winter, would have secured almost the whole of the through traffic. The open portions, indeed, of the Mont Cenis and St Gothard railways, in reaching altitudes on the colder northern slopes of 3793, and 3638 feet respectively above sea level, have approximately attained the limit of tolerable freedom from interruption of traffic amongst those lofty, precipitous, glacial regions, for the lines have occasionally been blocked by snow drifts. One of the advantages of the proposed Simplon Railway is that its open portion, on the northern slope, would only attain an altitude of 2690 feet above sea level, and would therefore be more secure from interruption by snow than the Mont

Cenis or St Gothard lines; whilst this lower altitude could be reached by easier gradients.

Another point of considerable importance, in selecting the route of these Alpine tunnels, is the internal heat that is encountered in rocks lying at a great depth below the surface; for this heat increases in proportion to the depth of the strata below the surface. Accordingly, it is probable that the heat experienced in working at a depth below the surface exceeding 6000 or 7000 feet, together with the confined space in a tunnel, the fumes from blasting, and the difficulty of affording adequate ventilation at a long distance from the outlet, would render it hazardous to attempt driving a tunnel at depths much greater than the limits named.

The Mont Cenis Tunnel.—The site between Fourneaux and Bardonnèche, under the Col de Fréjus, was indicated, as early as 1840, as the most suitable direction for an Alpine tunnel, to afford railway communication between France and Italy. It was not, however, till 1852 that the proposal was seriously entertained; and the works were only actually commenced in 1857. The driving of a tunnel more than seven and a half miles long, without intermediate shafts, through the hardest rocks, composed mainly of calcareous and carboniferous schists, with comparatively small thicknesses of quartz and of limestone, was in 1857 a work without a parallel in the annals of engineering. A somewhat similar undertaking, but of less magnitude, had indeed been previously commenced in the United States; for the Hoosac Tunnel, under the Green Mountains, on the line between Troy and Greenfield, was begun in 1854, to afford Massachusetts railway communication with the west. The Hoosac Tunnel, however, the longest tunnel in the United States, traversing mica schist and micaceous granitic gneiss, has a length of only $4\frac{3}{4}$ miles; it progressed very slowly, from one extremity only, till 1864, and was not finally completed till 1876. Moreover, this tunnel was constructed by the aid of a central shaft, 1028 feet in depth, and two or three minor ones, so that, except with regard to difficulties about funds, it was executed under more favourable conditions than the Mont Cenis Tunnel.

The three long Alpine tunnels, the Mont Cenis, the St Gothard, and the Arlberg, have all been driven in a perfectly straight line between their two extremities, and have been carried out simultaneously from the two ends towards the centre, with rising gradients inwards so as to provide for drainage. A very careful survey had to be made of the district, to fix the precise line of the tunnel, which was marked out along the surface; and observatories were placed on prolongations of the straight line, across the further side of the valleys, opposite each end of the tunnel, by means of which the exact direction was constantly checked as the work progressed. The maintenance of the correct line on each side was most important, as an error in direction would have prevented the meeting of the two headings of the tunnel near the centre, which would have involved great cost and delay in rectifying.

The Mont Cenis Tunnel was commenced at both ends towards the close of 1857; and the work of boring the holes for the blasting charges was carried on by hand till the end of 1860 at the southern heading, and till 1862 at the northern heading, when perforating machinery was introduced.[1] The progress with hand-boring was neces-

---

[1] A "heading" is the advanced gallery or passage which is formed a little in advance of the main excavation of a tunnel, and from which the tunnel is subsequently enlarged to the full size as the work proceeds.

sarily slow, so that the advanced heading had only reached a distance of 793 yards from the Bardonnèche end in 1860, and 1007 yards from the Fourneaux end in 1862, making an average yearly progress of about 440 yards. At this rate, the tunnel would have required about thirty years for its construction; but the introduction of rock drills, worked by compressed air, supplied by air compressors moved by water power at each end of the tunnel, accelerated the progress considerably. The rate of advance differed greatly according to the strata pierced, the least advance during a month with the machines having averaged at one of the faces only 1.17 feet per day when traversing quartz, and the greatest advance, 12.9 feet per day in carbonaceous schist. The average yearly advance after the introduction of the machines was 1286 yards, so that the average rate of progress was nearly trebled by the machines, and more than trebled during the last seven years of the works; the average daily progress throughout was 2.57 yards. The tunnel was enlarged by stages as the work proceeded, from the advanced gallery or heading at the base, $9\frac{1}{2}$ feet wide and $8\frac{1}{2}$ feet high, to the completed tunnel, arched at the top with brickwork and having masonry side walls, and of sufficient size for an up and down line. The advanced heading was driven by boring about eighty holes in the face of the rock, from $2\frac{2}{3}$ feet to $3\frac{1}{4}$ feet deep, by means of seven perforators, which were then filled with gunpowder cartridges, and the rock blasted. As the rock was more homogenous and easier, on the whole, to work along the southern, or Italian portion of the tunnel, the heading on that side was carried on more quickly than on the French side, so that the two headings met at a point 2107 yards nearer the French end than the Italian end. The wall between the two headings was perforated on Christmas

Day 1870, thirteen years and one month from the commencement of the work; and by the following day the aperture was sufficiently enlarged for the tunnel to be traversed from end to end, thus uniting France and Italy through the Alps.

The tunnel proved to be 15 yards longer than calculated from the surveys; and probably the error of 1 foot in level was due to this slight discrepancy in length. The direction of the two headings was perfectly correct, showing with what great care the alignment had been made from the two ends. Though the tunnel was driven in a perfectly straight line, two short curved tunnels were made subsequently, near each end, to connect the railway in the tunnel with the approach railways on each side, which have increased the actual length of the tunnel through which the trains run to very nearly 8 miles. From Fourneaux the line rises, with a gradient of 1 in $43\frac{1}{2}$, towards the centre of the tunnel, to make up for the lower level of the Fourneaux end; and it falls from the summit level towards Bardonnèche just sufficiently to provide for the efflux of the water dripping into the tunnel. Some attempt has been made to improve the ventilation of the tunnel by supplying compressed air, through an 8-inch pipe, from the Bardonnèche end, which can be let out by means of cocks where required, and by drawing out foul air by means of exhausters at the Fourneaux end. The main ventilation, however, is due to the natural current of air generally found in the tunnel, resulting partly from differences in atmosphere pressure at the two ends, subject frequently, from their positions, to different meteorological conditions, partly from the greater heat towards the centre of the tunnel tending to induce a draught, and sometimes from wind.

The highest temperature observed in the Italian portion of the tunnel, during construction, was 85° near the centre of the tunnel. This is a much lower temperature than would result from the increase in temperature of 1° for each 50 to 60 feet in depth below sea level, which has been observed in some places, considering that the highest part of the mountain directly over the tunnel is 5076 feet above the rail level. This observed increase in temperature, however, is due to the gradual approach towards the molten mass forming the central core of the earth; whilst the rocks pierced by the Mont Cenis Tunnel are further removed from this heated mass than at the sea level, though the great depth below the surface has caused them to retain to some extent their original internal heat. The actual opening of the Mont Cenis Railway for traffic took place towards the close of 1871, about a year after the headings of the tunnel were joined.

The St Gothard Tunnel.—Within a year of the completion of the Mont Cenis Railway, a still more formidable enterprise was undertaken, consisting, in addition to the heavy approach railways, of a tunnel 9¼ miles in length, and at a still greater depth below the surface than the Mont Cenis Tunnel, namely 5733 feet from the level of rails to the highest point of the ridge immediately above the tunnel. The driving of the tunnel from each end was commenced in September 1872; and the boring of the holes for blasting was begun by hand till the machines could be got ready. The machine drills were set to work at the northern end in April 1873, and at the southern end in July 1873. The advanced headings were, in this case, carried out along the top of the tunnel; and the enlargements were made first sideways, and then downwards. The greatest advance at both ends in a month was 53 yards by hand labour, and 304 yards with the machines. The rock drills of improved types were driven, as at Mont Cenis, by compressed air, obtained by aid of water power at each end of the tunnel. The advanced heading was about 8 feet $2\frac{1}{2}$ inches square; and its face was bored with about twenty-six holes, from $3\frac{2}{3}$ to 4 feet in depth, which were charged with dynamite cartridges, and exploded in three operations, from the centre outwards. The strata traversed consisted mainly of granite, schist and gneiss, with veins of other rocks intervening in places. The nature of the strata encountered varied, accordingly, somewhat frequently, and also their condition; and the chief difficulty in boring was experienced where a variation in condition caused the drill to diverge sideways to the softest rock, and thus jam itself in the hole. The headings were joined on the 29th of February 1880, being seven years and five months from the commencement, or $5\frac{2}{3}$ years less time than the same work occupied at the Mont Cenis Tunnel, though the St Gothard Tunnel is $1\frac{2}{3}$ miles longer than the other. The average daily advance of the two headings was 6 yards, in place of the $2\frac{1}{2}$ yards at the Mont Cenis, showing how much the more general adoption of drilling machinery, and its improvements, had expedited the work. The driving of the advanced heading was more rapid on the northern side, so that the junction of the headings was effected 613 yards nearer the southern end than the northern. A considerable amount of water came into the tunnel, when fissures were traversed, during the progress of the works, its influx being favoured by the nearly vertical dip of the strata; whereas very little water was met with in the Mont Cenis Tunnel.

The St Gothard Tunnel was found to be 8⅓ yards shorter than anticipated from the preliminary surveys. The centre lines of the northern and southern sections of the tunnel, though prolonged for over 4 miles from each extremity, differed only 13 inches in direction at their junction; whilst the error in level was only 2 inches, exemplifying a second time the great accuracy which can be attained in these long underground operations. As the difference in level of the extremities of the approach railways on each side is only 118 feet, it was quite easy to allow for this by a gentle rising gradient from Goeschenen to the summit level near the centre of the tunnel, whilst providing a sufficient fall from the summit to Airolo for drainage. Owing to slight modifications of the tunnel at each end, to facilitate the connections with the approach railways, the actual length of the tunnel traversed by trains is 9⅓ miles. Though the headings were joined early in 1880, the tunnel was not actually completed and ready for traffic till the beginning of 1882, as a longer interval was required between the driving of the top heading and the completion of the enlargement to the full-sized tunnel, than with the bottom heading adopted in the Mont Cenis Tunnel.

The temperature of the rock near the centre of the tunnel, before the junction of the headings, was naturally greater than at the Mont Cenis, owing to the greater distance from the surface, combined with a lower summit level, the highest temperature observed having reached $87\frac{1}{2}°$. Since, however, the opening of a free passage for the air from end to end, the temperature fell as much as $12°$ in $2\frac{1}{3}$ years. The high temperature experienced during construction was very trying to the workmen, in a damp atmosphere, and with inadequate ventilation; though the ventilation in the headings was gradually improved by introducing a better supply of air from the air compressors, and by using compressed air engines for removing the excavated rock, which furnished fresh air in place of the oppressive smoke of ordinary locomotives. The general ventilation of the tunnel is mainly dependent on the current produced by differences of atmospheric pressure at the two ends; though when this fails, some fresh air may be obtained by workmen in the tunnel from a pipe, laid along the tunnel, filled with compressed air.

The St Gothard Tunnel was not only executed more rapidly than the Mont Cenis Tunnel, but also, by help of the experience gained in the earlier work, it cost only £142 per lineal yard, instead of the £224 per lineal yard paid for the Mont Cenis Tunnel.

The Arlberg Tunnel.—A third tunnel has been driven under the Alps at the Arl Mountain, which, though shorter than its predecessors at the Mont Cenis and St Gothard, possesses the interest of greater rapidity in construction, combined with a smaller cost in proportion to its length. This tunnel, driven in a perfectly straight line, is $6\frac{1}{3}$ miles long, and was commenced in July 1880, only five months after the junction of the advanced headings of the St Gothard Tunnel. The boring was effected by hand during the first four months, whilst the drilling machinery was being prepared; and the progress was naturally slow during this period. However, as soon as the machines were set to work, they completed the driving of the headings in the short space of three years; for the headings were joined in November 1883, only $3\frac{1}{3}$ years from the commencement, giving an average rate of progress of nearly 2 miles a year. Similar drills were employed to those used for the tunnelling on the St Gothard Railway; but whilst a percussion drill, worked by compressed air, was employed at the eastern heading, a grinding rotary drill, worked by water pressure, was used at the western heading. The rock traversed by the tunnel is quartzous schist approximating to gneiss, and mica schist, so that the strata somewhat resemble those at the St Gothard. The rate of progress at both headings together averaged a little over 10 feet a day during the three years of work with the machines. The method adopted of driving the advanced heading along the bottom, and then making shafts upwards at intervals, so as to reach the roof and form an upper gallery, which could be advanced in both directions, enabled the enlargement to the full size and the lining of the tunnel to follow close upon the heading.

The railway was given a rising gradient of 1 in 72 in the tunnel from Langen, at the western end, to the summit, to make up for the higher level of St Anton, at the eastern end, and a falling gradient of 1 in 520 from the summit to St Anton, to ensure drainage on that side of the summit. Owing to the shorter length of the tunnel, and the smaller depth below the surface, than in the previous Alpine tunnels, the internal temperature was moderate, the highest temperature of the rock observed being $66\frac{1}{8}°$, so that no serious inconvenience in construction was experienced from this source. The railway was opened for traffic in September 1884, only four years and two months after the commencement of the works. The tunnel cost about £108 per lineal yard, being a considerable reduction on the cost of the St Gothard Tunnel, and less than half the proportionate cost of the Mont Cenis Tunnel, and in fact a rate of cost which has been attained by tunnels of the ordinary kind constructed by the aid of shafts through softer strata.

Proposed Simplon Tunnel.—It is possible that a fourth tunnel may be constructed; for the project of a railway across the Simplon, which was first proposed in 1859, has recently been revived, and has met with a good deal of approval. The route has been carefully surveyed, and the scheme reported on; and the railway, according to the most recent plans, would start from Visp, in the Rhone valley, and terminate at Domo D'Ossola, in Italy, with a total length of only about 30 miles. The gradients would not exceed 1 in 50 on the short north-western slope, and 1 in 40 on the longer south-eastern slope, descending to the plains of Italy; but a tunnel about 10 miles long would be required. This tunnel, laid out so as to form two straight lines, meeting near the centre at an angle, in order to avoid passing under greater mountain heights, would nevertheless be 6895 feet below the surface at the highest point, more than 1000 feet greater depth than the St Gothard. The internal heat would therefore be probably greater, especially as the tunnel would be at a lower level; and this has been estimated at a maximum of 100° to 104° in the central portion, which it is considered might be made bearable for the workmen by special arrangements for ventilation, and for cleansing and cooling the air near the faces of the advanced headings. The summit level of the line inside the tunnel, as designed, would be only 2773 feet above sea level, lower even than the summit of the Semmering Railway, which is the lowest of the existing Alpine lines, and 1720 feet lower than the summit of the Brenner Railway. This lower level would render the Simplon railway easier than either the Mont Cenis or St Gothard lines; and this route would also shorten the distance between Paris and Milan, and between Boulogne and Brindisi. The cost of the long tunnel, which would occupy about one-third of the whole length of line to be constructed, has been estimated at little more per lineal yard than the Arlberg Tunnel, even after making special allowances for ventilation and reduction of any extreme central internal temperature. The only apparent objections that could be raised against this scheme are, the uncertainty as to the heat that may be encountered at a depth below the surface 1160 feet greater than in the St Gothard Tunnel, and at a level 1010 feet nearer sea level, and to that extent nearer to the internal heat of the earth; and the doubt whether the traffic between Europe and Italy would be adequate to provide a reasonable return on the capital cost of another Alpine railway, considering that the Simplon line could only share the traffic at present possessed by the Mont Cenis and St Gothard, offering merely greater facilities to certain districts of north-western Europe. The question of internal heat, however, has received very careful consideration; it was correctly predicted for the St Gothard Tunnel; and it is not regarded by experts as an insuperable objection. As regards cost, it might be worth while for France to subscribe largely to the Simplon Railway, without looking to any direct return, in order to regain some of the trade diverted from her by the St Gothard Railway.

Two other projects for an Alpine railway, to compete with the St Gothard in the interests of France, have been proposed, one under Mont Maudit, of the Mont Blanc range, and the other under the Col de Ferret, near the Great St Bernard Pass. The Mont Blanc scheme, however, connecting Bonneville and Aosta, whilst laid out with easy gradients, and a summit level intermediate between the proposed Simplon and the St Gothard summit levels, would involve a tunnel 11½ miles long, at a depth of 9800 feet below the highest point traversed. The Great St Bernard scheme, going from Martigny to Aosta, would rise, by long, circuitous, and steep approach railways on each side, to a summit level of the great height of over 5300 feet above the sea, 800 feet higher than the Brenner Railway; but the tunnel at the summit would be barely 6 miles long, with a maximum depth below the surface of only 3480 feet. Neither of these schemes compares favourably with the proposed Simplon route; for an excessive heat would probably be experienced in the construction of the long Mont Blanc tunnel, at an unprecedented depth below the highest ridge traversed; and the long, steep approaches of the Great St Bernard scheme, reaching an altitude constantly exposed to snow drifts, would render it unsuitable for a competing line. Moreover, both these lines, though well situated for diverting traffic from the Mont Cenis Railway, would not follow nearly as suitable a direction as the Simplon Railway for competing for the traffic of the St Gothard Railway, which is the main object contemplated in the promotion of another Alpine railway to the west of the St Gothard.

CHAPTER V.

THE DETROIT, HUDSON, MERSEY, AND SEVERN TUNNELS, THE THAMES SUBWAYS, AND THE SARNIA TUNNEL.

THE tunnels under the Alps, described in the last chapter, presented great difficulties on account of the length of the tunnels, the hardness of the rocks pierced, the internal heat encountered, and the deficiency of ventilation. There is, however, another class of tunnels, passing underneath rivers, in the execution of which still greater and more unforeseen difficulties have to be overcome. In the Mont Cenis Tunnel the main obstacles were the hardness of the strata, and the absence of experience in boring machinery; but the progress having been greatly accelerated in the later Alpine tunnel works, there only remain the internal heat and the need of ventilation, impediments which are known and can more or less be provided against. In subaqueous tunnels, on the contrary, though the mere excavation presents little difficulty, the works are constantly liable to an inrush of water from an unknown source, and in an unknown volume, as the headings are pushed forward. It might naturally be supposed that this danger would be threatened from the river water overhead; but except in the case of the Thames Tunnel, which was carried across at only a slight depth below the river bed, and the Hudson River Tunnel, traversing silt, the water has generally come in from land springs, and not from the river.

The earliest example of a tunnel carried under a river was the notable Thames Tunnel, between Rotherhithe and Wapping, regarded at the time of its execution as a marvellous achievement, and remarkable for the difficulties encountered in its construction. The work was commenced in 1825, by sinking a shaft on the Surrey shore, 50 feet in diameter and 80 feet deep, from which the tunnel, 1200 feet long, was driven through a bed of clay, the top of the arch being about 16 feet below the bed of the river. Defects in the upper layer of clay led to the irruption of the river into the tunnel in 1827, when the work had reached 544 feet from the shaft, and again in 1828. These accidents, together with financial difficulties, delayed the completion of the tunnel till 1843, when it was opened for foot passengers. The cost of the tunnel amounted to £1137 per lineal yard, being a much larger cost per unit of length than any of the Alpine tunnels. Though the tunnel was made with a double roadway for vehicles, the necessary approaches were never constructed; and only foot passengers made use of it till the East London Railway purchased it in 1866, for the purpose of forming a connection between the railways north and south of the river at that part.

The serious accidents, the long period occupied in construction, the cost, and the financial results of the Thames Tunnel, offered little more encouragement to schemes of subaqueous tunnels than the unsuccessful attempts previously made to carry out similar works under the Thames by Mr Trevethick, in 1807, at Rotherhithe, and under the Severn at Newnham.

The two tunnels at Chicago, made under the Chicago River, in 1867-71, to afford improved communication across the river, were really constructed in the open air, on the 'cut and cover' principle, by enclosing the site within a cofferdam across one-half of the river at a time. Tunnelling, also, for railways in Japan under rivers whose channels have been gradually raised above the surrounding plains by the silting up of their beds and the raising of embankments on each side against floods, has been carried out by temporary diversions of the river channels. These instances, accordingly, of tunnels under rivers, are not strictly examples of subaqueous tunnelling. The construction, however, of the East London Railway, at a level suitable for passing in the Thames Tunnel under the Thames, necessitated the formation of approach tunnels on each side; and the tunnel on the northern side had to pass under the East Dock of the London Docks. Two tunnels, also, 5 and 7 feet in diameter, were successively made, in 1864-67 and 1872-74, extending 2 miles, and 2 miles 83 yards respectively, from Chicago, through blue clay under Lake Michigan, for the purpose of supplying Chicago with water from the lake, drawn off at a sufficient distance from the town to avoid pollution, through a vertical shaft sunk at the outer extremity of each tunnel. The success of the first of these tunnels led to the construction of a similar tunnel for the water supply of Cleveland, Ohio, extending to a distance of $1\frac{1}{4}$ miles under Lake Erie. This tunnel, commenced in 1869, proved a troublesome work, owing to layers of sand met with in the clay; and, on one occasion, sand and water poured into the heading in such quantities, through a seam, that the end of the heading had to be bricked up and abandoned, and the direction of the tunnel altered. A peculiarity attending these tunnel works was the influx of a natural inflammable gas, which occasionally could be lit at its point of issue with impunity; but this gas sometimes appeared in such quantities that on one occasion some men were suffocated by it, and on another a violent explosion resulted from lighting a match.

Recent subaqueous tunnelling operations have not invariably proved as successful as the above-mentioned lake tunnels; for, out of the five railway tunnels passing under rivers, commenced in the last twenty years, only three have been brought to a successful termination, namely, the Mersey, the Severn, and the St Clair tunnels. The Detroit River Tunnel, and the Hudson River Tunnel both remain submerged, unfinished works; but they illustrate very clearly the difficulties and uncertainties attendant upon tunnels passing under rivers which can neither be partially dammed off nor temporarily diverted. In subaqueous tunnels, in addition to the tunnel itself, exposed during construction, from its low-lying situation, to the inrush of springs, a small drainage tunnel has to be made to remove the water flowing down the descending gradients to the centre of the tunnel; and long approach tunnels have to be constructed at each end, in order to bring the railway up to the surface, from under the centre of the river.

The Detroit River Tunnel.—A tunnel under the Detroit River, flowing from Lake St Clair to Lake Erie, was commenced in 1872, with the object of connecting the Michigan Central Railway with the Great Western Railway of Canada. The total length of the tunnel, as designed, was to be $1\frac{2}{3}$ miles, of which a little over half-a-mile had to be constructed under the river. There was to be a minimum depth of 20 feet of material between the top of the brickwork of the tunnel and the bed of the river, 12 feet of which consisted of stiff clay. It was decided to drive two independent circular tunnels, $18\frac{1}{2}$ feet inside diameter, for the up and down lines; and a drainage tunnel, below the main tunnels, was to be formed right across the river, with the object, not merely of draining the main tunnels, but also of expediting the construction of these tunnels by upward shafts, so as to increase the number of faces from which the tunnels could be advanced. The drainage tunnel was commenced from each bank, on the completion of the shafts, in June 1872. When, however, an advance of 250 feet had been made from the Canadian side, an irruption of sand mixed with water took place, from a seam of sand in the clay, which had been pierced. Though this influx of sand gradually exhausted itself, and was cleared away, other similar irruptions took place, which could only be arrested by erecting bulkheads across the tunnel; and the difficulties and cost became so great, that the work was not carried further than between 300 and 400 feet from the Canadian shore. On the Detroit side, the work was carried out without much difficulty up to 1110 feet from the shore; but from this point, up to 1220 feet from the shore, nearly half way across, the influx of water greatly increased, and though attempts were made to push forward the main tunnel by means of upward shafts, the works were eventually abandoned in 1873.

The Hudson River Tunnel.—New York is separated from the mainland to the west by the Hudson River, so that communication with Jersey City, and the railways going to the west, is effected by ferries. As the river is about a mile in width, and 60 feet deep, and the bed is composed of silt, the erection of a bridge would involve great difficulties and cost. A tunnel was accordingly decided upon, to be carried through the silt by the aid of compressed air, following, as in all subaqueous tunnels, the slope of the river bed, and therefore descending towards the centre, with nowhere less than a depth of 15 feet of silt over the crown of the arch. The work was begun, in 1874, by sinking a shaft on the New Jersey side of the river, 30 feet inside diameter, to a depth of 60 feet; but this preliminary work was stopped for five years, owing to litigation, soon after its commencement. When the sinking of the western shaft was completed, and the bottom concreted, an air-lock was placed near the bottom, and an opening was formed in the side of the shaft, from which a temporary approach to the site of the tunnel was formed by a series of iron rings, so as to get beyond the adjacent silt, disturbed by the sinking of the shaft, before commencing the actual tunnel. The air-lock is an arrangement invariably employed in connection with compressed air, for providing a method of communication between the outer air and the chamber filled with compressed air. It consists of a small airtight room with two doors, placed at the entrance to the compressed air chamber, into which compressed air can be admitted and subsequently let out. To gain admission to the compressed-air chamber, a gang of workmen enter the air-lock by the outer door, which is then closed; and compressed air being then introduced into the air-lock, till the pressure is the same as in the chamber, the inner door can be opened, and the workmen pass into the chamber.[1] A reverse process enables them to return again into the outer air, or in this instance into the shaft of the tunnel. The tunnel was commenced at the end of the connecting chamber by building out segments of iron rings as the excavation in front proceeded,

---

[1] Men can work without injury to health in compressed air, provided they are in a healthy condition, and are temperate; but the work under pressure is more fatiguing than in the open air.

2½ feet long, fastened to the adjacent inner ones, the upper ones being pushed on in advance like a hood, so as to form a roof over the excavations at the face; and the lower ones were then gradually added as the excavation was carried down till the ring was completed, four or five incomplete upper segments being always fixed in advance. When four rings were thus finished, the silt was cleared out of them, and a circular ring of brickwork was built round the inside, thus completing 10 feet in length of the tunnel. The excavation in front was removed in benches or steps, the excavation being carried forward in advance at the top; and the silt and water were prevented coming into the work by the compressed air, which also supported the iron rings against external pressure. Two tunnels were driven parallel to one another, for the two lines of railway, in preference to one large one. The progress, after a short time, averaged nearly 5 feet of completed tunnel per day. The works were lighted by arc electric lights. The northern of the two tunnels had been extended 300 feet from the New Jersey shaft, the south tunnel was in progress, and preparations were being made for putting in the permanent entrance from the shaft to the completed tunnel, in place of the temporary connecting chamber, when, in July 1880, about ten months after the resumption of the work, a leak occurred at the junction of the shaft with the connecting chamber, the water finding a way through the loose filling adjoining the outer sides of the shaft, overlying the silt, which had been drawn downwards with the shaft in its descent. Some of the roof at the junction consequently fell, and jamming the inner door of the air-lock, barred the exit of twenty men in the connecting chamber; and the water rushed in, drowning the entombed men, and, passing through the slightly open inner door of the air-lock, soon filled the shaft, the outer door having been opened by six men in the air-lock to effect their escape. Attempts to pump the water out of the shaft proved unavailing, so a timber caisson, or diving-bell, open at the bottom, and made watertight above with lead and asphalt, was lowered alongside the shaft. The caisson was filled with compressed air, and could be entered from above by two small shafts and air-locks; it was gradually lowered on to the connecting chamber by excavating the material from under its edges. This is the ordinary method of employing compressed air for putting in the foundations of bridge piers or quay walls in rivers, where the water cannot be excluded from the site. The novelty in the work was using compressed air for effecting excavations horizontally for the tunnels. In October, three months after the accident, the caisson reached the connecting chamber, which was then cleared out; the old air-lock in the shaft was reached and put right, and a permanent piece of tunnel was built connecting the shaft with the two single line tunnels. This very difficult piece of work having been successfully completed, the tunnels could be again carried forward As, however, the variable nature of the silt rendered it impossible to carry on the iron rings, forming the outer framework of the tunnel, in a perfectly straight line, an iron pilot tube, about 60 feet long, composed of rings 4 feet long and 6 feet in diameter, built up in ten segments, was advanced about 30 feet in front of the tunnel heading, its rear being supported by the finished work. The rings for the tunnel were then kept in line, as they were built out, by being strutted against this tube with radial braces. The excavated material was conveyed in small trucks to the shore end of the tunnels, where, being tipped into a hole and mixed with water it was ejected through a pipe, by aid of the air pressure, to the surface, and removed. The north tunnel had reached 1550 feet, and the south tunnel 570 feet from the New Jersey side, and the work was proceeding rapidly and satisfactorily, when it had to be stopped, in November 1882, for want of funds.

The work on the New York side of the river was only commenced in July 1881; and profiting by the experience gained on the New Jersey side, a caisson was sunk for a starting point for the two tunnels, in preference to a shaft. The first part of the tunnels on this side had to be driven through gravel and sand which, being much less tenacious than silt, could not be kept in position by compressed air alone. Accordingly, an iron bulkhead, or shield, had to be placed against the face of the heading, being gradually extended from the top downwards as the excavation was carried down, and strongly strutted. The top, sides, and bottom, were lined as before with iron rings, which had to be reduced in width to $1\frac{1}{3}$ feet to diminish the temporarily exposed portion in putting the segments in place. The tunnels were carried forward in lengths of 10 to 12 feet at a time; and as soon as the brickwork was completed, the bulkhead was advanced piecemeal for closing the face of the next length. A blow out, or escape of the air under pressure, took place in August 1882, a plate in the iron bulkhead being forced out, owing to the air finding a vent during the construction of a section of the tunnel of the unusual length of 15 feet. The pressure being thus reduced, the water rushed in, and the workmen escaped by the air-lock. On partially expelling the water by a fresh admission of air, the disturbed plates were replaced, and work resumed. The north tunnel had been carried forward 147 feet from the caisson on the New York side, and the south tunnel 23 feet, when the work was stopped on this side for want of funds, in July 1883. The progress through sand did not exceed 1 foot of completed tunnel per day; but as the sand had been nearly traversed by the north tunnel, the future progress, in silt, should be the same as on the opposite side. The pressure of the air had to be adjusted according to circumstances; for when the pressure was rather too low, the silt at the face became damp, and water leaked in; and if the pressure was too high, the water was forced some way back from the face of the silt, which was then liable to lose consistency, and fall in. It was estimated that, if adequate funds were available, the work could be completed in $2\frac{1}{2}$ years; and operations have been recently resumed in the tunnel, with the help of a shield similar to that adopted for the Thames Subways. (*See page* 107.) Towards the end of 1890, a progress of nearly 50 feet per week was being maintained. The novelty of tunnelling through silt and quicksand, where the depth of water overhead attains 60 feet in places, renders this undertaking peculiarly interesting; the work exhibits a fresh method of employing compressed air; and the boldness of the attempt, almost bordering on the impossible, merits a successful termination.

The Mersey Tunnel.—The estuary of the Mersey, which is very wide between the mouth of the river Weaver and the Sloyne, flows in a comparatively narrow deep rock-bound channel between Liverpool and Birkenhead. The only connection formerly between these two adjacent towns was either by ferry across the river, or by a very circuitous railway journey round by Runcorn, where a bridge crosses the river at a narrow point. In order to provide regular railway communication between

MERSEY TUNNEL. LIVERPOOL.

BIRKENHEAD.

River Mersey.

DATUM LINE 240 FEET BELOW MEAN SEA LEVEL.

SEVERN TUNNEL.

NOTE. THE HORIZONTAL SCALE TO THE SEVERN TUNNEL IS HALF THAT OF THE MERSEY TUNNEL.

River Severn.

GRADIENT 1 IN 100.   GRADIENT 1 IN 90.

DATUM LINE 250 FEET BELOW MEAN SEA LEVEL.

the towns, and to connect the lines converging to both the towns and separated by the river, a scheme for a tunnel under the river at this part was designed, which was authorised by Parliament in 1866. The bed of this narrow portion of the estuary, underlying a surface layer of sand and clay, is sandstone rock, a very good material for tunnelling in, and one which, though porous, has in this case its surface pores choked by sand and silt. The only possible unfavourable contingencies were the existence of some fissure in the rock forming the river bed, or the tapping of extensive land springs by the land portions of the tunnel. No works were undertaken till December 1879, when a small experimental tunnel was commenced, to test the continuity of the new red sandstone across the river. On the satisfactory completion of this preliminary work, in 1881, the regular works were commenced. Shafts were sunk on the two shores down to 170 feet from the surface, a sufficient depth to draw off the water from the drainage tunnel, which had to be formed below the main tunnel, with an adequate fall from the centre towards each shaft, so as to keep the tunnel dry. (*See section, page* 96.) The distance between these shafts is 1 mile 10 yards, and between the quay walls on each side, or the actual width of the estuary at the site, three-quarters of a mile. Pumps were placed in both of the shafts, and served to keep the works dry during their construction, and to drain the tunnel since its completion. The drainage tunnel, 7 to 8 feet in diameter, was first driven from each shaft, rising towards the centre with gradients of 1 in 500 and 1 in 900; and more water was encountered under the land than under the river. The Liverpool drainage tunnel was driven by hand, at an average rate of about $11\frac{1}{2}$ yards per week; and the Birkenhead drainage tunnel was driven by a Beaumont boring machine, giving an average weekly advance of 14½ yards. The two portions of the drainage tunnel were joined at 1115 yards from the Birkenhead shaft, with a divergence of only 2½ inches between the two lines. The regular tunnel was then constructed, 26 feet wide and 23 feet high. To obtain a minimum thickness of material of 30 feet above the tunnel, at a place where the depth of the river at high-water of spring tides attains 100 feet, it was necessary for the tunnel to descend from the shafts with gradients of 1 in 27 to 1 in 30 on the Liverpool side, and of 1 in 30 on the Birkenhead side; whilst it rises with somewhat gentler gradients to the surface on the further sides of the shafts. The portion under the centre of the river, for about 2½ furlongs, has been given only just sufficient fall from the centre for drainage. A bottom heading (*see note on page* 74) was driven along the line of the tunnel, the water draining to the drainage tunnel through bore holes; and at the same time several upward openings in the roof of the heading, or 'breakups' as they are termed, enabled several faces to be worked at the same time. At one place, near the Liverpool shore, the top of the tunnel emerges 3 to 6 feet out of the sandstone, in an old main channel of the river, for a distance of 66 yards; but as the stratum reached was mainly clay, and there is a thickness of 70 feet of material intervening between the tunnel and the river at that part, only somewhat additional care, timbering at the top in advance in short lengths, and a thicker arch, were required to carry the tunnel across this gap in the rock. One fissure only was traversed, near the centre, filled with sandstone, *débris*, and clay; and the adjacent rock was somewhat broken.

For the local traffic between Liverpool and Birkenhead, it was important to have stations nearer the river than the points where the inclines from the river tunnel emerge into the open air. Accordingly, a station was formed on each side, in the rock, a little landwards of the pumping shafts, having the rail level on the Liverpool side, 92 feet, and on the Birkenhead side, 103 feet below the surface. A flight of steps and three hydraulic lifts provide access for passengers between each station and the street above. Each lift, worked by water under pressure, can convey 100 passengers, and perform the journey in about half-a-minute.

The ventilation of the tunnel is effected by two fans on each shore, worked by steam engines. The fresh air, which enters at both the underground stations down the shafts affording access to the stations, is drawn by these fans to openings situated about midway on each side of the stations, where the foul air enters air drifts, bored through the rock, and passes to the fans. A continuous current of air is thus maintained in the tunnel by the suction of air caused by the fans, passing in both directions from the two underground stations, which are thus constantly supplied with fresh air, to the ventilating passages leading to the fans.

The actual tunnel is rather over $1\frac{1}{2}$ miles in length; but, including a covered way in shallow cutting beyond Birkenhead, the railway passes underground, without a break, for more than 2 miles. The portion of the railway extending from a junction at Birkenhead with the London and North-Western, and Great Western railways to Church Street, Liverpool, about 3 miles long, was opened in February 1886, a little more than six years after the commencement of the works, having cost £500,000 per mile. The total proposed length of the Mersey Railway, joining other lines on the

Cheshire side, connecting the railways of the docks on both sides of the river, and terminating at the Central Station, Liverpool, is $5\frac{1}{4}$ miles; but only $3\frac{1}{4}$ miles are in operation.

The Mersey Tunnel possesses the interest of being the first subaqueous tunnel of importance designed and opened for railway traffic, though the Thames Tunnel preceded it in being used by a railway, and the Severn Tunnel was commenced earlier; it is also the first tunnel under a large river which has not been submerged at any period of its construction, owing to the capital material through which it passes.

The Severn Tunnel.—The river Severn flows into the largest and most exposed estuary on the English coast, with the highest rise of tide; and this estuary separates Bristol from the coalfields of South Wales. The Severn, like the Mersey, is crossed by a railway bridge at some distance from its mouth, opened in 1879, connecting the Forest of Dean with Bristol; and a steam ferry between New Passage and Portskewett gave Bristol its only direct access to the South Wales Railway, which passes by Newport, Cardiff, and Swansea, to Milford, and also to the railway going by Hereford to the north. The Great Western Railway Company had for a long time contemplated a more direct and convenient connection between their lines, on each side of the estuary, than round by Swindon or by the ferry. They eventually abandoned a scheme for a bridge across the river near Chepstow, which they had obtained powers to construct; and in 1871 they decided to carry a tunnel under the river a little below the site of the ferry, at a point where the deep channel of the river is comparatively narrow. The distance across the river at this site is a little over 2¼ miles, at high-water, from bank to bank; whilst the main low-water channel is only about 2½ furlongs wide. The maximum depth of the river at high-water spring tides is 95 feet, the rise of tide being 37 feet. (*See section page 96.*)

The tunnel passes at a minimum depth of 44¾ feet under the low-water bed of the river, being made level for a little over a furlong under the deepest channel, and then rising, with a gradient of 1 in 90 on the Monmouthshire side, and 1 in 100 on the Gloucestershire side, till it emerges into an open cutting on each shore. It traverses conglomerate, the carboniferous strata, sandstones, marl, and gravel, the dip of the strata being considerable.

Work was commenced, in 1873, by sinking a shaft on the Monmouthshire side, 15 feet in diameter, to a depth of about 200 feet, so as to enable the whole of the tunnel to be drained from this point, by a small drainage tunnel rising towards the lowest portion of the tunnel, under the low-water channel, which is near the Monmouthshire shore. (*See page* 96.) This tunnel was commenced as soon as the shaft had been sunk, and it was extended along the line of the main tunnel, rising towards the opposite shore. Another shaft was subsequently sunk on the Gloucestershire shore, and two more shafts, inland of the first Monmouthshire shaft; and timbered headings (*see note on page* 74), about 7 feet square, were carried forward in the line of the tunnel from all four shafts. The greater portion of the headings of the main tunnel had thus been carried out, in separate sections, with little trouble from water, the first heading having been extended nearly 2 miles from the original shaft, when, in October 1879, an underground spring was opened by the upper tunnel heading, proceeding landwards from this shaft, about a furlong and a half inland. The water flowed in so rapidly, in spite of every effort to arrest the flow, that the workmen had to make their escape; and the long tunnel heading under the river was soon flooded, the water pouring down into it, through the shaft and the drainage tunnel, from the main tunnel heading on the rising Monmouthshire slope. Before attempting to remove the water, two shields of oak were placed against the openings of the tunnel heading, on each side of the old shaft, and fixed firmly by struts across the shaft, to stop the influx from the spring. The pumps in the shaft were then set to work, but did not succeed, after numerous breakdowns of the pumps and fresh attempts, in lowering the water within about 25 feet of the bottom. It was then determined to try to close a door in the long heading under the river, about 1000 feet from the old pumping shaft, which had been left open in the rush at the time the spring burst out. An attempt was made by an experienced diver to reach the door, groping his way in the dark across the *débris* in the heading, with the help of three other divers to pass along his air tube. He found it, however, impossible to drag along his tube sufficiently far to reach the door. At last this diver was provided with a newly invented portable knapsack, containing compressed oxygen, enabling a diver to supply himself with the necessary gas for a certain period under water without the encumbrance of dragging along a constantly lengthening tube. After testing the apparatus, on the second attempt the man succeeded in making his way along the heading, across the *débris*, and reached the door, which he shut, closing also a valve regulating the flow of water, on the far side of the door, and returned in safety, after having been 1 hour and 20 minutes under water, with no supply of air beyond that contained in his knapsack. The water was then, at last, removed from the workings, after a submersion of over a year. Access was also obtained to the heading leading to the big spring, through a door in the shield; and a wall was built across this heading, at a suitable place, with a door in it, which was then closed, and the spring thus excluded from the rest of the works. A new shaft, 18 feet in diameter, was sunk on the Monmouthshire shore, a little in advance of the old one, and another shaft, for pumping, on the land side of the spring, with the object of keeping down the water.

After the flooding of the works, it was determined to lower the tunnel 15 feet, so as to give it greater security from an irruption of the river. A new drainage tunnel had, accordingly, to be driven below the original one, and the old tunnel headings became top headings instead of bottom headings; and, accordingly, for some distance the arch of the tunnel was built first, and the lower part of the tunnel was subsequently built by underpinning on lowering the headings. In other places, the more ordinary method of bottom headings, with 'breakups' to reach the level of the arch, and increase the number of faces, was employed. The works were ventilated by a fan placed at the top of the new deep shaft; the rock was bored by drills worked by compressed air; the blasting was effected mainly with cotton powder, or tonite, owing to its comparative freedom from obnoxious fumes; and the works were lit by Swan electric lights.

The lining of the tunnel with brickwork was commenced, in 1881, at three places; and the long heading from the Monmouthshire side was connected with the heading from the shaft on the other bank in September 1881. In the previous April, however, salt water came in suddenly through the roof of the tunnel at a point under the river, near the Gloucestershire shore, where the men were building the arch of the tunnel. This water was found to come through a deep hole in a part of the river nearly dry at low-water. The hole was filled with clay, which was weighted with clay in bags at the top; and the leak was thus stopped, and a thicker arch of brickwork was built over the tunnel at this place. The work progressed without any special incident throughout 1882, the tunnel having been completed for some distance under the river from the Gloucestershire shaft, the arch completed under the main channel, and the tunnel commenced on each side of the three shafts in the Monmouthshire approach tunnel. Considerable progress was made with the tunnel, from the ends of the completed portions, on each side of the five shafts, during 1883, the tunnel being completed nearly half way across the river from the Gloucestershire side, and the work under the main channel extended. Early in October 1883 however, the big spring broke out again, and flooded the workings a second time. The rush of water into the long heading under the river, down from the old shaft, was so sudden that the men were swept along through the open door. The door was subsequently closed again by the same diver in the same manner as before; the water was then pumped out, and the large spring excluded in less than a month. In the middle of October, a very high tide coinciding with a south-westerly gale, the water rose above any previously recorded level, and overtopping one of the inland shafts on the Monmouthshire side, poured down into the headings in communication with this shaft. Fortunately, the tide fell before the water had risen within 8 feet of the arch of the tunnel; and eighty-three men at work in this section of the tunnel took refuge in the upper headings, till they could be rescued by a boat let down the shaft, and launched upon the subterranean canal.

When the progress of the tunnel, in 1884, rendered it necessary to undertake the portion traversing the fissure of the large spring, a side heading was driven to intercept the spring at a lower point, so that by diverting the water into this heading the site of the tunnel could be kept dry. As, moreover, the spring was fed by water percolating through the fissured bed of a brook above, a concrete bed was formed for this brook, along a length of 4 miles. The final link of heading through this part was completed in October 1884, enabling the tunnel to be traversed from end to end; and the tunnel was practically completed at the close of the year, with the exception of this piece, which was only partially lined with brickwork. The fissure below the tunnel was filled with concrete; and the last length of the tunnel was completed in April 1885. An attempt was then made to imprison the spring, but after a time the pressure of the confined water on the tunnel became so great that the bricks began to break, and the water escaped through the cracks. Accordingly, a shaft, 29 feet in diameter, was sunk at the side of the tunnel, and pumps were erected, in 1886, sufficient to lift the whole of the flow of water from the spring. Altogether, the pumping power provided at this and other shafts, on the completion of the works, is able to raise 66 million gallons of water a day, which is more than double the maximum quantity that had been pumped. Ventilation is provided by two fans placed in the shafts on each side of the river, one of the fans having a diameter of 40 feet. The railway was opened for traffic in December 1886, the same year as the Mersey Tunnel, more than thirteen years after the first commencement of the works.

The total length of the tunnel is 4 miles 626 yards, and

it is therefore the longest tunnel in Great Britain; and indeed, after the Alpine tunnels described in the last chapter, and the Hoosac Tunnel in the United States, it is the next longest railway tunnel in the world; and the sudden and unforeseen difficulties encountered and surmounted have not been surpassed in any other engineering work. Trains traverse it in about seven minutes; and it has already proved a very important link of the Great Western Railway system, and is attracting an increasing traffic.

The Thames Subways.—It is evident, from the preceding pages, that subaqueous tunnels often have a most eventful, chequered history during their construction, little dreamt of by passengers who pass through them in comfort after their completion. Of those already described, the Mersey Tunnel alone has been happy in having no such history; whilst the Thames Tunnel, the pioneer of this class of works, furnishes a striking illustration of the difficulties that may be encountered. Two subways, however, have been since carried out under the Thames at London, one below, and one above London Bridge, which have attracted comparatively little attention owing to their uneventful history, resulting from the success of the system adopted, and the favourable nature of the stratum traversed. The first of these subways, known as the Tower Subway, crosses under the Thames near the Tower; it was constructed in 1869, traversing the London clay underlying the alluvial deposit in the bed of the river. The subway was driven from two shafts sunk from a convenient place on each bank, behind the wharves and buildings abutting on the river, down into the London clay, to depths of about 63 feet and 56 feet respectively below the surface. The subway consists of a cast-iron tube, 7 feet inside diameter, formed by a series of rings composed of three segments bolted together. It slopes down to the centre, where there is a thickness of material of 22 feet between the tube and the river bed; and the length of the subway is a quarter of a mile.

The construction of the subway was effected by means of a shield, pushed forward by six screws, following close upon a short heading excavated in front of it to prepare for its advance; and the successive rings were put together under the shelter of the rear portion of the shield, which supplies the place of timbering. The shield consisted of a circular wrought-iron tube, slightly larger in diameter than the rings forming the subway, with a sort of strengthened cutting edge in front, and partially closed near the outer end by a diaphragm of iron plates, leaving a central aperture for the passage of the men excavating ahead of it, and through which the excavated material was thrown back, to be removed by a skip, or little truck, running on a small tramway laid along the finished portion of the subway. The total length of the shield was $4\frac{1}{2}$ feet, of which $2\frac{3}{4}$ feet at the rear were quite clear of the diaphragm and stiffening plates, and provided a protecting lining to the heading, under the shelter of which the cast-iron rings forming the subway were put in place, each ring having a width of only $1\frac{1}{2}$ feet. The vacant space, of 1 inch round the outside of the rings, left by the advance of the shield was filled up by injecting liquid lias lime through little holes purposely provided in the rings, so as to guard against any settlement of the surrounding clay. The works were commenced in February 1869, and completed in the following November. A tramcar drawn by a rope along the subway, and hydraulic lifts in the shafts, were originally provided for the conveyance of passengers; but as the working expenses exceeded the receipts, these conveniences were removed; and the subway serves as a passage for foot passengers, with staircases in each shaft.

This second tunnel under the Thames furnishes a striking contrast, as regards rate of progress, to the old Thames Tunnel, owing, in a great measure, to its passing, at a greater depth from the surface, through undisturbed, homogeneous London clay, owing also to the simpler and more rapid method of progress for a comparatively small undertaking, and to freedom from delays through want of funds. The Tower Subway, however, resembles the Thames Tunnel (closed to foot passengers in 1869) in attracting only a small number of people beyond workmen, morning and evening, going to and returning from their work.

Another larger double subway has been recently constructed under the Thames, a little higher up, forming a portion of the City and South London Railway, designed to connect Clapham and Kennington directly with the city, by a subterranean tramcar service, worked by electricity, opened between the city and Stockwell in November 1890. This subway consists of two adjacent cast-iron tubes, formed with rings, 10 feet in diameter and $1\frac{2}{3}$ feet in width, composed of six segments and a key piece at the top; and it has been driven through the London clay by a similar method to that adopted for the Tower Subway. The cutter at the front end of the shield is of steel; and the shield is pushed forward by six hydraulic presses. The rate of progress has averaged 13 feet a day, and a maximum of 16 feet has been attained. The portion under the river, which was carried out three or four years ago, was accomplished without difficulty, and was remarkably free from water; indeed, less water was found there than at several other points along the route, compressed air having been required in one place, when piercing a layer of gravel, to keep back the water. Access to the subway, about 50 feet below the surface, is provided at the stations, by lifts working in large shafts.

Sarnia Tunnel, under St Clair River.—The boundary between Canada and the United States, from Lake Huron to Lake St Clair, is formed by the River St Clair which connects these two lakes. A tunnel has been constructed under this river, 2017 yards in length, to connect the Grand Trunk Railway of Canada, at Sarnia, with the United States Railways at Port Huron. The tunnel traverses 650 yards on the Canadian side; it then passes for a length of 767 yards under the River St Clair, and terminates at a distance of 600 yards beyond the American bank of the river. It consists of a cast-iron tube, 21 feet in diameter, built up in segments, and lined inside with masonry, providing accommodation for a single line of railway. The tunnel was driven from each end through blue clay, within the shelter of a shield pushed forward by hydraulic pressess, and by the aid of compressed air, in a similar method to the Thames Subways. This Sarnia Tunnel, opened in 1890, has superseded the ferry which formerly served as the means of communication between the railways of Canada and the United States at this point; and it is the first subaqueous tunnel which has been completed in America.

The Channel Tunnel.—A much-talked-of submarine tunnel has been proposed for some years past, designed to traverse the chalk stratum under the English Channel, at the straits of Dover, so as to connect England with the Continent by railway. The continuity of the chalk between the two coasts has been tested, as far as practicable, by comparing the strata on each side, as ascertained by borings, and by bringing up samples of the chalk bottom from various points across the Channel. Shafts, also, have been sunk on the English and French shores, and experimental headings driven to determine more exactly the nature of the chalk to be traversed; and a heading, from a shaft between Folkestone and Dover, has been carried 2000 yards under the sea. Two companies have been formed for undertaking the work; but owing to political considerations, and questions of military expediency, parliamentary sanction has been withheld.

The feasibility of the scheme depends upon the absence of any large fissures in the chalk in the line of the tunnel, which can only be determined with absolute certainty by driving a heading, or small tunnel, right across under the Channel. The whole, however, of the indications obtained from the various investigations give promise of continuity and compactness in the chalk. The shortest distance across the straits is about 21 miles; but one of the routes proposed would be $23\frac{1}{2}$ miles from shore to shore; and two or three miles additional would be required on each side to reach the level of the existing lines, so as to form a junction with them. The submarine tunnel, accordingly, between the shafts on each shore, would be from 21 to $23\frac{1}{2}$ miles long, without any intervening shafts. The continuous tunnel would therefore be more than double the length of the longest Alpine tunnel; but chalk is perhaps the best material in which a tunnel can be made; and, with control of the water, rapid progress could be effected. Besides the great cost, the ventilation of the tunnel would probably constitute one of the chief difficulties. The depth of water in mid-channel, at low-water, is from 160 to 190 feet; and the least thickness of chalk over the tunnel would be between 100 and 200 feet. The tunnel would descend from each shaft, with gradients not exceeding 1 in 80, till a suitable depth is reached in the chalk; and it would then ascend towards the central point, with gradients of 1 in 1000, to drain the tunnel from the centre to the end of these gradients, where drainage tunnels, with downward gradients to the shafts, would convey away the water to be raised by pumps at the shafts. These drainage tunnels would have to be first constructed to drain the main tunnel during its progress; and they would serve also afterwards as ventilation conduits, for drawing the foul air away from the centre of the tunnel towards the shafts.

Apart from considerations of political expediency, in relation to the piercing of the silver streak which guards our shores, there is apparently no insuperable impediment to the construction of the Channel Tunnel, owing to the favourable nature of the stratum to be traversed. A suitable return on the large capital expenditure may appear doubtful; but this is not a matter which concerns the general public, if a company is prepared to undertake the risk. Moreover, if the large expenditure on the Mersey and Severn tunnels, and the Forth Bridge, should prove adequately remunerative, an outlay of three or four times the cost of the last-named work would not appear excessive for securing the whole of the traffic between Great Britain and the Continent. It is quite possible that, in spite of the element of uncertainty which must always surround subaqueous operations, the Channel Tunnel might be constructed with much less difficulty than some of the tunnels described in the present chapter; and the magnitude of the work, and its position, would unquestionably make it rank as one of the wonders of the world.

CHAPTER VI.

THE PROGRESS AND PRINCIPLES OF MODERN BRIDGE CONSTRUCTION.

THE ordinary method of carrying a railway across a river is by means of a bridge, where all the work, with the exception of the foundations for the piers and abutments, is above ground, and in the construction of which the uncertainties and risks attending subaqueous tunnels are avoided. Accordingly, subaqueous tunnels have only been resorted to where the conditions of the site render it impracticable or inexpedient to erect a bridge across a river or estuary. As it is desirable, in crossing a navigable river, to impede the navigation as little as possible, and as in many cases piers in the alluvial deposit of the river bed are costly and difficult to construct, the spans of river bridges, especially across the deeper portion of the river, are made as large as practicable, consistent with due regard to cost.

PROGRESS OF BRIDGE CONSTRUCTION.

The earliest bridges were made of wood; and arched masonry bridges were subsequently adopted for most large spans, previous to the introduction of iron for bridge building in the last century. Masonry bridges, however, have not attained very large spans; for the Alma Bridge at Paris, over the Seine, built of concrete, has a central span of 141½ feet; London Bridge, 152 feet; Grosvenor Bridge, over the Dee at Chester, a span of 200 feet; and Trezzo Bridge, over the Adda, 251 feet, which appears to be the largest span of any masonry arched bridge hitherto built. Curiously enough, one or two timber bridges have been built with larger spans, the wooden Schaffhausen Bridge, across the Rhine, destroyed in 1799, having had a span of 193 feet; a wooden bridge, over the Connecticut River at Hanover, in the United States, built in 1796, had a single arch of 236 feet; whilst the Wittingen timber bridge, built in 1758, and destroyed by fire about the beginning of the century, had a span of 390 feet. Cast-iron was introduced for arched bridges towards the end of the last century, the first bridge of this construction, 100 feet in span, having been erected across the Severn, near Coalbrookdale, in 1779. A larger bridge, formed of cast-iron, was built across the Wear at Sunderland in 1796, with a single arch of 236 feet span; and Southwark Bridge, with a central arch of 240 feet, was erected in 1819. These cast-iron bridges, however, though cheaper than masonry bridges, and applying a purely compressive strain to the cast-iron, which it is specially fitted to sustain, do not exceed the spans of masonry bridges.

One or two suspension bridges were erected in the last century; but the first notable example of a suspension bridge of large span was the Menai Suspension Bridge, erected in 1819-25, for carrying a road across the Menai Straits, to facilitate communication with Anglesea, and thence to Ireland. This bridge has a span of 570 feet between its points of support, and affords a headway in the centre above high-water of 102 feet. This principle of suspension has since been extended to a number of road bridges, amongst the most notable of which are a bridge at Budapest, over the Danube, having a span of 666 feet, erected in 1842-49; the Freiburg Bridge, in Switzerland, erected in 1833-4, across the valley of the Sarine, having a span of 870 feet, and situated at a height of 167 feet above the river; and the Clifton Suspension Bridge, crossing the precipitous valley of the Avon below Bristol, at an elevation of 250 feet above high-water, with a span of 702 feet. The Clifton Bridge was erected in 1862-4, the chains of the old Hungerford Suspension Bridge having been used for a portion of the chains of the Clifton Bridge, when the Hungerford foot-bridge was superseded by the Charing Cross Railway Bridge. A suspension bridge also, nearly half-a-mile in length, crosses the Dnieper at Kieff, having four principal spans of 440 feet, which was erected in 1851.

Timber trusses, masonry and brick arches, and cast-iron arches and girders, were employed for the earlier railway bridges. When, however, a bridge with large spans was required for carrying the Chester and Holyhead Railway across the Menai Straits, a new departure was made in bridge construction by Mr Robert Stephenson. A suspension bridge like Telford's road bridge was deemed unsuitable, owing to the oscillations set up in an ordinary bridge of that type by a heavy rapidly moving load. One design proposed consisted of a cast-iron bridge, having two arches, and a central pier built on the Britannia rock in mid-channel, on which the central pier of the present structure stands. After numerous experiments, however, for ascertaining the strength of wrought-iron, particularly in the form of tubes, it was determined to carry the railway across the Straits in wrought-iron tubes, with cellular roof and floor forming the top and bottom flanges of these girders. This bridge, well known as the Britannia Tubular Bridge, consists of two parallel rectangular tubes, one for the up, and the other for the down line, with two central spans of 459 feet, and two shore spans of 230 feet, affording a clear headway of $103\frac{3}{4}$ feet above high-water of spring tides in both the channels on each side of the central rock. (*See page* 134.) The four tubes for the central spans were floated into position, and gradually raised by hydraulic presses to the required height, the supporting masonry of the piers being built up underneath, as no scaffolding was permitted to be erected in the channel. This bridge was commenced in 1846, and opened for traffic in 1850. A similar tubular bridge, with a single span of 400 feet, was erected about the same time for carrying the same railway across the Conway River at Conway, by the side of another roadway suspension bridge erected by Telford for the Chester and Holyhead road; and it was opened in 1848. Another much longer bridge of the same type was erected across the St Lawrence at Montreal in 1854-59. This railway bridge, nearly $1\frac{3}{4}$ miles long, has one central span of 330 feet, and twenty-four side spans of 242 feet; and it has piers with specially shaped cutwaters up stream to protect the bridge on the breaking up of the ice in spring. The Britannia Tubular Bridge is of special interest as being the first instance of a wrought-iron girder bridge; but without detracting at all from the merits of the structure, it is unquestionable that if a bridge had to be erected in a similar position at the present day, it would not, with the extended knowledge gained during the last forty years, be constructed in the same manner. The tensile strength of wrought-iron in the form of bars had long before been satisfactorily established in the construction of the chains of suspension bridges. The preliminary experiments, however, for the tubular bridge proved, and the success of the Britannia Bridge demonstrated to the world, that wrought-iron plates and angle-irons riveted together so as to form a beam, or girder, with strong top and bottom flanges, and a comparatively thin vertical connecting piece, or web, could resist considerable tensile and compressive strains, and thus that wrought-iron girders could bear heavy loads when merely supported at each end.

In later constructions of wrought-iron girders, the cellular flanges have been replaced by flat plates riveted together, and the sides of the tube by a single central web. In small girders, the web has generally been made of a solid plate stiffened at intervals; but in large girders, open trellis or lattice work in various forms, composed of struts and ties, has been substituted for the solid web. (*See page* 134.) The object of the web in these girders, or trusses, is to give depth, and consequently increased strength to the beam; and the web transmits the strains from one flange to the other, and thus unites the different portions into a single structure. Innumerable wrought-iron girder bridges of various dimensions and types have been erected for railways since the inauguration of the system by the Britannia Bridge; but only the two other bridges named above have been constructed on precisely the same tubular principle, though tubes have been employed for portions of bridges exposed to compressive strains.

Another wrought-iron bridge, having nearly as large spans as the Britannia Bridge, was erected soon after by Mr Brunel, across the river Tamar at Saltash, for the Plymouth and Cornwall Railway. A large arched tube above and suspension chains below, strongly braced together, carry the small girders underneath supporting the platform of the bridge across the two large spans of 455 feet, affording two clear spans of 436 feet between the piers, and a headway of 100 feet above high-water of spring tides. The total length of the bridge, including several small spans on both sides, is 2240 feet; and the bridge was opened for traffic in 1859.

Though the Britannia and Saltash bridges remained unrivalled as regards span in Great Britain for more than thirty years, the large size of the rivers of the Continent of Europe and North America necessitated the erection of large structures for conveying railways across them, approaching in many cases the spans of these bridges, and occasionally surpassing them. Thus, amongst wrought-iron girder bridges, a bridge erected across the Vistula at Dirschau, in 1856, has a span of 397 feet; another, erected in 1861, across the Inn at Passau, has a span of 420 feet; another, across the Rhine at Mainz, erected in 1862, has a span of 345 feet; whilst the Kuilenberg Bridge, across the river Lek in Holland, erected in 1868, has a span of 492 feet; and the Moerdyk Bridge, completed in 1880, carries the Antwerp and Rotterdam Railway across the Hollandsch Diep by fourteen spans of 328 feet. In the United States, two bridges were built across the Ohio at Louisville, in 1870, with spans of 368, and 396 feet respectively, the form of construction adopted being the Fink truss system, with cast-iron tubes for the flange in compression at the top, and the remainder being made of wrought-iron, with no continuous bottom flange. Two wrought-iron girder bridges were erected across the Ohio at Cincinnati, in 1872 and 1877, with spans of 420, and 519 feet respectively. More recently, the Henderson Bridge has been erected, with a span across the main river channel of 522 feet, and another bridge over the

Ohio at Cincinnati, with a span of 550 feet, which have the largest spans of any discontinuous ordinary girder bridges hitherto constructed. A continuous wrought-iron girder bridge was built across the Kentucky River, in 1876-7, having three spans of 375 feet at a height of 280 feet above the river bed. The Tay Bridge, besides being memorable on account of the overthrow of the large spans of the first structure by the wind in a storm in December 1879, only a year and a half after its opening, is remarkable as being the longest girder bridge in the world, the new bridge, built in 1882-7, having a total length of 10,700 feet, or rather more than two miles, though its largest openings, eleven in number, have a span of only 245 feet. Some bridges across deep valleys, though not having unusual spans, are worthy of notice on account of the general light appearance and gracefulness of their construction, of which the Crumlin Viaduct over the river Ebbw in Monmouthshire, the Portage Bridge over the Genesee River in the State of New York, and the Trisana Viaduct, on the Arlberg Railway, over the river Trisana, are instances. The Crumlin Viaduct, 1800 feet long, has ten spans of 150 feet; and the height of the rails above the bed of the Ebbw is 200 feet. The Portage Bridge, in the United States, originally constructed of wood, and burnt down in 1875, has been reconstructed in iron. It has a total length of 800 feet, having one span of 180 feet, two spans of 100 feet, and seven spans of 50 feet; and it is 230 feet above the river. The Trisana Viaduct has a central span of 377 feet, at a height of 282 feet over the river, and two side spans of 131 feet.

The use of wrought-iron for bridge construction has not been confined to girders and suspension bridges; for arched bridges have also been made of wrought-iron, as, for instance, at Coblentz, where the Rhine is crossed by three arches of 515 feet span. In the construction of the Victoria Bridge over the Thames at Pimlico, commenced in 1859, and completed in 1860, and also in its widening, in 1865-6, wrought-iron was preferred to cast-iron for the four arches. The most notable instances, however, of the employment of wrought-iron for arches are the two bridges over the Douro at Oporto, and the central span of the Garabit Viaduct, in France, over the river Truyère, completed in 1884. (*See page* 134.) These three open-work arches, built out from each side and joined in the centre without using any scaffolding, have spans of 525 feet, 571 feet, and 541 feet, and are raised 201 feet, 251 feet, and 390 feet above their respective rivers.

Soon after the completion of the Britannia Tubular Bridge, the suspension principle, which had been considered unsuitable for railway traffic across the large spans of the Menai Straits, was adopted for a railway, connecting Canada with the United States, over the Niagara River, below the falls, where the span required is $821\tfrac{1}{3}$ feet. An iron wire cable suspension bridge was erected in 1852-55, and carries a railway on the upper platform, and a roadway underneath, at a height of 245 feet above the river. This remarkable bridge, thrown across a river in which no staging could have been erected, is suspended from four cables, 10 inches in diameter, each containing 3640 wires; and it is stiffened by a series of auxiliary cables spreading out from the towers on each bank, and thus relieving the cables from the strain of the shore ends of the bridge for some distance from the towers. Though the suspended framework, originally made of timber, has required to be replaced by iron, and the towers strengthened, the bridge has successfully carried the railway traffic for thirty-five years. This bridge was for some time the only suspension bridge employed for railway traffic, as well as the longest span in the world. It was, however, nearly equalled by a suspension bridge, of 800 feet clear span, over the Monongahela River at Pittsburgh, opened in 1877. This bridge, however, serves only for a double line of tramway and footways, and is not more than 80 feet above the river. The Niagara Bridge has, in its turn, been surpassed by a suspension bridge of 1057 feet span at Cincinnati; and it has been eclipsed by the Brooklyn Bridge, over the East River at New York, with a span of 1595 feet, designed by Mr Roebling, the engineer of the Niagara Bridge. The Brooklyn Bridge, opened in 1883, is the largest suspension bridge in existence (*see illustration*); and till the opening of the Forth Bridge, in 1890, its span was the largest of any bridge in the world. It, however, is liable to share the fate of most of the celebrated engineering triumphs of modern times, in having its pre-eminence amongst suspension bridges diminished by a still more daring engineering feat. A bridge is, indeed, proposed for crossing the Hudson River at New York, which is designed to have a central span of 2860 feet, nearly double the span of the Brooklyn Bridge, and surpassing the two large spans of the Forth Bridge by 1160 feet. This new project is intended to serve the same purpose, of affording more direct communication between New York and Jersey City, as the tunnel in progress under the river (*see page* 89), which was originally started as a more feasible scheme than a bridge.

Wrought-iron, which gradually superseded cast-iron after the erection of the Britannia Bridge, is in its turn being superseded by steel. Cast-iron is much stronger than wrought-iron in resisting a compressive strain, but much weaker in resisting tensile strains; whilst wrought-iron is somewhat more able to resist tension than compression. Steel, however, is, in every sense, able to support much greater strains than wrought-iron; and therefore, for the same span, a lighter bridge, subjected from its smaller weight to less strains, can be constructed of steel than of wrought-iron, or a steel bridge of larger span than an iron bridge can be made with the same weight of material. For some time the great varieties of steel, and the uncertainties attending its manufacture, checked the general adoption of steel for bridges; but the great improvements effected in the manufacture of steel in recent years, and an extended knowledge of its qualities and reliability, as well as the reduction in its cost, have established its employment for large structures. The St Louis Bridge, over the Mississippi, constructed in 1867-74, was the earliest instance of the adoption of steel for a bridge of large span. This bridge has a central arch of 520 feet span, and two side arches of 502 feet, formed with tubes of cast steel. (*See page* 134.) Another large arched steel bridge has since been erected over the Harlem River at New York, with two spans of 510 feet, and a clear headway of 150 feet under the centre of the arch. The most notable and most recent adoption of steel for a bridge of large span is the cantilever Forth Bridge, with two spans of 1700 feet, over the Firth of Forth. (*See illustration.*)

PRINCIPLES OF BRIDGE CONSTRUCTION.

The preceding pages show what a great advance has been achieved in bridge construction within the last fifty years. The Britannia Bridge, with its spans of 459 feet, surpassed all previous railway bridges ; but of recent years several bridges of over 500 feet span have been erected. The spans of the Freiburg and Niagara suspension bridges have been doubled in the Brooklyn Bridge ; and the greatest span of the Britannia Bridge has been nearly quadrupled in the Forth Bridge. To realise fully, however, the magnitude of this advance, a brief reference to the general principles of bridge construction is indispensable.

When an increased span is given to a bridge, the resulting increased strains necessitate an enlargement of the different parts to support these strains, and consequently an increased weight, which, together with the larger load which a longer bridge may have to carry, adds to the strains which the mere increase in length involves Accordingly, an addition to the span, besides adding proportionately to the length of the bridge, and therefore to the weight to be supported, adds also to the weight of the bridge per unit of length, and increases the possible moving load, or length of train, that can be on the bridge at one time. The weight of a bridge therefore, and consequently its cost, increases much more rapidly with the span than the mere proportionate addition to its length. With a girder or arch of uniform depth, the maximum strain increases in proportion to the total weight supported multiplied into the length of the opening as the span is increased, and therefore in a somewhat greater ratio than the square of the span ; and the only method of reducing this rapid increase is by making the depth greater with the increase in span, as the strain varies inversely with the depth, or, in other words, if the depth is doubled the strain on the flanges is halved. The existing methods of spanning large openings are the various forms of girders or trusses, the suspension principle, arches, and cantilevers, examples of which have been already given. (*See page* 134.) It must be a matter of surprise to the uninitiated to observe, in comparing these types, that whilst suspension bridges, arches, and cantilevers get slighter from the abutments towards the centre, detached girders are always made higher, or their flanges thicker, in the centre.

Girders.—In ordinary girder bridges, supported at each end on abutments or piers, the bending strain, due to the total weight borne, is greatest in the centre of the span, tending to compress the top flange and to extend the bottom flange. The shearing stress on the web or bars, connecting the two flanges of the girder, or the transverse strain, tending to make the more loaded portion of a girder slide away and separate from the less weighted portion, is very slight in the centre, and increases towards the abutments, reaching a maximum close to either point of support. As the bending strain diminishes from the centre to the points of support, the height of the girder may be gradually reduced towards the abutments, or the thickness of the flanges reduced. On the contrary, owing to the increase of the shearing stress from the centre towards the ends, the stiffening of the solid web has to be increased, or the tension bars and struts have to be enlarged in section gradually, from the centre towards the extremities of the girder. Girders have to support both tensile and compressive strains, for their bottom flange and the alternate bars, or ties, of their trellis web are in tension, whilst their top flange and their remaining bars, or struts, are in compression. Accordingly, cast-iron is not a suitable material for girders, owing to its poor capacity for resisting tensile strains. Wrought-iron and steel, however, are well suited for resisting both tension and compression. The simple discontinuous girder is not well adapted for long spans, for the maximum central strain rapidly augments with the increase in span, and the strength, and therefore the weight at the centre, has to be proportionately increased. This may, indeed, be to some extent reduced by an increase in the depth of the girder; but this has a limit, owing to the necessity of greatly increasing the stiffness of long struts, to secure them against bending under compressive strains. (*See page* 134.)

A simple method of augmenting the strength of a girder for large spans is by making the girder continuous over two or more spans. In the simple case of a girder continuous over two equal spans, the bending strains are altered, both in position and magnitude, from what they are with two disconnected girders. The bending strain becomes a maximum over the central pier; and the top flange is in tension at this part, and the bottom flange in compression. When the girder is uniformly loaded, the bending strains, decreasing from the central point, become nothing at a point about one-third of the span distant on each side from the central pier; and this central portion of the girder, comprising about one-third of its length, acts as a sort of cantilever to the remainder of the girder on each side. The effective spans of these outer portions of the girder are thus practically reduced to the length of these portions, or about two-thirds of the actual spans; and the maximum strain in the centre of each of these sections of the continuous girder is proportionately reduced. Accordingly, the continuity of the girder places the maximum strain, and consequently the greatest weight, in the centre of the central pier, where it is easily supported, and reduces the strains on the end portions of the girder, over the openings, to those produced on a disconnected girder having a span two-thirds of the actual span. In fact, the effect of the continuity over the pier, on the two one-third portions of the girder at each end, is as if girders were substituted for them, resting on each abutment, and on brackets extending out for one-third of the actual spans on each side of the central pier. (*See* Hooghly Bridge, *page* 134.) The strains on the central portions of girders continuous over more than two spans would be still more reduced; but the necessity of providing for expansion and contraction renders any great extension of the principle inapplicable for large spans.

Suspension Bridges.—The principle of suspension for bridges possesses two great advantages, namely, that every portion of the structure is in tension, and therefore requires no additional strengthening, as in long struts, to provide against bending, and enables the whole strength of the materials to be fully utilised; and also that, with wire cables, which are used for very large spans, the resistance of the metal, in the form of wire, to tension is much greater than the average strength of the metal, owing to the great tensile resistance of the outer skin of the wire. Unlike a simple girder bridge moreover, the strain on a suspension bridge is least in the centre of the span, increasing towards the piers; and the weight, also, of the bridge per unit of length is least in the centre, and increases towards the sides, owing to the increasing divergence of the chains from the horizontal, and the greater length of the suspending rods on approaching the piers from which the cables hang. The anchor cables, which carry down the strain of the supension cables to solid anchorages imbedded in the ground on the land side of the piers, are a necessary addition to the actual bridge spanning the opening. In suspension bridges, also, which have smaller shore spans on the land side of the piers, the strain on the main cables can be reduced by auxiliary cables spreading out on each side of the piers, which also stiffen the bridge, and are equipoised by supporting the land span on one side of the pier and the nearer portion of the large span on the other side. This arrangement has been adopted with advantage at the Brooklyn Bridge. (*See illustration.*) Even, however, when the large span extends right across the opening, as at the Niagara Bridge, and the strains on the cables have to be wholly borne by corresponding shore cables, this form of bridge is very economical, and is well suited for crossing deep ravines, as it can be erected without any central staging between the piers. The deflection of a suspension bridge under a moving load, owing to the flexible chains modifying their curvature according to the position of the load, is of much less importance in bridges of large span, in consequence of the small proportion the moving load bears to the fixed load in a very large bridge; and it is also reduced by the introduction of auxiliary cables, acting as stiffening ties, radiating from the piers. A danger to which wire cables are peculiarly liable is their unperceived deterioration by rust, from moisture penetrating to the interstices between the wires; but great precautions have been taken of late years to guard against this insidious corrosion, by so coating the cables as to render them impervious to wet, and also by so arranging the cables that the renewal of a damaged cable can be easily effected.

The dip of the cables, or the vertical distance between the level of their suspension on the piers and their lowest central point, corresponds to the depth between the flanges in a girder bridge, and to the rise of an arched bridge, and increases with the span. Accordingly, the height of the suspension towers from the bottom level of the bridge, which is 52 feet in the Menai Bridge, is 60 feet in the Niagara Bridge, and 150 feet in the Brooklyn Bridge; whilst the height of the towers, as designed for the proposed Hudson River Suspension Bridge, is 500 feet above the water, or very nearly the height of the spires of Cologne Cathedral, and rising about 380 feet above the bridge.

Arches.—An arch is the exact converse of a suspension bridge; for whereas in a suspension bridge all the parts are in tension, in an arch all the parts are in compression. The cables in the one correspond to the arched ribs in the other; the suspension rods are replaced by the spandrils, which transmit the weight of the roadway to the arch; and in place of anchor cables bearing the tensional strains of the cables, there are solid abutments to support the thrust of the arch. The parts, however, of an arched bridge, being all in compression, have to be given much greater rigidity to avoid flexure, and therefore an arched bridge is much heavier and more costly than a suspension bridge of the same span; but, for the same reason, it is less liable to deflection under a moving load. Arched bridges, also, are more costly to erect; and the great rise required with large spans would preclude their adoption, except across deep gorges, or over rivers with high banks. They are, moreover, not nearly so well suited for being constructed without scaffolding; though the arched bridges of largest span have had to be erected by building out. Owing to the great rise attainable with arched bridges (*see page* 134), and the decrease of the strains from the abutments to the centre of the arch, the spans of arched bridges have equalled, and even somewhat surpassed, the spans obtained hitherto with ordinary girder bridges;

though the spans of both those types of bridge have, up to the present time, found a limit between 500 and 600 feet. Neither arch nor girder bridges have as yet much exceeded one-third of the span attained by the Brooklyn Suspension Bridge.

Bowstring girders are really arches, in which the abutment is dispensed with by the help of a horizontal tie connecting the two extremities of the arched rib, and thus taking its thrust. The High Level Bridge at Newcastle furnishes a good example of this form of arched structure; and the Saltash Bridge is similar in type, the chains taking the place of the horizontal tie. This arrangement converts the arch into a self-contained structure, like a girder, which can rest on piers, and obviates the necessity of abutments to sustain the thrust of the arch. The Saltash Bridge, however, remains the longest span of this type; whilst the simple arch has been given increased spans within the last thirty years.

Cantilevers.—A cantilever,[1] in the engineering sense, is an overhanging bracket or truss. The word might possibly be applied to the central portion of a continuous girder, for if a girder, continuous over two spans, was separated in imagination into three equal parts, the central third might be regarded as a double bracket or cantilever, supporting at its two extremities the outer ends of the two other portions, which actually bear the same strains as independent girders of the same length would be subjected to. The term cantilever is, indeed, given to continuous girder bridges by American writers, the Kentucky River Bridge being described as the first cantilever bridge of importance erected in America, though it is really a con-

---

[1] Cantilever, from *cant*, old French for angle, and *lever*, to raise.

tinuous girder bridge of uniform depth over three spans, without any appearance of a bracket at the piers. This bridge, however, formed a cantilever during its construction, being built out without scaffolding; and from this point of view the St Louis, Douro, and Garabit bridges were cantilevers during erection, though this description ceased to be applicable on the completion of the arches. The term cantilever appears to be only suitable strictly to structures which increase in depth over their piers, giving the appearance of a bracket with a symmetrical overhang on the shore side of the pier to counterbalance the other, or where the projecting portions are really independent of the girders whose ends they support. (*See page* 134.)

The principle of the cantilever, for increasing the span of bridges, was known long ago; for bridges formed with timbers deeply embedded into the abutments or banks on each side, and with central beams resting on the ends of these timbers, were constructed for crossing rivers some centuries ago in India and Japan; but the application of the principle to metal bridges of large span is quite recent.

The Niagara Cantilever Bridge, crossing the Niagara River a short distance upstream from the Suspension Bridge was the first true metal cantilever bridge erected, having been opened in 1883. (*See page* 134.) The bridge rests upon two light braced steel piers, which, with the masonry foundations, rise 180 feet above the surface of the river on each bank. Two cantilevers, 395 feet in length, spread out on each side of the piers at the top, the shore portion of each cantilever forming the shore spans, and the river portions supporting between them a central girder, 120 feet in length, which, together with the river cantilevers, spans the gap of 495 feet between the two piers. The Fraser River Bridge of the Canadian Pacific Railway, opened in 1885, is a structure of similar type, with a central opening having a clear span of 315 feet. Counterpoise weights at the shore ends of the cantilevers, or shore anchorages, enable the river ends of the cantilevers to support the additional weight of the central girder between them, with its proportion of the moving load. The cantilever system is specially well adapted for building out from the piers; for the additions on each side, as the work proceeds, balance each other, and the shore anchorage counterbalances the half portion of the central span. The bracket form, moreover, of the cantilever, with its increased depth near the piers, is particularly suited for supporting the projecting arms during construction; and it is only necessary, in addition, to make the ends of the central portion capable of bearing the increased strains during building out till they are joined in the middle.

Another form of cantilever bridge, approximating to a continuous girder bridge of varying depth, has been adopted for the Kentucky and Indiana Bridge over the Ohio at Louisville, erected in 1883-6, and for the Poughkeepsie Bridge, quite recently constructed. In these bridges, a girder across a central span was built on scaffolding, and a projecting portion was built out from the ends of this girder beyond the two piers supporting the girder, and these projections formed cantilevers for the adjacent spans, true cantilevers being built out towards them from the further piers. The Kentucky Bridge has two cantilever spans, of 480, and 483 feet respectively between the centres of the piers. The Poughkeepsie Bridge has two cantilever spans on each shore of 523 feet, and a central cantilever span of 521 feet, situated between two ordinary girders of 500 feet span, with projecting ends forming cantilevers.

The cantilever system, though of recent adoption for long span bridges, has been rapidly developed; for the Sukkur Cantilever Bridge, crossing the Rori branch of the river Indus at Sukkur, with a single span of 790 feet, was opened in June 1889, and eclipsed in span all previous bridges of rigid construction. Within nine months, however, of the opening of the Sukkur Bridge, the completion of the Forth Bridge put all previous achievements in bridge building in the shade, by exhibiting a bridge with two spans of 1700 feet, more than double the span of the Sukkur Bridge, and exceeding the previously unrivalled Brooklyn Suspension Bridge by 105 feet in span.

In view of this rapid advance, it may well be wondered what the future may have in store in regard to bridge construction. The recent extension of the span of rigid bridges is due partly to the use of steel, and partly to the judicious adaptation of the cantilever principle with a great depth over the piers. There is no prospect at present of the discovery of any metal stronger than steel and equally cheap, nor is there any known untried principle available for still larger spans. With our present knowledge, therefore, the suspension system or cantilevers seem likely to be resorted to for bridges of unusual span; whilst continuous girders of varying depth appear capable of being extended to greater spans than girder bridges have hitherto attained.

CHAPTER VII.

THE HAWKESBURY, ST LOUIS, GARABIT, HOOGHLY, BROOKLYN, FORTH, AND TOWER BRIDGES.

AMONGST the great number and variety of bridges erected within recent years, there is some difficulty in selecting representative examples of the several types, from different countries, for description, with two exceptions. The Brooklyn and Forth Bridges stand out pre-eminent examples of the suspension and cantilever systems in their grandest forms. Of the others, several similar bridges are equally worthy of mention; and those chosen must be regarded merely as specimens of their class. The Hawkesbury Bridge furnishes an instance of a large girder bridge recently erected in a British Colony, with exceptionally deep foundations for the piers, and where the girders were floated into position. The St Louis and Garabit bridges are two of the largest arched bridges in the world, very different in form, erected, in the United States and in France, by building out from the piers. (*See page* 134.) The Hooghly Bridge, in India, affords an instance of a very peculiar form of cantilever bridge, in which two of the three spans were put in position by rolling out. The Tower Bridge is an uncommon example of a bascule bridge, or drawbridge, with a footway overhead, and is of interest to Londoners

BRIDGES WITH LONG SPANS.

Britannia Tubular Bridge.

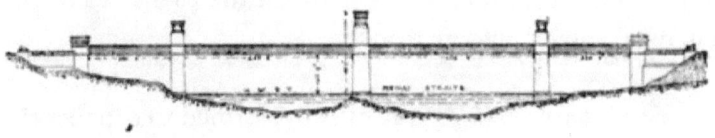

Hawkesbury Bridge, New South Wales.

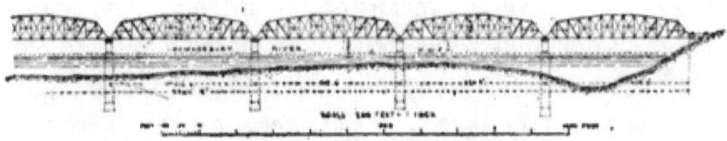

St. Louis Bridge.

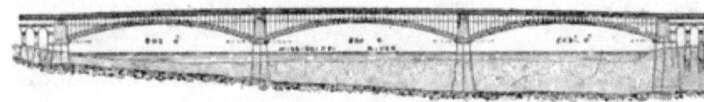

Garabit Viaduct, Cantal, France.

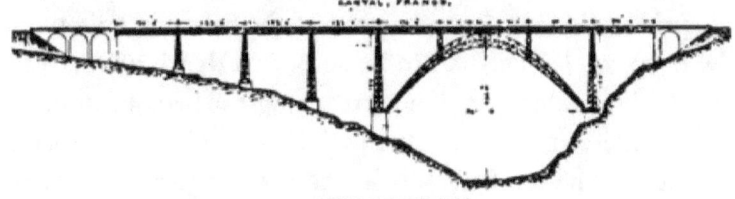

Niagara Cantilever Bridge.

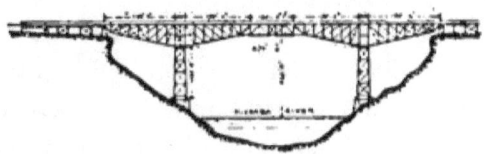

Hooghly Bridge.

Comparative lengths of large spans.
Sukkur Bridge.
Brooklyn Bridge.
Forth Bridge.

as providing communication between the two sides of the Thames below London Bridge.

Hawkesbury Bridge.—A railway, formed to connect the two systems of railways of New South Wales, crosses the Hawkesbury River by means of this bridge. The bridge has seven openings between its piers placed about 416 feet apart, centre to centre, on which the steel girders rest. (*See page* 134.) As the bottom of the river consists of a stratum of mud of considerable thickness, steel plate caissons were sunk at the site of the piers, the mud being removed from the bottom of the caisson by dredging, and the descent of the weighted caisson thereby accomplished. The depth of the river varies from about 20 feet to 77 feet; the rise of spring tides is 7 feet; and one of the caissons, adjoining the deepest channel, had to be sunk to a depth of 162 feet below high-water level before reaching the firm stratum of sand, underlying the mud, on which the piers have been founded. The next caisson, in shallower water, and reaching the sand at 144 feet below high-water, had to traverse the maximum thickness of mud of about 120 feet; and owing to difficulties experienced in sinking, though this caisson was begun the first, its sinking was completed the last. The dredging was effected in three circular wells, 8 feet in diameter, inside the caisson, and splayed out at the base; and the caisson was weighted with concrete placed between the wells and the outer skin of the caisson. As soon as the caisson rested firmly on the sand, the wells were filled with concrete, and the piers built up with masonry from near low-water level. As the bridge crosses the main channel of the estuary of the Hawkesbury River only seven miles away from the sea, the site is considerably exposed, and it was accordingly decided to float the girders into position on a large pontoon. The pontoon was constructed with a staging on it, so that, when floating on the pontoon, the bottom of the girder might be slightly higher than the top of the piers at high-water. After launching the pontoon, it was stranded on a gridiron in a sheltered bay; and the girders of one span were erected on the staging. The pontoon was then floated off, by closing its valves at low-water, during favourable weather; and being hauled out to the site of the bridge, it was moored between the piers at high-water, and, as the tide fell, the girders were deposited on the piers. The same operations were then repeated successively for each of the spans. The pontoon on one occasion was driven by the current on to some rocks during low tide, and was in danger of being wrecked with its load of girders, but was got off at high-water. The steel girders are of an American pattern, and the connections are made by bolts; they are 410 feet long between their pin supports, and 58 feet high in the centre. They afford a clear headway of 40 feet at high-water. The foundations of the bridge were commenced in 1886; and the bridge was opened for traffic in May 1889. The bridge carries two lines of railway, and has a total length of 2900 feet; and its contract price was £327,000.

St Louis Bridge.—Several lines of railway converge together on both banks of the Mississippi at St Louis, necessitating the erection of a bridge across the river at this point, in order to complete the lines of communication. The width of the river is about 1540 feet at a narrow part, opposite the centre of the town, which was the site selected for the bridge. The bed of the river is composed of shifting sand, overlying a stratum of rock which dips from 32 feet below the water level on the St Louis side to 107 feet on the Illinois side. As the sand which accumulates in the bed in the summer is scoured away to a considerable depth in flood time, when the current in the narrowed channel attains a velocity of $8\frac{1}{2}$ miles an hour, all foundations in the river had to be carried down to the solid rock; whilst the working season only lasts from August to December. As, therefore, it was important to reduce the number of piers in the river to a minimum, a bridge was designed by Mr Eads, crossing the river by three arches, the span of the central opening being 520 feet, and of the two side openings 502 feet, with rises from the springing to the crown of the arch of 47 feet and $43\frac{2}{3}$ feet respectively. (*See page* 134.) The foundations of the St Louis abutment, where the rock was near the surface, were laid in the open air, under the shelter of a cofferdam for excluding the water. The foundations, however, of the two river piers, and of the Illinois abutment, were laid on the rock at depths of 76, 102, and 108 feet respectively, by means of caissons sunk by the help of compressed air. The sinking of the caisson for the deepest pier occupied 133 days; whilst the filling with concrete the working chamber at the bottom of the caisson, in which the excavations had been carried out during the sinking, occupied 53 days.

The four arched ribs supporting the superstructure of the bridge across each opening consist each of two steel tubes, one above the other, $1\frac{1}{2}$ feet in diameter and 12 feet apart, centre to centre, and braced together; and the tubes, formed in lengths of about 12 feet bolted together, increase in thickness from the centre to the springing. As scaffolding for erecting the bridge would have impeded navigation, and would have been difficult to maintain in shifting sands, and liable to injury from floods and floating ice, the superstructure was built out from the piers and abutments. For a quarter of the span out from each pier, the arched ribs could bear their own weight, acting like a cantilever. The end of each rib was then supported by iron link chains, passing over wooden towers erected on the piers, and attached to another similar projecting rib on the opposite side, or anchored to the shore at the abutments, which enabled some additional lengths of tubes to be built out. This additional portion was then supported at the end by link chains, passing over a mast standing up on the centre of the projecting rib, and fastened at the opposite end to the springing plate against which the arch abuts ; and by this means the portions of the tubes in the centre of the span could be built out and joined in the centre, completing the arch. At certain stages of this work the chains above and the tubes below, far apart over the piers, and converging to the outer extremity of the projecting rib, presented a remarkable resemblance, on a smaller scale, to the cantilevers of the Forth Bridge when in course of erection.

The arches carry a double line of railway below, between the two pairs of ribs, and a roadway at the top, 54 feet wide, for carriages and foot passengers. The work was commenced in 1867, and completed in 1874 ; and its cost was £1,307,000. This bridge, at the time of its construction, had the largest span of any arched bridge in the world, and its foundations reached a greater depth than previously attempted ; but it has since been exceeded in span by the Douro and Garabit arched bridges ; and a greater depth of foundations was required for the piers of the Hawkesbury Bridge. Nevertheless, in spite of the progress that has been achieved in bridge construction during the last quarter of a century, the St Louis Bridge remains one of the finest examples in existence of an arched bridge, both in respect of the size of its spans, the symmetry of its construction, the double load it has to support, and its position on a large river with a shifting bed.

Garabit Viaduct.—It would be difficult to imagine a structure combining more gracefulness and boldness than the beautiful viaduct which has been erected across the precipitous valley of the river Truyère, in the south of France, from the designs of the engineer of the Eiffel Tower. (*See page* 134.) This viaduct, constructed for the railway between Marvejols and Neussargues, has a total length of 1849 feet; and the rail level on the viaduct is at a height of 401 feet above the water level of the river. The main portion of the viaduct is constructed of steel, and has a length of 1469 feet, divided into four openings on one side, and one on the other side of the large arched span, each having a width of 170 to 182 feet between the centres of the piers. These openings are spanned by lattice girders resting upon piers formed of four slightly converging columns braced together and founded on a masonry base. The girders, carrying the single line of railway, are continued across the large main opening; and they are supported by the two high piers on each side of the large opening, from the masonry base of which the arch springs, by two intermediate piers standing on the arch, and by the top of the arch itself at the centre. The trellis parabolic arch, stretching across the lower portion of the valley, has a span of 541 feet, a rise of 170 feet, and a clear height in the centre, above the river Truyère, of 356 feet. The arch itself has a depth at the top of 33 feet, and a width of 20⅔ feet, spreading out to the springing to 65⅔ feet, with a great corresponding reduction in depth. The girders supporting the roadway, and between which the trains run, are placed 16½ feet apart, and have a depth of 17 feet.

The design resembles the first bridge across the Douro erected at Oporto, by M. Eiffel, in 1877; and the central arch of the Garabit Viaduct was similarly built out from the springing on each side, like a cantilever, making use of the horizontal roadway girders, carried forward at the top, together with wire ropes suspended from a temporary erection on the top of each side pier right across the gap. The panels of the arch were thus built out by degrees, on each side, till they reached the centre, where they were joined, forming a complete arch. Scaffolding raised to such a height would have been impracticable, and therefore the only method of erecting the large arch was by building out from each extremity. The viaduct was commenced in 1879, and the work was completed in 1884. The crescent-shaped openwork arch, spread out laterally at the springings to resist the wind pressure, rising to a height of about 390 feet above the bottom of the valley, and flanked on each side by a light-looking viaduct on lofty tapering openwork piers, forms a remarkable feature in the picturesque landscape. Some idea may perhaps be formed of the scale of this structure from the consideration that if Antwerp Cathedral was placed at the bottom of the valley, the top of its spire would be just level with the top of the girder resting on the summit of the arch; and the arch would only fail by 10 feet to clear the highest point of St Paul's Cathedral if this building was standing underneath it. Its span exceeds the largest spans of the Britannia Bridge by 82 feet, and has been surpassed by very few bridges; whilst its height is unrivalled.

Hooghly Bridge.—The river Hooghly has a width of 1200 feet at low-water at Hooghly, being narrower there than for some distance above, and than anywhere lower down; and this site was selected for a bridge to carry the East Indian Railway across the river. The main channel lies near the right bank, or Hooghly side of the river, and is 66 feet deep, shoaling gradually towards the opposite bank. The erection of a bridge with three equal spans would have necessitated placing the river pier on the Hooghly side in a depth of 40 feet of water at low tide, where, owing to the floods of the river and the tidal bore, the stranding and sinking of a large caisson would have been a hazardous operation. Accordingly, the central span was given an opening of only $95\frac{1}{2}$ feet between the river piers, leaving clear openings of 520 feet on each side of the river. (*See page* 134.) This arrangement, besides placing the Hooghly pier in shallower water, rendered the erection of the girders over the central span on staging comparatively easy, and provided wider channels on each side for the navigation, the larger vessels preferring the deep channel along the right bank, and the local craft selecting the shallow channel where the stream is not strong.

The wrought-iron caissons for the river piers were floated into position, deposited on the river bed in about 30 feet of water, and then sunk by dredging inside, through about 60 feet of silt, down to a stratum of solid clay. The caissons were then filled with concrete below, and brickwork above, to form the piers, being surmounted by steel pedestals to carry the girders. The central girders were then erected on staging between the two piers; and a somewhat novel expedient was adopted for spanning the two side openings, 520 feet in width. The central girders were built out beyond the piers, on each side, by means of derricks, so as to form cantilevers, projecting about 113 feet beyond the piers. The shore girders on each side, 420 feet in length, were then so placed as to span the remainder of the opening, resting at one extremity on the shore abutment, and at the other on the end of the cantilever. These girders were put in place by rolling them out along an approach viaduct of brickwork, on which they were erected, and supporting their outer ends over the river by pontoons, with staging erected on them to the required height, so that the ends of the girders could be deposited on the ends of the cantilevers. The erection of the bridge was, accordingly, partly effected by staging, and partly by a combined system of rolling out and floating out, both of which methods have been often separately employed for the erection of bridges. The adoption of the cantilevers enabled the girders of the large shore spans to be reduced about one-fifth in span, thus realising in a conspicuous manner the practical reduction in span resulting from continuous girders. The shore ends of the girders rest on steel pins supported by suspended links, so as to allow of the forward or backward movement required by the expansion and contraction, resulting from changes in temperature, and amounting to about 3 inches at each end. The cantilever girders, $30\frac{2}{3}$ feet apart, to provide for a double line of railway between them, are 52 feet high at the centre; and the shore girders are 47 feet high, being all of steel, with curved tops; and the bridge affords a clear headway of 53 feet under the girders at low-water. The works were commenced in 1883, and completed at the end of

1886; and the cost of the bridge, including the viaducts, was £261,000. Though the spans of this bridge have been very greatly exceeded in the Sukkur Bridge over the Indus, the bridge possesses an interest from the peculiar method in which the cantilever system has been introduced for modifying the position of the piers, and facilitating the crossing of the large openings; whereas the Sukkur Bridge presents too great a resemblance in principle to the gigantic cantilevers of the Forth Bridge to render a separate description expedient. The Hooghly Bridge is quite a special type in the arrangement of its side spans; though the same kind of central cantilever, extending over two piers, has been since adopted on the Kentucky and Indiana, and the Poughkeepsie bridges for lightening the girders across the adjacent spans.

Brooklyn Bridge.—The insular position of New York, and the difficulties of communication between the north and south of Manhattan Island before the construction of the elevated railways, led to the extension of Brooklyn and Jersey City as residential quarters for men engaged in business in New York. Means of access, accordingly, across the East, and Hudson rivers were obtained by ferries, pending a more convenient means of communication being achieved. The East River, however, is considerably narrower than the Hudson River, and consequently the bridging of the former was undertaken in 1870, when the erection of a bridge across the latter was considered impracticable, though proposals have recently been made for accomplishing this still bolder feat. (*See page* 120.)

The Brooklyn Bridge, connecting New York and Brooklyn across the East River, has a total length of

5989 feet, or rather over a mile and a furlong. The bridge has a central span of 1595½ feet between the two towers, over which the suspension cables are hung; two side spans of 930 feet each between the towers and the shore; and approach viaducts, having lengths of 1562½ feet on the New York side, and 971 feet on the Brooklyn side of the river. (*See illustration.*) The suspension towers stand on two piers founded in the river within caissons, by the aid of compressed air, on the solid rock, at depths of 78 feet and 45 feet below high-water; and they rise 277 feet above the same level. There is a clear headway under the centre of the bridge of 135 feet, and near the piers of 118 feet above high-water, thus affording ample clearance for the masts of vessels passing underneath. There are four suspension cables, 15½ inches in diameter, each composed of 5282 galvanised steel wires placed side by side, without any twist, as close together as possible, arranged in nineteen strands, bound up with wire. This method of forming the cables was preferred to the plan often employed of twisting the wires together, as in an ordinary rope, on account of the greater tenacity possessed by the unbent wire. These cables, having a dip in the centre of the large span of 128 feet, rest on moveable saddles on the top of the towers, to allow for the slight movements of the cables due to changes of temperature and load; and they are held down at each end by very massive masonry anchorages built on shore. Supplementary cables extend out like a fan on each side of the towers, and both assist in supporting the two shore spans, and the portion of the long span roadway nearest the towers, and brace the roadway to reduce its deflection under heavy loads. After the foundations of the piers had been laid, the piers built, and the towers erected, the

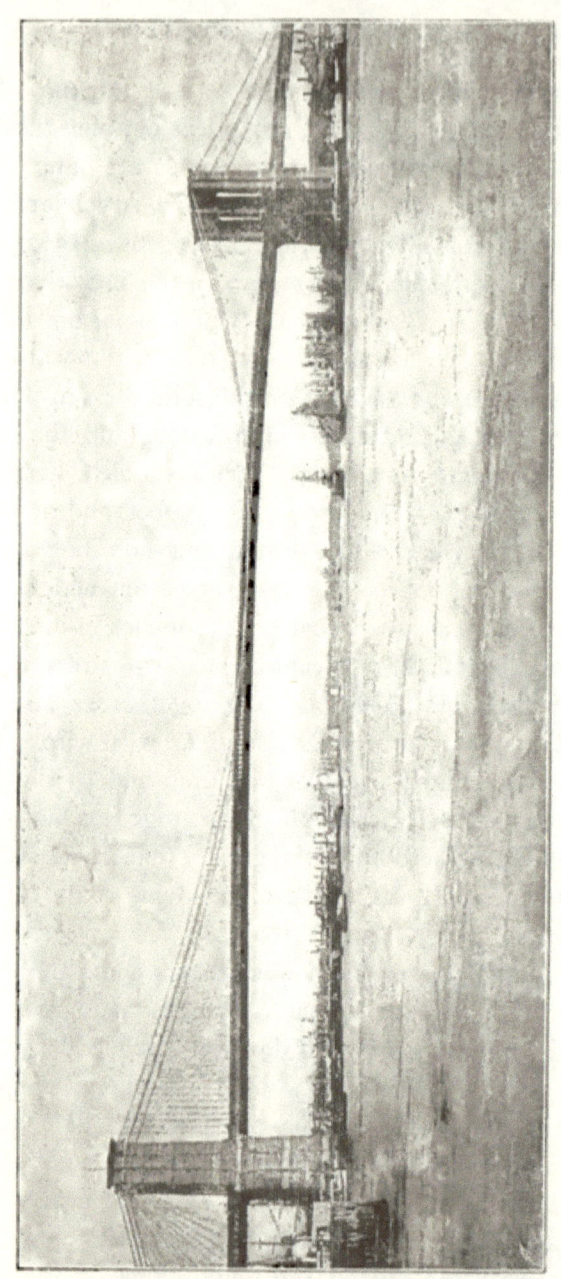

BROOKLYN BRIDGE, ACROSS THE EAST RIVER AT NEW YORK

first travelling wire rope was passed over one of the towers in 1876, conveyed by a steamboat across the river, and after being passed over the other tower, the rope, which was allowed to drop to the bottom of the river whilst its end was carried across, was drawn tight at a moment when the channel was free from shipping; and the first step towards connecting Brooklyn with New York was thus accomplished. A second travelling rope was similarly established and connected with the first; and by aid of this continuous wire rope, a temporary suspended platform was erected, on which the strands of the cables were then gradually put in place; and, lastly, the suspending ropes, and the platform of the bridge were fixed.

The bridge has a width of 85 feet, separated into five divisions; the centre one, $15\frac{1}{2}$ feet wide, and raised 12 feet above the rest of the bridge, forms a footway, on each side of which there is a line of rails for a rope railway, worked by a stationary engine on the Brooklyn side; and on the outside there is a roadway for carriages and carts, 19 feet wide, on each side. The bridge, therefore, carries two roadways, two lines of railway, and a footway. The bridge was opened in 1883; and it cost about £3,100,000, about three times the original estimate.

For seven years the Brooklyn Bridge remained the bridge with by far the largest span in the world; but the Forth Bridge deprived it of this pre-eminence, on its completion in 1890, by having two spans exceeding the large span of the Brooklyn Bridge by 115 feet. The Brooklyn Bridge, like most suspension bridges, is a graceful structure; and it has rendered a very important service to both Brooklyn and New York by providing an easy means of communication between the two towns. In the proposed bridging of the Hudson River by a monster suspension bridge, the Brooklyn Bridge is threatened by a formidable rival, on the opposite side of New York, which, if erected as designed, would outstrip the large Brooklyn span by as great a proportion as the Brooklyn Bridge surpassed any of its predecessors.

The Forth Bridge.—The railways from England converging to Edinburgh were prevented from following a direct route to Perth, Dundee, Aberdeen, and other large towns on the east coast of Scotland, by the Firth of Forth, so that the traffic had either to make a long detour by Stirling, or to be conveyed across the Firth of Forth by ferry. The Firth, which is very broad opposite Leith, the port of Edinburgh, is contracted to about a mile in width at Inverkeithing, where a ferry had been long established between North and South Queensferry; and, moreover, the small island of Inchgarvie, situated in mid-channel at this narrowed part, divides the channel into two equal portions. The idea of bridging the Forth at this point is said to have been first put forward about 150 years ago, and in 1805 a double tunnel was proposed for effecting the crossing; whilst in 1818 a design for a suspension bridge over the site of the present bridge, and with very similar spans, was published. Nothing further was done in the matter till the erection of a railway bridge, higher up the Firth, with spans of 510 feet, was authorised in 1865, which project was subsequently abandoned. In 1873 a company was formed and authority obtained for the erection of a steel suspension bridge at Queensferry, with two spans of 1600 feet, a clear headway of 150 feet, and towers, 550 feet above high-water, on Inchgarvie Island and the two shores, for supporting the chains. This bridge had been actually commenced, when the overthrow, by a gale in 1879, of the large spans of the Tay Bridge, erected by the designer of the Forth Suspension Bridge, led to a reconsideration of the plans. Eventually, after a comprehensive inquiry into the original design, other forms of stiffened suspension bridges, the cantilever system, and a tunnel, a modified design, on the cantilever principle, proposed by Messrs Fowler and Baker, was approved in 1881, and has now been carried out. The land rises rapidly from each shore at Queensferry, and the site was therefore specially suitable for the approaches to a bridge which had to be constructed at a high level to afford adequate headway for vessels to pass underneath. For the same reason, combined with the great depth of water, exceeding 200 feet, in the two channels between Inchgarvie Island and the shore, the site was not favourable for a subaqueous tunnel.

The bridge, as erected, consists of two approach viaducts; three double cantilevers, resting on two piers near the shore and on a central pier on the island; and two pairs of ordinary girders, spanning the intervals between the ends of the central and side cantilevers over the two deep channels. (*See illustration.*) The approach viaducts are formed by girders, from 168 to 179 feet in length, resting upon masonry piers, spanning five openings on the north side, and ten on the south side, together with masonry arches at the extremities. The cantilevers are symmetrical steel structures, rising 361 feet above high-water, composed of a central portion over the piers, from which two cantilever arms extend out on each side, 680 feet in length, and tapering to their extremities both vertically and horizontally. The central portions of the cantilevers consist of four vertical columns, each resting upon a circular granite pier, which are 120 feet apart at the bottom, and 33 feet apart at the top across the bridge. Longitudinally, the columns of the two side piers are 145 feet apart from bottom to top; whilst the columns of the central pier on Inchgarvie Island are 260 feet apart. This considerably greater width has been given to the central pier to enable it to resist the leverage produced when one end of its cantilever arm is fully loaded by two trains meeting on one of the central girders, and the other consequently unloaded, which leverage cannot, in the case of the central cantilever, be provided against by a counterpoise weight, such as is placed at the shore ends of the other two cantilevers which are encased in, and rest on the shore abutments. The vertical columns are connected at the top and bottom, and strongly braced together horizontally and vertically. The cantilever arms are the same in all the cantilevers, except that the fixed counterpoised shore arms are somewhat heavier in construction. They are composed of two circular curved steel tubes at the bottom in compression, and two flanged lattice steel ties at the top in tension, braced together horizontally and vertically ; and the top ties and the bottom tubes converge vertically from 330 feet at the piers to 34 feet at the extremities, and from 120 feet at the bottom and 33 feet at the top at the piers, to 32 feet and 22 feet respectively at the extremities horizontally. The cantilevers, accordingly, form very strong balanced double brackets, with such a great depth over the piers and so strongly braced as to be able to support a considerable load on their extremities. Accordingly, the ends of the cantilevers, stretching over the channels, serve as piers for girders of 350 feet span, completing the communication between the cantilevers over the

THE FORTH BRIDGE.

two channels; and the cantilevers and girders together compose a bridge affording two clear openings of 1700 feet between the piers. The road for the double line of way is supported by cross girders between the central girders; and longitudinal roadway girders, resting on uprights borne by the cantilevers, carry the railway, with a uniform width of road and at a uniform level, between the cantilevers. The widening out of the cantilevers vertically towards the piers is required to enable them to resist the strains involved in so great a span as 1700 feet; and the horizontal increase in width affords stability against wind pressure, increasing in proportion to the surface exposed, which, in the cantilever system, is greatest at the piers and least in the centre of the span. The shore ends of the side cantilevers, besides being counterpoised sufficiently to counterbalance the train load on their outer extremities, are also provided with an adequate additional weight to counterbalance half the weight of the central girder.

The total length of the bridge, together with the approach viaducts, is 8098 feet, or a little over a mile and a half; the length of the cantilever portion is 5349 feet, or rather more than a mile; the total length of the central cantilever is 1620 feet, and of the two side cantilevers, $1514\frac{3}{4}$ feet; and the clear headway under the central girders, at high-water, is 150 feet. The actual bridge, exclusive of the approach viaducts, consists of three piers, two clear spans of 1700 feet over the two channels on each side of the island, and two openings at the sides of about 680 feet each, spanned by the counterbalancing arms of the shore cantilevers, the northern one stretching over the land, and the southern one over a shallow foreshore bordering the southern channel. The central girders are attached at one end to the adjacent side cantilevers, but are left free at the other end on the central cantilever, to allow for the movements resulting from expansion and contraction.

The works were commenced at the beginning of 1883; and preparations were made for founding the twelve piers, in groups of four, on the island and each bank, on which the vertical columns of the cantilevers rest. The two northern piers on the Fife shore were built on land without difficulty, and rested on a rock foundation; and the two other piers on the Fife shore, and the two northern piers on the island, were built under the shelter of watertight casings, or cofferdams, enclosing each site. The two southern piers, however, on the island, and the four southern or Queensferry piers, had to be constructed by the aid of caissons, with compressed air, which were sunk gradually till a solid level foundation was reached, when the working chamber and caisson were filled with concrete to form the foundation for the granite pier. The chief difficulty experienced in sinking the two Inchgarvie caissons resulted from the dip of the rock, so that whilst one portion of the caisson rested upon firm rock, the other side, being unsupported, was liable to sink to a lower level and tilt the caisson, which had, accordingly, to be propped up with concrete piers and sand bags to keep it level, till the rock on the higher side could be cut away. The Queensferry caissons were sunk through from 33 to 45 feet of silt, boulder clay, and hard ground, to a solid foundation, the deepest foundation being 89 feet, and the shallowest 71 feet below high-water. Comparatively little excavation had to be effected in sinking the Inchgarvie caissons, beyond levelling the rock; so that, though owing to the greater depth of water at this site than at the Queensferry piers, the foundations were 64 and 72 feet below highwater, the launching, placing, and sinking the caissons only occupied about four months. Three of the Queensferry caissons required from five to six months for the same operations; and, owing to the accidental grounding, tilting up, and submergence of the fourth caisson, fourteen months elapsed between its launching and final sinking to its full depth.

As soon as the piers were completed, the central portions of the cantilevers were erected, and the arms were then built out in both directions without staging; and the central girders were also built out from each end of the adjacent cantilever arms, till they met in the middle and were finally connected. The work of erection of such long heavy pieces to a great height, and to great distances from the piers, without any fixed staging, involved very considerable difficulties. Special machinery and special plant were required for carrying out, adjusting, and connecting the various parts; the slanting positions of the columns and struts caused them to bend under their own weight; a high wind forced the long detached portions out of their proper lines; and even the heat of the sun led to temporary deflections; all which deviations had to be readjusted before the various parts of the structure could be joined together. The bridge was opened in March 1890, about seven years after the commencement of the works. The weight of steel used in the cantilever portion of the bridge was about 51,000 tons. The total cost of the works in connection with the bridge has been about £3,250,000, which is about double the original parliamentary estimate.

The bridge is devoid of any extraneous architectural

adornments, and is a model of simplicity and utility combined. It has been described by some persons as ugly; and when looked at from the shore ends, the convergence of its sides gives it a peculiar appearance. When viewed, however, from the water, the grandeur of its proportions is more thoroughly realised; and the massiveness of its columns and struts is lightened by the apparent slender network of cross bracing, whilst the convergence of its sides is not seen. The large sizes of its several parts are best observed from the footways, running along each side of the railway across the bridge, from whence also the great height and width of the cantilevers over the piers can be most advantageously perceived, at an elevation of about half their height. It is difficult from any other point of view to grasp the real magnitude of the structure; for the central girders, of 380 feet span, which in any other bridge would be regarded as considerable, appear quite diminutive in comparison to the gigantic cantilevers on each side of them.

The two cantilever arms alone of one span of the Forth Bridge, exclusive of the central girder, are 250 feet longer than the height of the Eiffel Tower; and the cantilevers rise over the piers, above high-water, to within 5 feet of the height of St Paul's. Each of the large spans is about 200 feet longer than the total length of the Britannia Bridge, with its four spans, and longer than Waterloo Bridge, with its eight arches including its shore spans; and one span alone would stretch across the Thames at Woolwich, or the Mississippi at St Louis. The two spans of the Forth Bridge would traverse the East River at the site of the Brooklyn Bridge; and the cantilevers are about 85 feet higher above the water than the towers of the

Brooklyn Bridge, though their height is very much masked by their great proportionate length, the length of the central cantilever being four and a half times its height. The Forth Bridge has not the light appearance of the Brooklyn Bridge, in which particular suspension bridges excel, but it possesses greater rigidity; and though it has not nearly the width of roadway of the Brooklyn Bridge, it exceeds it by 105 feet in span. The two large spans of the Forth Bridge correspond approximately in length to the large span and two shore spans at Brooklyn; but the counterbalancing cantilever spans, with the approaches, at the Forth Bridge are longer than the Brooklyn Bridge approaches; so that the Forth Bridge, altogether, is about 3 furlongs longer than the Brooklyn Bridge, whilst it provides less accommodation in width. These two bridges, far excelling all others in span, though not really comparable, happen to have cost very nearly the same amount, which in both cases largely exceeded the original estimates; and this result may lead to hesitation in undertaking the construction of long span bridges. The Forth Bridge has proved very firm under heavy loads, and has already attracted a large quantity of traffic. Its successful completion has demonstrated the advantages of the cantilever system for large spans.

The Sukkur Bridge resembles the Forth Bridge in having a central girder, with a span of 200 feet, supported at the ends of two cantilever arms, each 310 feet long; but the cantilevers of the Sukkur Bridge are less symmetrical, and their parts are more massed together than in the Forth Bridge.

The Tower Bridge.—The bridge which, after long discussion of various schemes, was designed for providing a connection between both banks of the Thames below London Bridge, is still in course of construction just below the Tower. The most uncertain portion, however, of the work, namely, the foundations of the river piers, has already been accomplished, so that only the erection of the towers on the piers, and the superstructure of the bridge remain to be carried out; and it is anticipated that the bridge will be finished at the end of 1892. The bridge is not remarkable for any specially large span; but it possesses an interest from the peculiarity of its design, which distinguishes it from all bridges hitherto erected over the Thames, and also as solving the problem of providing a convenient roadway across the river below London Bridge without unduly impeding navigation. Schemes have been proposed for a tunnel under the bed of the river, or a high-level bridge over the river; but the long, steep approaches required in either case on each side, in a densely crowded and valuable part of the metropolis, have proved an insuperable obstacle. The present design obviates that difficulty by providing an opening central span for vessels, and thus enabling the approaches on each side to reach the bridge from the main thoroughfares with less rise than at London Bridge. (*See illustration.*)

The distance between the two abutments of the bridge, on each side of the river, is 880 feet, divided into three openings by two river piers, 70 feet in width, the two side openings being 270 feet in width, and the central opening 200 feet. The roadways of the two side openings are to be suspended from chains hanging from the high towers on the river piers to the lower towers on the abutments. The central opening is to be spanned by a double bascule or drawbridge, the two halves being pivoted in the piers, and when down forming a flat arch across the

opening, with a headway in the centre of 29½ feet above high-water. These two halves are counterbalanced at their tail ends, extending inside the piers, and can be raised by machinery to a vertical position against each tower, so as to be quite clear of the opening, the tail ends revolving in segmental recesses provided in the piers, and the roadway portions going partially into vertical recesses in the faces of the towers on the piers. When the bascule bridge is open, a clear headway of 139½ feet will be afforded between high-water and a light fixed upper roadway for foot passengers, resting on the upper part of the river towers, and spanning the central opening between the towers. Access to this upper roadway is provided by staircases and hydraulic lifts inside the towers; so that foot passengers will always be able to cross the river, even when the bridge is closed to vehicles for the passage of vessels. The width between the parapets will be 50 feet in the opening span, and 60 feet along the approaches and side spans. The approaches have been built on brick arches; and the gradient nowhere exceeds 1 in 40. Hydraulic power will be supplied by engines on the Surrey side; and hydraulic accumulators, which are weighted cylinders for maintaining the water pressure, are to be placed in the piers, so as to store up power for working the machinery for opening the bridge and raising the passenger lifts. Most of the metal work in the bridge and towers is to be steel; the weight of each leaf of the bascule bridge, with its counterpoise weight, will be 950 tons; and the weight of iron and steel in the bridge will amount to 15,000 tons.

The foundations for the river piers were laid within wrought-iron caissons, sunk to a depth of 27 feet below the river bed, and 60 feet below high-water; but the foundations of the two piers could not be carried on simultaneously, as the amount of staging allowed in the channel at one time was restricted on behalf of the navigation, so that the progress of the work was thereby delayed. Parliamentary sanction for the construction of this bridge was obtained in 1885; the foundation stone was laid in 1886; and progress is now being made with the towers and superstructure. The length of the bridge and abutments is 940 feet, and of the approaches 1700 feet, making a total length of 2640 feet; and the estimated cost of the work is £750,000. Wooden bascule bridges are very common in Holland, especially in Amsterdam, over the numerous canals intersecting that city; but they have been rarely employed for large spans. Bridges turning horizontally on a pivot, known as swing bridges, are much more common, but would have been unsuited for the centre of a crowded river, owing to the space occupied by them when open.

The Tower Bridge, with its suspended shore spans, its high river towers, its high-level footway, and its bascule bridge, will have features of novelty and architectural merits not always possessed by engineering works, and will also be a great advantage in facilitating communication below London Bridge.

Proposed Channel Bridge.—The success of any large undertaking generally leads to proposals for the construction of works of still greater magnitude. It is proposed, as previously mentioned, to follow up the Brooklyn Bridge by the erection of a much larger suspension bridge across the Hudson River; and the completion of the Forth Bridge has imparted fresh vigour to schemes for bridging the

English Channel, in place of the Channel Tunnel. The promoters of the latest design naturally adopt the cantilever system, selecting the principle of the Kentucky and Indiana Bridge, across the Ohio, of girders supported on two piers, and projecting beyond them as cantilevers on each side, supporting smaller central girders at their extremities over the intermediate or cantilever spans. The bridge, traversing the Channel at the Straits of Dover, would have a length of 24 miles, nearly twelve times the length of the Tay Bridge. It is to be borne on 120 piers, the piers in the main deep channel attaining a depth of 180 feet below high-water, and supporting the girders at a height of 180 feet above high-water, to afford that clear headway for vessels navigating the Channel. The large cantilever spans in mid-channel are to have openings of 1640 feet; whilst the distance between the piers of the intermediate supporting girders is to be 984 feet. Other spans, of from 328 to 830 feet, are to be formed in the shallower and less frequented parts of the Channel. The estimated amount of metal required is 1,000,000 tons, or about forty times the quantity used in the Forth Bridge; and the estimated cost is about £34,000,000. The height of the largest girders is to be 213 feet, so that the total height of the highest portion of the structure would be about 570 feet above the sea bottom, or 40 feet higher than the top of the spires of Cologne Cathedral, the highest building in the world with the exception of the Eiffel Tower. A bridge across the Channel is not dependent upon the continuity of the chalk stratum like a tunnel, and passengers on the Channel Bridge in a stormy night would be in no need of ventilation; but in other respects a bridge would involve much greater difficulties in construction, in the open sea at such a depth, than a tunnel through chalk.

Moreover, the much greater cost of a bridge, and the danger presented to shipping in fogs or storms by a number of piers in mid-channel, appear to render a Channel bridge inexpedient, unless a tunnel should prove to be impracticable.

CHAPTER VIII.

SUBMARINE MINING AND BLASTING.

EXCAVATION under water, known by the general term of dredging when soft material has to be removed, is generally cheaper than excavation on land, owing to the large floating dredging machines that can be employed, and readily moved about, and owing to the economy with which the carriage of the lifted material to a suitable place of deposit can be effected by water. When, however, rock impedes the widening or deepening of a navigable channel, its removal is attended with difficulty, and involves a considerable expense. Blasting on land is a slow and somewhat costly operation; but blasting under water, where the boring of the holes has to be effected in an unseen rock, and the blasting charges have to be inserted and fired under water, is much more tedious and expensive. As the execution of such works depends in great measure upon questions of cost, a large rocky shoal presents a very serious impediment to the improvement of a channel. Rocks under water have, however, been removed when not large in extent, and when they have presented a serious danger to shipping, as for instance in Holyhead and Alderney harbours. Rocky shoals, also, extending across river channels, and limiting the improvement in depth that can be obtained by dredging, have been lowered in recent years by drilling from special rafts, the explosive being deposited in the holes either through tubes or by divers, as in the Tees, the Yarra River in Australia, and elsewhere. Dynamite and nitro-glycerine have been employed for the blasting, being fired by fuses or electricity, with the help of a detonator such as fulminate of mercury, which, by causing a concussion, ensures the completeness of the explosion. Drilling machines, also, worked by compressed air, have been used for drilling the blasting holes from a barge. Sometimes dynamite has been employed for shattering subaqueous rocks, by being exploded when simply in contact with the rock; but a good deal of the power of the explosive is wasted by this arrangement, and it is not advantageous when the rock is massive. These are the ordinary methods of removing rock under water; but there are three other systems for effecting this object, one of which has enabled a gigantic operation for deepening a channel to be accomplished.

Compressed Air Diving-Bell.—A peculiar form of floating diving-bell, into which compressed air can be introduced, has been employed for facilitating the removal of rocks in Brest and Cherbourg harbours. The lower portion of the apparatus consists of a large plate-iron caisson, 33 feet long, $26\frac{1}{4}$ feet wide, and 23 feet high, which is divided into two parts by a watertight horizontal diaphragm, about $6\frac{1}{2}$ feet above the bottom which is left open. The lower division forms the working chamber, which can be filled with compressed air by a pipe leading from air compressors on shore. The upper division makes the apparatus float when full of air, or sinks it when water is admitted. The sides are carried up, somewhat converging, above the caisson to a sufficient height to place the platform at the top above high-water when the caisson is sunk in position. A staircase, in a large central shaft, leads from the top platform to the air-locks on the roof of the working chamber; whilst two smaller shafts, on each side, serve for the removal of the displaced rock. The caisson is ballasted near the bottom with masonry and pig-iron to make it float upright. The caisson is floated out to the required spot, and sunk by admitting water into the air chamber above the working chamber. The men then enter the working chamber, lit by electric light, from which the water is excluded by compressed air; and when the holes have been bored in the rock and charged, the men retire into the air-locks for the blast. The men can thus mine and blast the submarine rocks as if they were out of water; and at the termination of the work, compressed air being let into the air chamber, forces out the water, and floats the apparatus.

Rock-breaking Rams.—Another system of dealing with rock under water is by first breaking the rock up by a succession of blows, delivered by a heavy falling weight, and then removing the shattered loose rock by raising it in the buckets of an ordinary dredger. The rock-breaking rams are made of iron, about 42 feet long and 9 inches square, with a steel-pointed wedge-shaped end or cutter, and weighing 4 tons. The rams are raised, by hydraulic power, within a staging erected over the bottomless well of a bucket dredger, and are dropped from a height of 10 to 20 feet upon the rock. These rams, with their wedge-shaped ends, gradually shatter the rock after a series of blows on the same spot, and thus dispense with the cost and delay of boring and blasting rock under water. Ten rams have been used in one set, capable of giving about 500 blows in an hour. This system has been successfully applied to the widening of the portion of the Suez Canal which traverses rock, as much as 1000 cubic yards of solid rock having been raised in sixteen hours at Chalouf. The method appears primitive, but it has proved more effectual, more rapid, and cheaper, on the Suez Canal widening in 1888, than the ordinary methods of blasting rock.

Blasting Operations at Hell Gate, New York.—The channels of the East River, leading from Long Island Sound to New York Harbour, were obstructed by a number of scattered reefs, which both imperilled navigation, and also rendered it difficult owing to the rapid currents produced in the contracted channels. (*See page* 164, *fig.* 1.) Wrecks, accordingly, frequently occurred, which led to the ominous name of Hell Gate being given to the locality. The first proposals for improving the channels, made in 1848, only contemplated the removal of the highest pointed reefs by surface blasting (which was carried on from 1851 to 1853), owing to the great cost of extensive removals of submarine rocks; and nothing further was done for several years. At last, in 1868-69, some larger and wider detached rocks were lowered by drilling and blasting, the drilling being effected from a very strong barge at a considerable cost. A more comprehensive scheme, for the general removal of the rocks in the channels to a depth of 26 feet below low-water, was proposed in 1869; and a commencement was made in the same year at Hallett's Point, from which

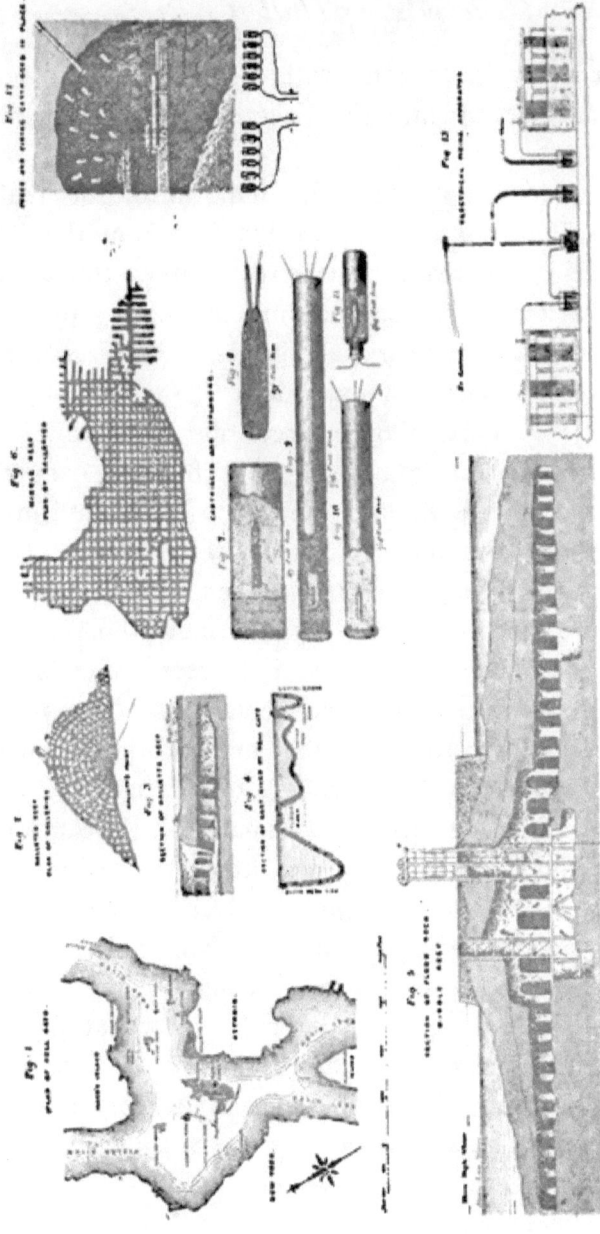

BLASTING OPERATIONS AT HELL GATE, NEW YORK.

a reef extended, connected with Long Island, but jutting out inconveniently into the East River at an awkward bend.

The plan adopted for the removal of the reef at Hallett's Point, extending out 325 feet from the shore, and covering an area of 3 acres rising above the depth of 26 feet at low-water, consisted in undermining the whole of the area with a network of galleries, and then shattering the roof and supports by explosives. (*See page* 164, *figs. 2 and* 3.) A portion of the reef above low-water was enclosed by a watertight casing, or cofferdam, connected with the shore at both ends; and a shaft was sunk in this enclosure to a depth of 33 feet below low-water. Large galleries or headings were then driven in radial lines by boring and blasting from the shaft under the reef; and smaller intermediate galleries and cross galleries were formed in the rock under the whole area of the reef to be removed. Accordingly, a regular network of galleries extended under the reef, having a total length of nearly a mile and a half, resembling on a small scale the catacombs of Rome and Paris; and the roof, from 6 to 20 feet thick, separating the galleries from the river overhead, rested upon 172 pillars of rock, left in piercing the galleries, about 10 feet thick and from 8 to 22 feet high. The boring of the holes in forming the galleries was done at first by hand, and afterwards by steam drills; but the work progressed slowly, owing to the hardness of the rock, consisting of hornblende, gneiss, and quartz, the shallow holes and small charges necessary to avoid injuring the roof, and the inadequate sums yearly voted by Congress for the work, so that the galleries were not completed till the middle of 1875. Holes were then drilled in the roof and piers for the cartridges required in the final explosion, mostly about 3 inches in diameter and 8¾ feet long. Cartridges filled with dynamite, vulcan powder, and rendrock, solid compounds of nitro-glycerine, were inserted in about 4460 holes, provided at the end with detonating charges of fulminate of mercury. Altogether 49,900 lbs. of explosives were employed for shattering the 63,100 cubic yards of rock in the roof and piers of the galleries. Provision for the simultaneous firing of all these mines was made by placing twenty-three galvanic batteries at the spot, and connecting each of them with a group of the mines. Twenty-three brass pins, each connected with one of the poles of a battery, were suspended by a cord over twenty-three mercury cups in connection with the other poles of the batteries. When everything was arranged, the galleries and shaft were flooded by the admission of the water from the river, through a syphon, on the 23d of September 1876, in order to increase the energy of the explosion by somewhat closing the vent of the holes, or tamping as it is termed, by the pressure of the water. The following day, September 24, 1876, the final explosion was effected by firing a dynamite cartridge, attached to the cord suspending the brass pins, by electricity from the shore. The cord was thus severed; and the brass pins dropping into the cups containing mercury, completed the circuit of the batteries, and caused a simultaneous explosion of all the mines. Spray was thrown up by the explosion to a height of 123 feet; but no windows were broken by the shock, and the landtremor produced was small. All the shattered rock which lay above the 26 feet depth had to be subsequently removed by grapple dredgers; and blocks which were too big to be thus lifted had to be broken up smaller by surface blasting. The removal of the broken rock lying above the requisite level on the reef, amounting to 45,300 cubic yards, was not completed till 1882; so that the work occupied about twelve and a half years, and it cost £250,420.

Before the final explosion at Hallett's reef had been effected, a still greater undertaking was commenced, namely, the removal, in the same way, of the Middle Reef, situated in mid-channel between Astoria and New York, and covering an area of 9 acres above the depth of 26 feet at low-water requisite for navigation. (*See page* 164, *figs.* 1, 4, 5, *and* 6.) Two shafts were begun, in 1875, on a portion of the rock above high-water level, and were sunk to about 60 feet below low-water level. Parallel galleries were driven from the shafts in each direction, together with galleries at right angles, extending in a network, as at Hallett's reef, under the whole area of the reef to be lowered. The total length of these submarine galleries was a little over 4 miles, about 10 feet square in section generally, but in some places as low as 4 feet, and in others 33 feet high. The roof, from 10 to 20 feet thick above the galleries, was supported by 467 pillars of rock, about 15 feet square, and 25 feet apart, and varying in height with the height of the galleries. Some fissures in the rock were traversed in driving the galleries, which let in a good deal of water, but they were closed with cement. The great care required in blasting for forming the galleries, so as not to injure the roof, and the inadequacy of the yearly grants, delayed the progress of the works; but the drilling of the holes in the roof and pillars for the final explosion was begun in 1882, though the galleries were not completed till 1885. There were 12,560 of these holes, about 3 inches in diameter and 9 feet deep, arranged from 4 to 5 feet apart, and extending down the pillars to 33 feet below low-water, so that all the rock might be shattered down to this depth. The charging of these holes with explosives was commenced in July 1885, about two and a half months before the final blast was fired.

The arrangements for this much larger explosion, expending 282,730 lbs. of explosives in shattering 270,700 cubic yards of rock, differed in two important particulars from the previous one at Hallett's Point; for a new explosive was used, and the mines in the roof and pillars were not connected with the batteries. Rackarock, which was mainly employed for charging the cartridges, consists of a mixture of 79 parts of potassium chlorate, which is a solid, with 21 parts of nitro-benzol, which is a liquid, and which are therefore readily mixed, as the solid absorbs the liquid. These ingredients are harmless before admixture, and therefore can be stored in large quantities without danger of explosion; and the mixing is effected without the great risk attending the admixture of two solids to form an explosive compound. Moreover, rackarock is not so readily exploded as dynamite; whilst its explosion under water is more effective.

The holes were filled with rackarock cartridges, in the top of each of which an exploder was inserted, consisting of a tube filled with dynamite, containing inside it a small tube filled with fulminate of mercury; and at the outer end of each hole a dynamite cartridge, 15 inches long, containing a fulminate exploder, was inserted, projecting about 6 inches out of the hole. (*See page* 164, *figs.* 7 *to* 11.) All these precautions were necessary to insure the explosion of the charges by sympathetic detonation, resulting from the concussion produced by the explosion of cartridges placed in the galleries and fired by electricity. These initial exploders, 592 in number, were placed on boards across the galleries, at intervals of 25 feet, and consisted of dynamite cartridges provided with fulminate detonators connected with the batteries. (*See page* 164, *fig.* 12.) These exploders were connected with the twenty-four batteries in separate groups, so arranged that no two adjacent exploders should be on the same circuit, in order that if one battery failed to act, the exploders connected with it might be exploded by sympathy by the neighbouring exploders. To secure the simultaneous firing of all the exploders placed in the galleries, some mercury, contained in an iron bowl, was connected with the negative poles of all the batteries; and a thin glass tumbler was put in the bowl, with some mercury in it connected with all the positive poles of the batteries, so that the glass of the tumbler alone prevented the closing of all the circuits. A long iron rod, with a pointed end, was placed in a vertical position, with its point resting on the bottom of the tumbler; and on the top of the rod, a flat plate supported a small cartridge which could be fired by means of wires leading to a battery on the shore. (*See page* 164, *fig.* 13.)

Water was let into the galleries, by two syphons, on the 9th of October 1885; and when they were filled with water on the following day, October 10, 1885, the movement of a handle by General Newton's little daughter on shore, at Astoria, completed the circuit of the shore battery, and firing the small cartridge at the Middle Reef, drove down the iron rod, which, breaking the glass tumbler, completed the circuits of the twenty-four batteries. The exploders along the galleries were thereby fired, and by the shock of their explosions fired the detonators in the cartridges projecting from the pillars and roof, and produced a simultaneous explosion of the mines. A dull rumble was heard; the water rose in a mass over the site of the reef; and spray shot up in peaks, from 100 to 200 feet high, as illustrated by the instantaneous photograph of the explosion, taken end on from Blackwell's Island. (*See illustration.*) The explosion produced no loud report or great shock; and little damage was done, beyond the breakage of a few panes of glass in the nearest buildings. The earth-wave produced by the explosion was carefully recorded at various places; and the rate of transmission of the shock was found to be more rapid and more uniform when the shock passed northwards through rock, than when it passed through drift in an easterly direction. In travelling through drift, it reached Goat Island, a distance of 145 miles, in 59 seconds, and Harvard College Observatory, $182\frac{3}{4}$ miles off, in 3 minutes 40 seconds; and in travelling through rock, it reached West Point, $42\frac{1}{3}$ miles distant, in 11 seconds, and Litchfield Observatory, $174\frac{1}{3}$ miles away, in $45\frac{1}{3}$ seconds.

Considerable economy was effected at Middle Reef by the use of rackarock, and the explosion by sympathy; for whereas the blast there was six times the blast at Hallett's Point, the expenditure on the final explosion was only about a third larger. The amount of shattered rock lying above the depth of 26 feet at low-water was about 294,000 cubic yards, which has been gradually removed by grapple dredgers. The total cost of the work was about £1,070,000, for which expenditure New York has got a communication with the sea by the East River and Long Island Sound, with a minimum depth of 26 feet at low-water, where formerly there were numerous shoals im-

EXPLOSION OF MIDDLE REEF AT HELL GATE, NEW YORK, OCTOBER 10TH, 1885.

perilling the navigation. Though headings for mines have occasionally been carried, at a considerable depth, beyond the coast under the sea, the system of submarine mining had not previously been adopted for lowering reefs; and though costly, the removal of such large reefs could not have been well accomplished in any other way. The lowering of the Middle Reef was effected by the firing of the largest explosion ever attempted, which was completely successful, and has provided the shipping trade of New York with an excellent direct channel to the ocean.

CHAPTER IX.

THE PORTS OF LONDON, LIVERPOOL, ANTWERP, MARSEILLES, AND NEW YORK.

THE foreign trade of a country may, to a great extent, be measured by the size of its ports. This is absolutely true of Great Britain, Australia, New Zealand, India, and other countries separated from foreign lands by the sea or mountain barriers. It is true, also, though to a somewhat less extent, of continental nations possessing a convenient seaboard; for trading nations do not confine their trade within the narrow limits of adjacent countries, if they can obtain a sea-going trade with the various countries of the world. Seaports, accordingly, form an important element in the commercial prosperity of nations; and their development is essential to the increase of trade. Many ports are of ancient origin, but their development is in all cases of recent date; and several ports have only come into existence within the present century. For instance, the large ports of Hull, the Tyne, Glasgow, and Havre, possessed very little accommodation for shipping previous to the present century; whilst Cardiff, Barrow, and Middlesborough have sprang into existence as ports in the last fifty years.

Port of London.—At the beginning of the present century London possessed only one dock, namely, the Greenland Dock, constructed in 1660, forming part now of the Surrey Commercial Docks, with an area of 12 acres, and quays along the river having a total length of rather under a mile. Considerable additions to the dock accommodation along the Thames were made early in the century, by the construction of the East and West India Docks, the London Docks, the Surrey and Commercial Docks, and lastly, in 1828, the St Katherine Docks, close to London Bridge. All the important subsequent dock extensions have been made during the last thirty-five years.

A tendency has been manifested, in most of the more recent large dock extensions of recent times in the Port of London, to place the docks lower down the river, where more open space is available, land is cheaper, and the river is both broader and less crowded with shipping. The first large addition to the dock accommodation of London since 1828 was the opening of the Victoria Dock and Basin in 1855, adding 90 acres of water to the dock area of the port. This dock, like most of the earlier docks, is situated in a low-lying tract of land between two bends of the river, where the excavations from the docks could be utilised for raising the adjacent land to form quays, and where an entrance lock could be easily made to open on the river from the extremity of the docks. The Victoria Dock, nearly opposite Woolwich, is lower down the river than any of the earlier docks; it is 3000 feet long, and 1050 feet wide, and is provided with several jetties on the north side, to increase the quay accommodation for vessels; and, like most of the other London docks, it has a basin between the main dock and the entrance lock, which joins the river a little beyond Bow Creek below Blackwall. The lock was given a width of 80 feet, 20 feet wider than any previous lock on the Thames; and its length of 350 feet was greater than the length of the earlier locks. An interesting feature of this dock is the arrangement of the repairing, or graving docks in connection with it. Usually these graving docks are made sufficiently deep for a vessel of the largest size to be floated in; the gates at the entrance are then closed, the water is pumped out, the vessel is propped up, and the repairs are executed. The Victoria graving docks, however, are made shallow; and the vessel, on entering the channel leading to the graving docks from the main dock, passes over a pontoon sunk at the bottom of the channel, which is then lifted out of water, by hydraulic rams underneath, raising the vessel suitably supported on it. The water flows out of the open valves of the pontoon, which are then closed; and the rams, descending again, leave the vessel resting on the floating pontoon, which is hauled into one of the shallow docks for repairs.

The Millwall Docks, in the Isle of Dogs, were next opened in 1868, having a water area of 35 acres, and an entrance lock of the same width and depth as the Victoria Dock lock, but 450 feet long, being an increase of 100 feet. In 1870, the opening of the South West India Dock added 32 more acres to the water area of the docks of London. This dock, which stretches across the Isle of Dogs, has a lock at each end like the other West India docks, the lower and larger lock serving for the entrance of large vessels, and the upper lock being used by the river barges, which convey goods from the vessels up to wharves alongside the river. This dock is also provided with a basin between the main entrance lock and the dock, which facilitates the entrance and exit of a number of vessels by being made level with the river outside near high-water, so that vessels pass in or out without the delay of locking; whilst the level of water in the dock is not altered. The chief novel feature in the Millwall, and South West India docks was the employment of a large proportion of concrete at the back of the face of brickwork in the quay walls surrounding them, which, owing to the abundance of good river gravel found in the excavations, reduced considerably the cost of the walls.

The Albert Dock, forming an extension of the Victoria Dock, and, though a distinct dock, connected with it by a channel, was opened in 1880. This dock, 6500 feet long and 490 feet wide, is narrower than the Victoria Dock, and has no jetties. Including a basin, it has an area of 84 acres, and with its basin and entrance lock, extends to the further side of the bend of the river which passes by Woolwich; so that the two docks stretch right across this very wide bend, with entrances into the Thames at each end about 3 miles apart. The Albert Dock lock, though given the same width of 80 feet as the Victoria Dock lock, was made 550 feet long instead of 350 feet, and was given a depth of 30 feet at high-water spring tides instead of 28 feet, indicating the advance considered expedient in the lapse of twenty-five years. When, however, the Tilbury Docks were in progress, holding out a prospect for shipping to enter the docks at any state of the tide, the Victoria and Albert Dock Company deemed it advisable to increase their accommodation by a deeper lock, which was accordingly constructed, near the first Albert Dock lock, with a depth of 36 feet at high-water spring tides, but with a length and width similar to the first lock. The quay walls round the Albert Dock were built entirely of concrete, made with the gravel from the excavations, mixed with an eighth part of Portland cement. Concrete under such conditions is very economical; it also requires little plant or skilled labour, and can be rapidly built up. In order to connect the new lock and a small extension with the basin, 520 feet in length of the basin wall had to be removed, which, after it had been reduced at the back by blasting to a uniform thickness of about 6 feet, was effected by drilling a number of holes at the back in the remaining front portion of the wall, filling them with gelatine dynamite, and firing all the charges simultaneously by electricity. There were 1450 holes, placed 4 feet apart, filled with 2900 lbs. of explosive; and the charges were fired on Good Friday morning 1886, which was chosen on account of the absence of men from work, giving greater security against injury, and to avoid interfering with the dock traffic. The explosion produced a loud report, but did not cause any damage to adjacent property; and the wall fell, broken to pieces, in a heap in the water. The Victoria and Albert docks form part of the dock property of the London and St Katherine Dock Company.

The Tilbury Docks were commenced in 1882 by the East and West India Dock Company, with the object of offering more ample accommodation lower down the Thames than the other dock companies. They are situated on low-lying land at Tilbury, opposite Gravesend; and they consist of an outer tidal basin of $19\frac{1}{4}$ acres, communicating directly with the river; a lock, 700 feet long and 80 feet wide, leading from the basin to the docks; and a main dock leading to three parallel branch docks, each 1500 feet long, with sheds and sidings along each side, having a total area of $57\frac{1}{4}$ acres. The basin has been excavated to a depth of 26 feet at low-water spring tides, so that vessels can always remain afloat in it; and as the outer sill of the lock is only 1 foot higher, or 45 feet below high-water spring tides, vessels can enter or leave the docks at any state of the tide. Two channels, parallel to the lock, each contain a pair of graving docks; and the largest and deepest channel could be used as a lock in case of necessity. Owing to the silty, alluvial nature of the soil, the foundations for the walls had to be carried to a considerable depth, and in some cases were founded upon piles; and as the bottom of the dock is 38 feet below high-water spring tides, the walls, made of concrete with brick facing, had to be raised about 44 feet above the dock bottom, higher than any previous dock walls on the Thames. These docks were opened in April 1886.

Hydraulic machinery for opening and closing the dock gates, the sluice gates, and the swing bridges, for moving the cranes and lifts, and for turning the capstans, was provided at the South West India Dock on its opening in 1870; it has been extended also to the older docks, and has always been supplied to the more recent docks in the Port of London. Hydraulic power is specially adapted for the intermittent work of docks; for the power can be gradually stored up by means of accumulators, to be employed more rapidly than it could be generated at periods of a press of work, such as at high-water.

The construction of docks, like that of the foundations of bridges, involves a great amount of difficult work; and the quays, sheds, sidings, swing bridges, and tops of the gates, which are alone visible when the docks are filled with water, furnish a very inadequate impression of the hazardous and intricate works required in making a dock. Temporary cofferdams have to be made for keeping out the water; large pumping machinery has to be constantly working to keep the foundations dry; deep foundations have to be excavated to reach a reliable stratum; great care has to be taken to prevent the sliding forward of the wall in filling up at the back of high dock walls before the water is let into the dock; the masonry in the locks has to be very accurately dressed to receive the gates; the gates have to be very carefully fitted, secured, and made watertight; sluiceways have to be formed through the walls of the lock, built so as to resist the pressure and rush of water through them; and the foundations of the floor of the lock have to be made secure against pressure and percolation under a head of water. The superstructure and piers of bridges and viaducts are always in evidence to attest the skill of their designers; whereas docks, and to a great extent waterworks, can be only justly appreciated during construction, the works being in great measure hidden from view after their completion; whilst breakwaters, being built mostly under water, can be only judged of by their effects.

The water area of the docks of London has been nearly doubled since 1855, and at present amounts to 558 acres, exclusive of shallow timber ponds; whilst the facilities for the admission of vessels of large draught, and for loading and unloading, have been immensely increased during the same period. Moreover, whereas the Port of London, fifty years ago, only reached as far as Blackwall, $6\frac{3}{4}$ miles from London Bridge, it now extends to Gravesend, 26 miles below London Bridge.

Port of Liverpool.—Though the first dock was commenced at Liverpool in 1709, the port progressed very slowly up to the beginning of the present century, as it only possessed 34 acres of water area in 1816. Whilst increasing more rapidly after this period, so that its dock area reached 108 acres in 1846, its chief advance has occurred within the last fifty years; for the Port of Liverpool now possesses docks with a total water area (including Birkenhead, which was incorporated with it in 1855) of 521 acres. Thus, the dock accommodation of the port is nearly fivefold what it was fifty years ago. Docks have been gradually extended north and south of the older docks, on the Liverpool side; whilst docks have been constructed at Birkenhead, on the opposite side of the Mersey, on the site of Wallasey Pool. The docks extend at Liverpool, along the Mersey, in a continuous line of nearly 6 miles, only broken near the centre by the approach road to the great landing-stage. The most recent dock extensions on the north side, nearest the sea, where the largest docks are situated, have been made on land reclaimed from the river foreshore, and surrounded with concrete quay walls. The southern extensions, on the contrary, encroach upon rising ground, so that excavations have been needed in forming portions of the quays; whilst the docks have been excavated out of the solid sandstone rock, so that in some places it was only necessary to face the rock with ashlar masonry, instead of building a dock wall. The earlier Liverpool docks were of small area, rarely exceeding 10 acres; but the more recent docks are larger, of which the biggest are the Canada, Langton, and Hornby Docks, of about 18 acres each; the Huskisson Dock, of 30 acres; and the Alexandra Dock, of 44 acres, opened in 1880. The East and West Docks at Birkenhead are larger, however, than any of the Liverpool docks, having areas of $59\frac{3}{4}$, and 52 acres respectively; but they are not so large as either the Albert or Victoria docks on the Thames, of 71, and 74 acres;

whilst the Cavendish Dock at Barrow exceeds them all, with an area of 102 acres.

The docks at Liverpool are all connected together by passages or entrances to the north and south of the landing-stage approach, which divides them into two distinct groups; and, instead of being approached by locks, as on the Thames, access is provided generally along the Mersey, at a few places, through entrances with a single pair of gates, which are opened a short time before high-water, and closed on the turn of the tide. These entrances are in some cases approached through a tidal basin, which shelters the vessels, and facilitates their entry or exit. There are entrances and locks at Liverpool and Birkenhead 100 feet in width, provided originally for paddle-wheel steamers which have been superseded by screw-steamers; and the largest new entrances are 65 feet wide. The largest lock at Liverpool is 498 feet long, leading to the Canada Dock; and the deepest entrances at Liverpool and Birkenhead are 2 feet below the lowest low-tide, affording a depth of $23\frac{1}{2}$ feet at high-water neap tides, and 31 feet at spring tides; but the construction of deeper entrances is in contemplation, to allow of a longer period for the entrance or exit of vessels.

The large quantity of sand and silt carried in suspension by the Mersey readily deposits in the sheltered tidal basins leading to the docks, and would soon impede the access if not cleared away; and a bank of sand, known as the Pluckington Bank, stretches across the entrances of the older docks, on the southern side, rising above low-water level. In constructing the deep Langton Dock entrances, opening into the Canada Tidal Basin, four iron pipes, 8 feet in diameter, encased in concrete, were carried under the concrete floor of the basin in front of the entrances, having several vertical outlets, 3 feet in diameter, on a level with the floor, spread over this area. By opening sluice gates at low-water spring tides, the water from the docks is admitted into one or more of these pipes, and issuing with great force from the outlets on the floor, sweeps away the accumulation of silt, and keeps the passage clear. Another set of sluices, with numerous horizontal outlets at a low level, are placed along the jetties on each side of the entrance to the tidal basin; and the current of water from the docks, let out at low-tide from these sluices, maintains the passage between the basin and the river. Another series of sluices higher up the river, fed with water from the southern docks at low tide, keep the northern end of Pluckington Bank from extending under the floating landing-stage. As many as twenty-three of the largest steamships, of an aggregate burden of 34,200 tons, and thirty-five smaller vessels, have been let in or out of the docks, through the Canada Basin, in a single tide during $2\frac{1}{3}$ hours before high-water.

The huge floating landing-stage forms a prominent feature in front of the Liverpool Docks. Rising and falling with the tide, it is connected with the land by seven hinged girder bridges, which vary in inclination with the height of the stage, and by a floating bridge, 550 feet long and 35 feet broad, which provides an inclined roadway suitable for carriage traffic at any state of the tide. This stage, 2063 feet long and 80 feet wide, supported on 138 iron pontoons, affords a platform 4 acres in extent, and is used by about two million persons in a year, for steamers and ferryboats come alongside it. There are two similar, but smaller, floating stages on the Birkenhead shore.

The ports of London and Liverpool stand unrivalled amongst the ports of the world, both in dock accommodation and trade. They are very considerably ahead of the other ports of Great Britain in the tonnage of vessels trading with them, the Tyne ports coming third; whilst they are much more in advance in respect of the values of their merchandise, for Hull stands third, with a fifth of the value of the Liverpool trade. London is first as regards imports, and Liverpool as regards exports; but, on the whole, London is the first port of the world, both in the tonnage of its vessels and in the value of its trade, as well as in its dock accommodation and facility of access.

Port of Antwerp.—The good depth of the Scheldt and Flemish enterprise made Antwerp one of the principal ports of Europe from the 13th, to the middle of the 17th century, when it was closed to vessels, by treaty, till the end of the last century. It was provided with two docks and some river quays early in the present century; but, like London and Liverpool, its main development as a port has been accomplished within the last fifty years. Indeed, there are few ports which show as remarkable a progress in recent years as Antwerp. Up to 1860, it only possessed two docks, having an area of about 21 acres, and some quays along the river; it now has 120 acres of docks; and its river quays, entirely remodelled, reconstructed, and extended, have a total length of 2 miles $1\frac{1}{2}$ furlongs. The Kattendyk Dock was opened in 1860; and shortly afterwards the removal of the lines of fortification to a greater distance from the town enabled the space of the old demolished fortifications to be utilised in extending the city and port. The docks were accordingly extended, and the Kattendyk Dock was prolonged, making its area 32 acres; and in 1880 the dock area had reached 120 acres. Two new docks were begun in 1883, on the site of the old North Citadel, namely, the Africa Dock, for large transatlantic steamers, and the America Dock, for the petroleum trade, having together an area of 50 acres, with a depth of 30 feet at high-water. These docks will raise the dock area of the Port of Antwerp to 170 acres. Meantime the river quay walls were built along a rectified line of the river, which necessitated the building of a great portion of the wall in the alluvial bed of the river, at some distance from the bank in the upper part. The foundations of this portion of the quay wall were excavated down to a solid bottom, and brought up to low-water by aid of caissons, furnished with a working chamber supplied with compressed air. These caissons were 82 feet long and $29\frac{1}{2}$ feet wide, with a bottomless chamber, $6\frac{1}{2}$ feet high, at the bottom, and plate-iron sides enclosing the area above the roof; and they were floated into position between two long barges, having a stage erected over them, from which the caisson was suspended by chains. The upper part of the caisson was then filled with concrete, and the wall built upon it, under the protection of the plate-iron sides; and the caisson gradually sank under the increasing weight till it touched the bed of the river, when its position was carefully adjusted, and the building of the wall continued above, till sufficient weight was attained to prevent the compressed air raising the caisson. The working chamber was then filled with compressed air, access for the men and materials to this chamber being provided by seven shafts furnished with air-locks at the top; and the men entering the working chamber, lit with electric light, proceeded with the excavations till the caisson reached a firm bottom, from 34 to 52 feet below low-water. The wall having, in the meantime, been built up, the working chamber and shafts were filled with concrete; and the plates surrounding the wall above the roof of the chamber, and the barges and staging, were removed to serve for another length of wall. The portion of the river bed between the wall and the old river bank was filled in, and formed a quay. The quays along the river have been very well equipped with sidings, sheds, and hydraulic travelling cranes.

The trade of Antwerp has responded to the improved accommodation afforded, for it has augmented rapidly since 1881; and the tonnage of vessels trading with the port about equals that of the Tyne ports, which stand third in this respect amongst the ports of the United Kingdom, and exceeds the tonnage of vessels entering any of the French ports.

Port of Marseilles.—The foremost port of France is Marseilles, which, as regards the tonnage of its vessels, is only exceeded by four English ports, namely, London, Liverpool, the Tyne ports and Cardiff. Like the ports already described, Marseilles, though an ancient port, has been only really developed within the last fifty years; for up to 1852 its accommodation consisted merely of the natural shelter provided by the Old Harbour, an inlet from the coast of 67 acres, to the southeast of the present port, which had been surrounded by quays, as well as a small canal and basin opening out of it, which raised the total water area of the port to 72 acres.

The Port of Marseilles, unlike the river ports of London, Liverpool, and Antwerp, just described, is situated upon the shore of a tideless sea. Shelter inside rivers is denied to the ports of countries bordering tideless seas, owing to the deltas formed by the rivers flowing into them, which obstruct their outlets. Accordingly, ports on the Mediterranean Sea have to be situated on the sea-coast; and artificial shelter has to be provided where, as in most cases, natural shelter is deficient. This shelter on the sea-coast has to be furnished by breakwaters, which protect an area between them and the shore in which vessels can lie in safety, and discharge and take in cargoes. At Marseilles a detached breakwater has been constructed parallel to the coast, commenced near the Old Harbour, and extended towards the north-west, which both serves in places as a quay on its sheltered side, and also protects a considerable water area between it and the coast, which is divided into a series of basins by jetties projecting from the shore. These basins are surrounded by quays, constructed upon the breakwater, the wide jetties, and quay walls along the shore, and serve like docks for the purposes of trade. They differ, however, from the ordinary form of docks adjoining tidal rivers in not requiring gates to keep the water at a uniform level, owing to the absence of appreciable tidal oscillation. They differ, also, in the method of construction of the quay walls; for the breakwater and jetties, having to be built in the sea, consist of a mound of stones deposited in the water, surmounted by a quay bordered by concrete walls, faced with stone above the water line. On the sea side of the breakwater, a high parapet wall takes the place of a quay wall; and large concrete blocks protect the sea slope. The first addition to the port was the Joliette Basin, commenced in 1844, and opened in 1852, having an area of 54 acres, and entered by a canal from the Old Harbour, and direct from the sea, through a partially sheltered outer harbour of 56 acres. The adjoining Lazaret and Arenc basins, 51 acres in area, and the Railway Basin, of 41 acres, were opened in 1863; and the National Basin, with an area of 105 acres, was completed in 1881, raising the total sheltered area of the port to 325 acres. The extension, moreover, of the breakwater, nearly half-a-mile beyond the National Basin, forms a partially sheltered outer harbour of 44 acres at this end, facilitating and protecting the entrance to the National Basin. Wide passages between the breakwater and the ends of the jetties furnish communication between the basins; whilst two swing bridges across the passage between the Joliette and Lazaret basins, and a railway swing bridge across the passage between the Arenc and National Basins, connect the quay along the breakwater with the land. The breakwater has a length of about $2\frac{1}{4}$ miles. Six graving docks have been constructed, opening out of an inner basin; and the quays are well equipped with warehouses, sheds, sidings, and hydraulic machinery.

The works commenced in 1844 have quite transformed the Port of Marseilles, for they have not only more than quadrupled the sheltered area of the port, but they have also added very extensive and thoroughly equipped quays, compared with which the Old Harbour provides very imperfect accommodation. The prosperity of the port has been established during this period; and the growth of its trade has followed so closely upon the enlargements of the port, that fresh extensions are under consideration.

Port of New York.—The City of New York is most favourably situated for a maritime trade, on account of its insular position, with deep water on each side along the Hudson and East rivers, and also because its water frontage is well sheltered from storms, whilst close to the ocean.

The docks of New York, as they are termed, are really merely quay walls, or bulkheads, extending continuously along the river fronts of the southern part of New York, with projecting timber jetties. No artificial shelter is required, as protection is afforded by Long Island to the east, and by the mainland to the west; and as the mean tidal rise is only 4⅗ feet, floating docks shut off from the sea by gates are quite unnecessary. Wharves have been gradually extended with the growth of the city; but, owing to the varied ownership of the river frontages, the walls and jetties were constructed at first according to the ideas of each individual owner, without any systematic arrangement or control. Though some supervision was introduced early in the present century, in the interests of the public, it was only in 1870 that a special department was constituted for reconstructing the wharves according to a comprehensive, definite plan. The city is gradually acquiring the river frontages; and the line of quay wall is being carried out far enough into the water to form a street alongside the river to accommodate the trade. Timber jetties are being erected at right angles to the quay wall, with intervals between them of 150 to 200 feet; and they extend from 400 to 500 feet into the river on the west side of the island, with a width of 60 to 80 feet; but on the east side they are rather smaller. Owing to the soft alluvial nature of the beds of the East and Hudson rivers, light quay walls of concrete and masonry have been built on piles, surrounded by a mound of rubble stone to keep the piles in place. On the East River, and on part of the Hudson River, the piles reach a solid stratum, and afford a firm foundation for the wall; but in parts of the Hudson River the silt was proved to exceed 200 feet in thickness, so that at these places the piles have to bear the weight of the wall by the adherence simply of the enveloping silt, which prevents any movement of the pile after being left undisturbed for some hours. By the new system, the length of wharfing is being increased from 28 miles, which was its length in 1870, to 37 miles; and the area afforded by the piers is being trebled, in addition to the gain of a street alongside the quay.

More than half the foreign trade of the United States passes through the Port of New York; and New York is only excelled in the value of its exports and imports by London and Liverpool.

CHAPTER X.

THE BREAKWATERS OF TABLE BAY, ALEXANDRIA, BOULOGNE, COLOMBO, DOVER, AND NEWHAVEN HARBOURS.

THOUGH some small artificial harbours were formed in ancient times, and the breakwater protecting the large harbour of Cherbourg was commenced towards the close of the last century, the development of breakwater construction has taken place in the present century; and most of the prominent examples of breakwaters have been constructed within the last fifty years. The harbour works of Plymouth, Kingstown, and Howth, and the extensions at Algiers Harbour, were, indeed, carried out in the early part of this century; but these breakwaters are of the simplest type, such as was adopted in earlier times, namely, a mound of rubble stone, protected by masonry pitching on the exposed face, or, in the case of Algiers, with large concrete blocks. A great impulse was given to the construction of harbours of refuge on the coasts of Great Britain by a letter from the Duke of Wellington, in 1842, on the unprotected and defenceless state of the shores of the country, which resulted in the commencement, about 1847, of the harbours of Dover, Portland, Holyhead, Alderney, and St Catherine's, Jersey, by the Government. Numerous harbours, also, have been more recently formed in various parts to provide shelter for accommodating and developing trade, as for instance Madras, Colombo, Newhaven, Boulogne, Brest, Genoa, Odessa, Alexandria, Table Bay, Charleston, Galveston, and the lake harbours of Chicago, Oswego and Buffalo.

The size and form of a harbour depend upon the natural conditions of the site, and the capital that is available, or can profitably be expended upon its construction. Sometimes a bay is sufficiently sheltered by the land to need only a detached breakwater across its wide outlet, in order to convert it into a harbour, with entrances between the ends of the breakwater and the shore, of which Plymouth, Cherbourg, and Delaware harbours are examples. Occasionally a single breakwater, carried out from a projecting point of a bay, affords adequate shelter to the water area partly enclosed between it and the shore of the bay, a method adopted at Holyhead, Alderney, Colombo, Alexandria, and Table Bay. The absence of any suitable sheltered bay in the neighbourhood of the place for which a harbour is required, sometimes necessitates the formation of a purely artificial harbour on a straight line of coast, entirely sheltered by two or more breakwaters, as exemplified by Kingstown and Madras harbours, and the complete design of Boulogne Harbour, as yet only partially carried out. The arrangements, accordingly, of breakwaters for forming a harbour are mainly dependent upon local circumstances, and are not capable of much modification. The chief progress has therefore been effected in the form and materials of

SECTIONS OF BREAKWATERS.

TABLE BAY

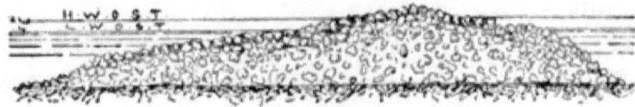

ALEXANDRIA.

BOULOGNE.

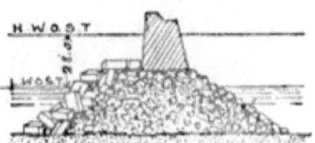

COLOMBO.

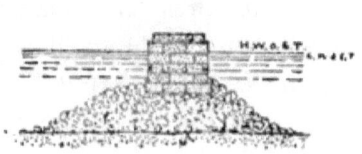

DOVER.

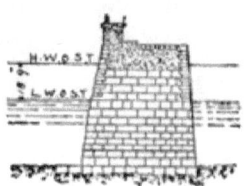

SCALE 1:300

Types of Breakwater Construction.

breakwaters, and in the methods adopted for their construction.

There are three types of breakwaters, namely, the rubble stone or concrete block mound, where a heap of hard material is deposited in the ocean along the line chosen for the breakwater; a mound of rubble stone to form the base, surmounted by a thick upright wall; and, lastly, a solid wall carried up from the bottom. Table Bay and Alexandria breakwaters illustrate the first type; Boulogne and Colombo breakwaters show two different forms of the second type; whilst the most notable instance of the third type is the Admiralty Pier at Dover. (*See page* 192.) The first type follows the old method of construction, and may be adopted where materials are abundant, where the width occupied by the breakwater is immaterial, and where no quay is required. The second type requires less material than the first; but its superstructure has to be solidly constructed to resist the waves breaking against it. The third type requires least material; but it involves still more careful construction, and diving work. It is chiefly adapted for a hard bottom, in no great depth of water; and, like the second type, it provides a quay accessible in fine weather.

Table Bay Harbour.—This harbour has been formed by a breakwater carried out, in a north-easterly direction, from a projecting point in Table Bay to the north of Cape Town, so as to afford some shelter from the north-west, in which direction the bay is open to the Atlantic Ocean. The breakwater runs out in a straight line due north-west for about 2400 feet, and then bends a little towards the east, to protect the water area bordering the adjacent coast more effectually from the north. The breakwater consists of a mound of rubble stone (*see section, page* 192), deposited from staging, which the sea has levelled on the exposed side to a slope of about 1 in 9 for some distance below low-water. The stone has been excavated from a neighbouring site, part of which has already been utilised for an inner basin. The work was begun in 1860, and reached 1900 feet from the shore in 1868, in a depth of 30 feet; and an extension was commenced in 1881, which will give the breakwater a total length of 3700 feet, and carry it into a depth of about 50 feet of water. This breakwater furnishes a recent example of the simplest form of breakwater, constructed in the simplest possible manner, but with a large expenditure of material, which, however, is close at hand.

Alexandria Harbour.—A new harbour was commenced, in 1870, by sheltering an extensive bay to the south-west of Alexandria, by means of a breakwater, which starts near Eunostos Point, at the south-western extremity of Pharos. After running parallel with the shore for about 3500 feet, the breakwater bends towards the shore in a nearly southerly direction, reaching a total length of 9675 feet, and leaving an entrance between its extremity and the shore, 3340 feet in width, with a maximum depth of 60 feet. A sheltered area has thereby been obtained of 1400 acres, possessing a minimum depth of 30 feet.

The breakwater is composed of a mound of large concrete blocks, 20 tons in weight, on the sea side, with rubble stone on the harbour side. (*See section, page* 192.) The concrete blocks were deposited first on the outside of the mound; and the rubble stone was placed at the back, under their shelter. The blocks forming the lower part of the mound were let down into the water along an inclined plane on the deck of a barge; but the blocks near, and above the water level were deposited by a floating steam derrick or crane. The block was lifted by the derrick from an attendant barge, by means of slings, which clasped the block at its four side edges, and which readily released the block, when brought into its proper position, by a slight pull of a rope which unloosed the clutches. The concrete blocks, made of broken stone, sand, and Portland cement, reduced the amount of material required for the mound, and increased its power of resisting the sea, owing to the size of the blocks. The rubble stone was deposited from barges, through trap-doors in the bottom and sides. The breakwater was completed in 1872, about two years only from its commencement, or nearly at the rate of a mile in a year, a very remarkable rate of progress when compared with the many years occupied in the construction of Cherbourg and Plymouth breakwaters, and even with the progress of breakwaters of more recent date.

Boulogne Harbour.—The condition of the harbours of Boulogne and Calais are always of interest to England, as they are the nearest ports to the English coast; and any improvements in their depth or accessibility facilitates communication with the Continent. The access to the Port of Calais has been improved by a rectification of its entrance channel, which is guided by parallel jetties on each side; by a large sluicing basin of 220 acres, formed on the strand, from which a powerful scouring current is discharged at low tide into the entrance channel to maintain its depth; and lastly, by the deepening of the approach channel, through the sandbanks outside, by dredging with sand-pumps, whereby a depth is now maintained of 13 feet below low-water of the lowest spring tides, where, up to 1875, the depth did not exceed $2\frac{1}{2}$ feet below the same level. Accordingly, Calais Harbour can be entered by the mail steamers from England at any state of the tide; whereas formerly steamers, drawing only $7\frac{1}{2}$ feet of water, could not enter the port near low-water of spring tides.

At Boulogne, works on a much larger scale than at Calais have been partially constructed, with the object of transforming Boulogne Harbour from a small jetty harbour, like Calais, inaccessible near low-water, into a spacious harbour, sheltered by breakwaters, affording ample depth for vessels of the largest draught at any state of the tide. This harbour was commenced in 1879; and a breakwater has been constructed, starting from the shore about $1\frac{1}{4}$ miles to the south-west of the old jetty harbour, and, after being carried out about 4500 feet from the shore, curving round and going towards the Old Harbour, nearly parallel to the coast. Some quays have also been formed under the shelter of the breakwater, extending a short distance out from the land. The breakwater already built is only the south-western portion of the design; and it is proposed to carry out another breakwater from the shore, in the line of the north-eastern jetty of the Old Harbour, a little more than $1\frac{1}{8}$ miles from the land, and then to close the wide gap between the outer extremity of this breakwater and the end of the return arm of the south-western breakwater by a detached breakwater, leaving entrances between each end of it and the extremities of the two other breakwaters, facing north and west respectively, 820 and 490 feet in width.

The breakwater is composed of a mound formed with small stones in the interior, surrounded with larger stone, and concrete blocks of 24 tons on the sea slope, surmounted by a solid masonry superstructure founded about 10 feet above low-water of spring tides. (*See section, page* 192.) The section of this breakwater exhibits a marked economy in material in proportion to the depth of water, when compared with the section of Table Bay breakwater, and even with the Alexandria Breakwater section. The material forming the mound was at first tipped from waggons run out from the shore; but afterwards barges were employed for depositing it to increase the rate of progress. The mixed type of mound and upright wall, to which this breakwater belongs, has been adopted for a large number of breakwaters; but generally the wall, or superstructure, is commenced at, or below the level of low-water, which reduces still further the amount of material required.

The cost of this harbour has been estimated at £1,280,000; but when it is completed, it will be second only to Cherbourg amongst the French ports on the Channel. The south-west breakwater affords some protection, and shelters the entrance to the Old Harbour from south-west gales.

Colombo Harbour.—Colombo is the port for the large and increasing trade of Ceylon; but, till the breakwater works were commenced in 1874, the bay in which the harbour is situated was exposed to the monsoons, greatly impeding the unloading and lading of vessels by the swell which they cause. The south-west monsoon, which prevails from May till November, is the worst wind; and, accordingly, a western breakwater has been carried out from a projecting point at the western extremity of the bay, running nearly parallel with the shore on the other side of the bay, for a distance of 4212 feet, in a straight line, except towards the end which is slightly curved inwards to increase the shelter afforded. The water area, at low-water, sheltered by the breakwater is 502 acres, of which 242 acres have a minimum depth of 26 feet, part of which has been obtained by dredging some shallow portions to that depth. Some wharves and jetties have been constructed under the shelter of the breakwater, along the southern shore of the bay.

The breakwater consists of a rubble mound, deposited from a barge, with a concrete block wall built upon it, 34 feet wide, and founded from 16 to 20 feet below low-water of spring tides, the rise of tide at Colombo being only 2 feet. (*See section, page* 192.) The mound was carried out 700 feet, on the average, in advance of the wall, so as to allow it at least a year to consolidate under the action of the sea before erecting the superstructure upon it, to guard against the settlement of the wall. The depth at which the wall was founded secured it against being undermined by the waves; and the mound, moreover, was raised on each side of the wall, above the foundations, by tipping stone over the sides of the wall, and was further protected on the sea slope by concrete bags laid close alongside the sea face of the wall. The concrete block wall, or superstructure, was built by depositing the blocks in a series of sloping rows, with the bottom of each row in advance of the top, so that each section of the breakwater, having the thickness of one block, leaned to some extent on the adjacent inner section, but was free to slide if unequal settlement of the mound occurred. Each block was laid in an inclined position from the overhanging arm of a counterbalanced crane, which travelled along the completed breakwater as the work progressed. This system of construction, which dispenses with staging liable to be injured by storms, and provides against cracks from unequal settlement, was inaugurated at the Kurrachee Harbour works in 1870, and was subsequently adopted at Madras Harbour in 1876; and it has also been employed for breakwaters at Reunion Island, and at Mormugao on the west coast of India. The concrete blocks in each section at Colombo are from $16\frac{1}{2}$ to 31 tons in weight; they are laid at an inclination of 1 in 3, and have a thickness of $5\frac{1}{2}$ feet. Each section contains three or four tiers of blocks; and the sections, or rows, were eventually connected together, after settlement had ceased, by filling grooves left in the face of each row with concrete in bags, and by a concrete-in-mass capping along the top of the breakwater.

The work was completed in 1885, having cost £705,200; and the revenues of the harbour in 1883 and 1884 averaged about £34,000 a year. The harbour, being open to the north, is still exposed to the north-east monsoon; and a detached northern breakwater has been proposed for sheltering it from this quarter, leaving an entrance of 800 feet between the two breakwaters for the passage of vessels.

Dover Harbour.—The position of Dover, at the

narrowest part of the English Channel, and the nearest point of the English coast to France, has been always regarded of great strategical importance. When, therefore, in 1845, measures were being taken by the Government to establish harbours at important places on the coast, both for refuge and defence, Dover was naturally one of the sites selected for a harbour; and the form, extent, and shelter of the proposed harbour, were the subject of the most careful investigations. Dover is situated in a slight indentation of the coast, protected somewhat from the south-west by the projecting part of the coast from which the Admiralty Pier starts, and under the shelter of which the old port was formed. The approved scheme, commenced in 1847, consisted of an oblong harbour of about 600 acres, enclosed by breakwaters extending as far to the east of the Castle as the Admiralty Pier is to the west, having a maximum length parallel to the coast of about 7300 feet, and a maximum width out from the coast of about 4200 feet. The present breakwater or pier represents the short, western, most exposed side of this grand scheme; and of the five harbours commenced in 1847, Dover, the most important, remains also the most incomplete. This breakwater, however, has been of great service for the continental traffic, and shelters vessels on its inner side during southerly or westerly gales, and on its outer, or south-western side during easterly gales. It is also of great interest as having been the first large breakwater built, in an exposed situation, on the upright wall system from the bottom, without any mound. (*See section, page* 192.)

The breakwater has been built of a series of courses of concrete blocks up to high-water level, and concrete-in-mass hearting above; both sides of the wall being faced with granite throughout for the greater part of the wall, but only above low-water level at the outer part, to reduce the cost. The foundation courses were laid upon the solid chalk bottom, very carefully levelled by divers in a diving-bell, entailing a considerable expense and a large amount of time. The wall has been given a slight inclination, or batter, on each face, and is surmounted by a parapet wall, which, during westerly gales, protects the paved quay on to which the trains run alongside the mail steamers. The breakwater was terminated, at its present length of 2100 feet, in 1871, extending into a depth of about 45 feet at low-water. The total amount paid to the contractors for the construction of the breakwater was about £679,300.

The Dover Breakwater is larger in section, and extends into deeper water than any breakwater hitherto constructed as a simple, solid, upright wall resting directly on the sea bottom. The advantages of the system are, that the smallest possible amount of material is required for its construction; that, when resting on a firm bottom, it is not liable to settlement like a superstructure built upon a mound of rubble stone; and that it is not nearly so subject to injury from waves as a loose rubble mound. The disadvantages of slow progress and large cost, experienced at Dover, are not necessarily inherent in the system; and there is no doubt that, with the progress in the methods of breakwater construction achieved in recent years, any extension of the Dover Breakwater could be effected at a much cheaper and more rapid rate.

Newhaven Harbour.—The Port of Newhaven, the

nearest port on the English Channel to London, has established a considerable trade with Dieppe, the nearest port to Paris. It has been formed at the mouth of the river Ouse, in Seaford Bay, a part of the coast which has at various times been suggested as a suitable site for a harbour of refuge. Though the depth at the mouth of the river was improved at various times by the erection and extension of jetties, which directed and concentrated the outflow across the beach, aided by the straightening of the river in 1863-64, the bar of shingle was only forced a little further out; so that only a tidal service could be obtained. In 1878, however, authority was obtained for constructing a breakwater a little to the west of the mouth of the river, under the shelter of which a channel, 12 feet deep at low-water spring tides, could be dredged across the bar, and the port, with its quays alongside the river, could be made accessible for vessels of moderate draught at all states of the tide.

The breakwater proceeds out straight from the shore, in a southerly direction, for 1000 feet, and then curves gradually towards the east, so as to protect the entrance to the river from west round nearly to south. The breakwater was designed to have a length of 2800 feet, of which 1482 feet have been carried out at a cost of £89,000. The bottom is chalk, as at Dover; but instead of spending time and money in dressing the chalk under water to a level bed for the concrete blocks, the concrete-in-mass, of which the breakwater is built, has been fitted to the irregular bottom. The portion of the breakwater up to low-water was built of concrete in bags, deposited by opening flap doors at the bottom of the well of a barge; and each bag, filled with 100 tons of concrete, extends right across the whole width of the break water. The special steam hopper-barge, for depositing the bags, having been brought alongside the quay in the river, its well was loosely lined with jute canvas; and after the concrete had been rapidly placed in the well, the sacking was sewn together over the concrete, whilst the barge steamed to the place of deposit for forming the breakwater. As soon as the flap doors closing the bottom of the well of the barge were released, the concrete bag fell through the water into position, being protected from the wash of the water by the canvas lining; whilst the loose bag, before the concrete had set, adjusted itself to any irregularities of the bottom, or of the previously deposited bags. As soon as a sufficient length of breakwater had been thus raised about 2 feet above low-water, the upper portion of the breakwater was formed by depositing concrete-in-mass inside timber framing enclosing the space above the bag foundations. The breakwater, accordingly, forms a solid upright wall, with a slight inclination on each face, composed of a series of heavy bag blocks below, laid right across the breakwater, and a monolithic mass of concrete above low-water. This system, which was introduced for the foundations of the Aberdeen Harbour breakwaters, on a rocky bottom, in 1871, is economical for long breakwaters, is rapid in execution, and forms a compact breakwater. The inevitable absence of a perfect connection between the bags below low-water is rendered immaterial by their large size; and, moreover, the weight of the continuous mass of concrete, forming the portion of the breakwater above low-water, effectually consolidates the lower portion.

The construction of breakwaters capable of successfully withstanding the continuous shocks of waves hurled against them with apparently irresistible force during storms, requires the utmost skill and experience of the engineer. The sea, like the most insidious of foes, infallibly discovers any weak point in a breakwater, and rapidly extends any damage it may have produced. The force of the sea cannot be measured with precision like the strains on a bridge; but its power has been demonstrated by the injuries structures in the sea have experienced during storms, and by the way in which huge masses of masonry have been dislodged by waves. The size of the waves, however, in any particular locality, and therefore the force to be controlled, depends upon the depth of water in front, the direction of the strongest and most prevalent wind, and the distance this wind may have travelled over a continuous stretch of sea.

The three types of breakwaters, namely, the old rubble mound system, the mound with superstructure, and the modern upright wall system, are all employed at the present day. The rubble mound, however, has been strengthened by the use of large blocks of stone or concrete on its exposed upper sea slope; and its construction has been greatly expedited by suitable appliances. The mixed type of breakwater, which is available for considerable depths of water, has been freed from the dislocation, and the consequent injury in storms, due to unequal settlement of the superstructure upon a yielding mound, by the adoption of the sloping-block system; and the use of an overhanging crane for depositing the blocks has enabled staging in the sea to be dispensed with, and has very materially increased the rate of progress attainable. The upright wall system, so costly in its first employment at Dover, has been greatly facilitated and cheapened by the use of concrete in large bags under water for large works, and concrete-in-mass deposited within frames under water for small piers, where the cost of the special plant required for the bags would be prohibitive.

Breakwater construction has, accordingly, made rapid strides in recent years; and the employment of Portland cement concrete has enabled numerous fishery piers to be constructed, with great benefit to the fishery trade and the seafaring population, which could not have been contemplated in former times.

CHAPTER XI.

IMPROVEMENT WORKS ON THE TYNE, THE SEINE, THE MAAS, THE DANUBE, AND THE MISSISSIPPI.

RIVERS afford access to sheltered ports, and also to the interior of a country; and the class of trade they can accommodate depends on the navigable depth of their channels. A broad distinction has to be drawn between rivers flowing into tidal seas, like the rivers of Great Britain and of the north and west coasts of France, and rivers discharging into seas like the Black Sea, the Mediterranean, and the Gulf of Mexico, in which the rise of the tide is barely perceptible. The volume of water flowing through the outlet of a tidal river is very greatly increased by the tidal water from the sea, so that the estuary and outlet channels of a tidal river are much larger than the freshwater discharge alone of the river could maintain. Thus the Thames, the Severn, the Mersey, and the Seine have estuaries quite out of proportion to the flow from the basins which they drain. The outlets, however, of rivers discharging into tideless seas can only be maintained by the volume of freshwater coming down these rivers, which is proportionate to the amount of the rainfall which reaches the watercourses, and the area of their basins. Tidal and tideless rivers also differ essentially in the nature of the

RIVER IMPROVEMENTS.

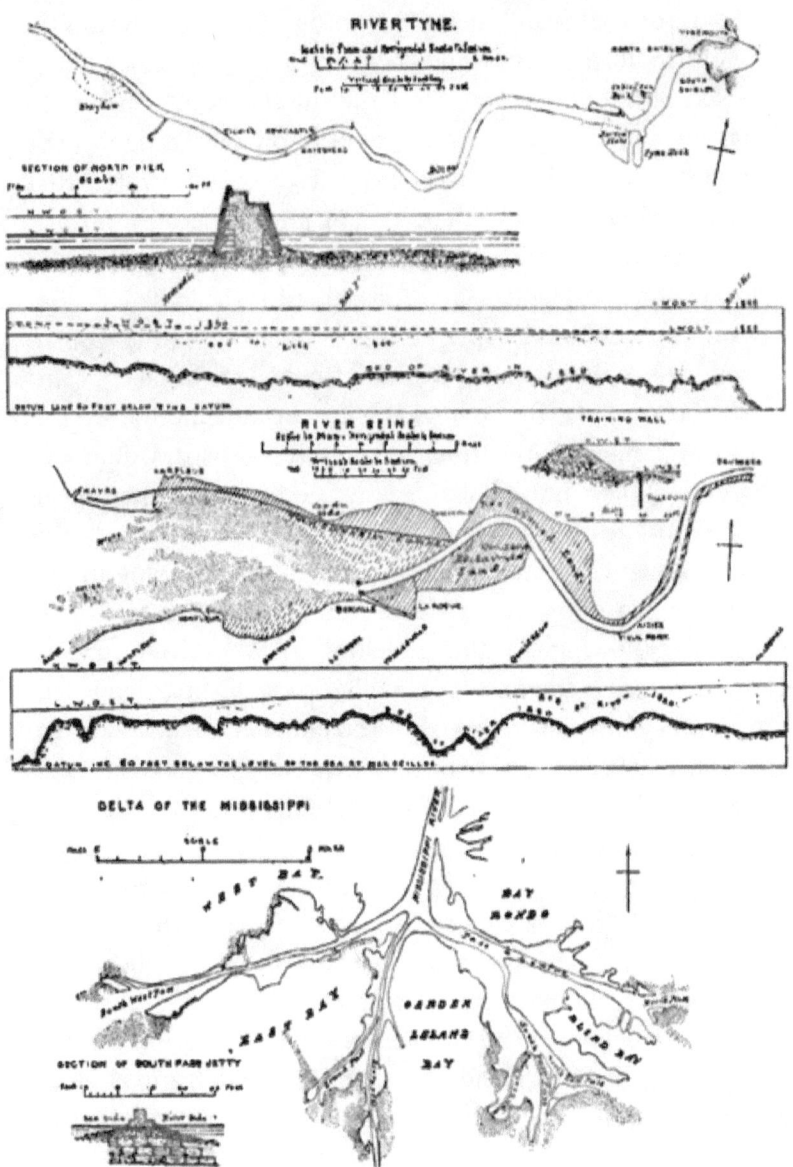

shoals, or bar, found at their mouths. The sea constantly tends to form a continuous beach along the coast, composed of the detritus of the adjacent shores, which is only partially prevented by the ebb and flow of the tide at the mouths of tidal estuaries, aided by the freshwater discharge of the river; so that, except under specially favourable conditions of the form of the estuary, the outlet is frequently obstructed by a shoal. In the case of tidal rivers, the material brought down by a river, in its course from the uplands, is prevented from depositing in any particular place by being kept in constant motion by the ebb and flow of the tide, so that it is dispersed in the large estuary into which many tidal rivers open near their outlet, or is gradually carried out to sea. All the detritus, however, brought down by a river flowing into a tideless sea is gradually deposited beyond the mouth of the river, owing to the checking of the river current when entering the open sea. The material thus deposited forms a fan-shaped shoal, protruding into the sea in advance of the coast line, constantly progressing seawards by the accession of fresh sediment; and through it the enfeebled river current finds an outlet, through shallow, diverging channels to the sea, to which the term delta has been applied, on account of the shape assumed by the channels and shoal. Well-known instances of such outlets are furnished by the deltas of the Nile, the Rhone, the Danube, and the Mississippi. (*See page* 208.) Shoals, moreover, are found in various parts of rivers, where ridges of hard material or rock across the channel prevent the natural deepening by scour, and cause rapids, or where a great expansion in width leads to a corresponding reduction in depth. The object of all river improvement works is to form a tolerably uniform channel, with a minimum depth adequate for the requirements of navigation; and the most important part of a river, and the portion in which the chief difficulties are generally experienced, is at the outlet, and for some distance above, where a deep channel is requisite to provide access for sea-going vessels.

River Tyne.—The first works undertaken on the river Tyne for obtaining an improved channel between Newcastle and the sea, a distance of $10\frac{1}{2}$ miles, were commenced in 1843. At that time there was a depth of only 2 feet, at one place, in the deepest channel at low-water spring tides, and $14\frac{1}{2}$ feet at high-water; and at some parts the shoals rose above low-water level in the centre of the river. Between 1843 and 1858 the river was regulated by carrying out projecting jetties or groins from the banks, joined eventually at their ends by longitudinal mounds of rubble stone, called training walls, with the object of improving the depth by the increase in scour thereby produced. A small amount of dredging was also carried out every year, at first by one dredger, and eventually by three dredgers, up to 1860. A moderate amount of improvement had been thereby effected; but even in 1860 there was a depth of only 6 feet over the bar at the mouth at low-water of spring tides; and no vessels of over 20 feet draught could enter or leave the Tyne, even at high-water spring tides. A series of shoals, moreover, existed between Shields and Newcastle, so that vessels of 15 feet draught could only get up to Newcastle, even at high-water spring tides, by following a winding channel between the shoals.

Piers, or breakwaters, were commenced at the mouth of the river in 1856, for protecting vessels in easterly gales; and these piers, by the shelter afforded, have facilitated the removal of the bar at the mouth. These piers are now approaching completion, having been carried out gradually, in proportion as the Tyne Improvement Commissioners could periodically allot funds for the purpose. They consist of a superstructure, built of concrete, and faced with masonry, founded upon a low rubble stone mound, deposited from barges, and protected on the top of the sea slope by concrete blocks. (*See page* 208.) The superstructures were at first constructed by the help of staging; but during the last few years the blocks have been laid by an overhanging balanced crane on each pier, differing from the Titans used at Kurrachee, Madras, and Colombo, in being able to revolve, as well as travelling backwards and forwards. These Goliaths can set blocks of over 40 tons, with an overhang of 75 feet. The converging piers form a harbour of refuge, in front of the mouth of the river, for vessels overtaken by storms, and have enabled the river channel to be easily extended across the bar, into deep water, by dredging. A sufficient width is to be left between the pier-heads to ensure that the flood tide shall not be at all restricted in entering the river.

Dredging with large bucket-ladder dredgers, upon a greatly extended scale, was commenced in 1861, for the first two years with four dredgers, and afterwards with six; and in 1866 a maximum quantity of 5,273,500 tons, or about 3,515,600 cubic yards, was raised and removed from the bed of the river between Newcastle and Tynemouth, in one year. Altogether, the amount of material taken out of the river channel, between 1861 and the end of 1888, was 54,670,000 cubic yards, or an average yearly excavation of nearly 2 million cubic yards. By this means the depth over the bar has been increased from 6 feet to over 20 feet at low-water of spring tides; and a wide channel, with a minimum depth of 20 feet at low-water, has been obtained right up to Newcastle, in place of the former shallow, tortuous channel, almost dry in places at low-water. The river has also been deepened to 18 feet below low-water of spring tides for 3 miles above Newcastle; and the deepening of the river is proposed to be eventually extended $5\frac{3}{4}$ miles higher up. These works, together with some straight cuts, and the removal of a projecting rocky point, have entirely transformed the condition of the river in the last thirty years; so that vessels of larger draught can reach Newcastle at low-water than could formerly get up on the highest tides; and there is an ample depth for vessels of the largest class to go 3 miles above Newcastle at high-water. These works have also placed the Tyne in the position of the third port of Great Britain as regards the tonnage of its vessels, and the fifth in respect of the value of its imports and exports. A number of vessels, also, of from 2000 to 4000 tons, enter the river now which could not possibly have found access in 1861. The increased capacity given to the river channel for the purposes of navigation has, moreover, had the beneficial effect of reducing the height of the river floods, which formerly used to overtop the river banks and quays between Wylam and Newcastle, as the freshwater discharge finds a much freer outflow through the enlarged and unobstructed channel.

The river Tyne has been selected for description as illustrating the improvement of a tidal river by dredging, for this method of improvement has been carried out on the Tyne to a greater extent than elsewhere; but many other tidal rivers of Great Britain have had their navigable channels deepened considerably by dredging, of which the Clyde and the Tees are notable examples. Dredging, indeed, has become, within the last fifty years, one of the principal means of artificially improving river channels and entrances to ports, and thus forms a very powerful agent in developing trade.

River Seine.—The most important river of France, the Seine, presents a great contrast to the Tyne, both in its natural condition and the principles adopted for its improvement. It is tidal up to 15 miles above Rouen; and by the introduction, in the non-tidal portion up to Paris, of locks and weirs at nine places (entirely remodelled since 1878) a minimum depth of $10\frac{1}{2}$ feet has been provided up to Paris, 226 miles from its mouth. A permanent navigable depth, moreover, of $6\frac{1}{2}$ feet has been secured above Paris, up to Montereau, a distance of 62 miles, by the erection of twelve locks and weirs since 1860. The Seine has a basin of 30,370 square miles, about twenty-nine times the area of the Tyne basin, and nearly six times the size of the Thames basin. It is, accordingly, a comparatively large river near its mouth; and it opens into a wide estuary. Unlike the Tyne, very little dredging has been carried out in the tidal Seine, beyond removing some hard shoals; and the improvement of the lower portion of the tidal river where very deficient in depth, between La Mailleraye and Berville, has been effected by restricting its irregular channel by mounds of chalk or stone on each side. Whereas the upper portion of the tidal river, between La Mailleraye and Rouen, had an ample depth and stable channel, the channel below was unstable, shallow, and winding, so that vessels of 200 tons had frequently some difficulty in getting up this part of the river, and wrecks often occurred.

Though various schemes were proposed from time to time for remedying the perilous condition of the Seine estuary, it was only in 1846 that training works were commenced, confining the river in a stable, uniform channel by solid mounds along each side, widening out gradually towards the sea. (*See page* 208). The scour of the ebbing current in the narrowed channel deepened the channel as the works proceeded; and the works were completed down to Berville in 1870. These works increased the minimum navigable depth to 18 feet at high-water neap tides, and enabled vessels of 2000 tons to get up the river; and Rouen was thereby raised to the position of the fifth port of France. The training works have been consolidated by additions of stone and pitching in the last few years (*see section, page* 208); and various proposals have been made to extend them to deep water at the mouth, about 10 miles beyond their present termination. Considerable accretion, however, has taken place, from material brought in by the flood tide settling down behind the training banks, and at the sides of the estuary beyond, owing to the enfeeblement of the ebb current outside the trained channel; so that, in the interests of the ports of Havre and Honfleur, it has been determined to carry out some experimental investigations, with a working model on a small scale, with the view of ascertaining the most favourable lines for the prolongation of the training banks before commencing any extension works. Training works, by concentrating the ebb and flow into a definite, narrowed channel, effect, by natural scour, the deepening which is produced artificially by dredging; but whereas dredging is very serviceable in a narrow river, like the Tyne or the Clyde, it could not produce a permanent, deep, and stable channel in a wide, exposed estuary like the Seine without the assistance of training works. Moreover, whilst the depth obtained by dredging requires periodical maintenance, the deepening by natural scour is maintained by the same force which causes it. Dredging, however, can be used for increasing the depth of a channel to any desired extent, or in proportion to the requirements of a growing trade; whereas training works can only produce a certain amount of deepening, depending on the current, the nature of the river bed, and the contraction in width between the training banks. The necessity, also, of not checking the tidal ebb and flow in a river renders it inexpedient to put the training banks very close together, and therefore limits the extent to which natural scour is available in tidal rivers. Considerable improvements in depth can be effected by training works alone, especially in a river with a large freshwater discharge like the Seine; and still more can be accomplished by supplementing training works by dredging, particularly in rivers having a small freshwater discharge, as, for instance, in the works on the Clyde below Glasgow, and the Tees below Middlesborough.

River Maas.—The mouths of the river Maas exhibit some of the features characteristic of the mouths of rivers flowing into tideless seas, owing probably to the flatness of the country through which the outlet channels flow, and the small rise of tide, of only $6\frac{1}{2}$ feet, in the North Sea on that coast. The river Maas, however, differs from most of the large tideless rivers in not bringing down any large quantity of material in suspension to deposit at its mouths. The position and depth of the outlet channels have varied from time to time; and some of the most direct channels have become shallow, owing to reclamations diminishing their tidal capacity. The trade of the Port of Rotterdam, situated on the most northern, or Scheur branch of the Maas, was forced gradually to seek circuitous southern outlets, which was very detrimental to its interests; and, accordingly, it was decided, in 1862, to form a new direct northern outlet for the Scheur branch, by making a straight cut, nearly 3 miles in length, across the Hook of Holland into the North Sea, and to improve the channel above by training works. The works were gradually carried out in the following years; the river was trained from Krinpen, above Rotterdam, towards the sea, with a gradually expanding channel; the cut was made across the Hook of Holland, in continuation of the trained channel; the channel was prolonged out to deep water, between parallel jetties, or breakwaters, formed of mattresses of fascines weighted with stones; and the old outlet to the south of the Hook of Holland was closed. Dredging has been carried out in the new channel to increase its depth, so that vessels of large size can now go up to Rotterdam, the minimum depth to be maintained being 23 feet at high-water. The improved channel has greatly increased the trade of Rotterdam, and the port has been considerably extended; and the remarkable change which has occurred in the general condition of Rotterdam bears unmistakable evidence of the advantages it has derived from its new maritime channel.

River Danube.—The Danube is the largest river in Europe; but though it has a basin about fifty-eight times the size of the Thames basin, it had a maximum depth of only 12 feet at the deepest of its mouths at the most favourable period; so that its great discharge was unable to form an outlet channel at all approaching the depth at the mouth of the Thames at high tide. The very unsatisfactory condition of its outlets was the result of the formation of a delta at its mouth, by the deposit of the silt carried in suspension by the river, gradually extending into the Black Sea which is devoid of tidal oscillations. At the commencement of the delta, 45 miles from the Black Sea, the Danube, which has a single channel above, 1700 feet wide and 50 feet deep, splits up into three diverging channels. The northern and largest of these channels forms a second delta near its outlet, passing into the Black Sea through several very shallow mouths; and this delta advances at the rate of a mile in about twenty-five years, as the channel discharges nearly two-thirds of the sediment-bearing waters of the Danube. The central, or Sulina Channel was selected for improvement, for, though the smallest of the three branches, it possesses a better depth over the bar at its mouth than the other two. Moreover, as the Sulina Channel only discharges about one-thirteenth of the whole flow of the Danube, the advance of its delta seawards is the least rapid of the three, having been about 94 feet, on the average, in a year before the execution of the improvement works.

The amount of material brought down by large delta-forming rivers is much too great to be controlled by dredging; and therefore the only methods of affording the inland navigation of silt-bearing tideless rivers an outlet to the sea consist, either in narrowing one of the mouths by jetties extending straight out from the shore towards the bar, and thus making the concentrated current scour the bar, and carry the material in suspension into deeper water, or in avoiding the delta altogether, by forming a canal connecting the river above with the sea at a point beyond the influence of the river mouths. The former method has been adopted for the Danube and the Mississippi, and the latter for the Rhone, by means of the St Louis Canal, constructed in 1863-73.

Two piers were built out from the shore on each side of the Sulina mouth, and carried across the bar in a parallel direction, 600 feet apart, into a depth of 18 feet of water. These piers were commenced as temporary constructions in 1858, and completed in 1861; and eventually, when their results had been manifested, and the Sulina Channel was finally adopted as the permanent outlet, they were strengthened and consolidated in 1868-71. The piers are composed of mounds of rubble stone, surmounted by a concrete block wall, and protected on the outer slopes by 20-ton concrete blocks. The northern pier is rather over a mile in length; but the southern pier, starting rather further out, is somewhat shorter.

The influence of the increased current over the bar, created by the piers, was felt as early as the end of 1860; and the floods, instead of raising the bar by the deposit of the material brought down by them as before, scoured away the bar, and carried the material in suspension into deeper water; and a minimum depth of $16\frac{1}{2}$ feet, with a width of 500 feet, was attained in 1861. The southern pier was extended, in 1869, out as far as the northern pier; and in 1870 a depth of 22 feet was obtained over the bar, where, in 1858, the depth had only averaged about 9½ feet. The river, of course, eventually deposits its material in the sea; but though a portion of this material is accumulating further out in front of the mouth, some of the discharge from the river has been brought under the influence of a littoral current flowing southwards, which carries away a portion of the material in suspension; so that the rate of the advance of the delta in front of the Sulina mouth is only about half what it was previous to the works. By degrees, the material which is accumulating in deep water beyond the piers will form another bar outside, which will sooner or later necessitate an extension of the jetties to scour it away. Hitherto, however, the piers have maintained an outlet channel having double the depth which it formerly possessed.

The Danube, in a point of its course much higher up, encounters an obstacle to navigation of a totally different nature, in the form of reefs of limestone, granite, and other rocks, which create dangerous rapids, and render the passage of the river difficult for vessels. These shoals, known as the Iron Gates of the Danube, are situated below Orsova, in the portion of the river flowing between Hungary and Servia, and are in course of removal at the present time by blasting, to improve the channel for navigation.

River Mississippi.—Though the Danube is the largest of European rivers, it appears small when compared with the large rivers of the American Continent, such as the Amazon, the La Plata, and the Mississippi. Thus the Mississippi has a length of more than two and a half times that of the Danube, and a basin four times the size of the basin of the Danube. Like the Danube, the Mississippi brings down a large quantity of alluvium in flood time, which it deposits at its outlet, forming a very extensive delta, stretching out into the almost tideless Gulf of Mexico, with an area of 12,300 square miles. The material which the river brings down in flood time amounts to 2800 cubic feet of solid matter per second, which is equivalent to a cube of about 207 yards in a day, or more in ten hours than the maximum dredged out of the Tyne in a year. Owing to the greater depth of the sea in front of the Mississippi delta, the average rate of advance of the delta, of about 220 feet in a year, is not much more than the advance of the Danube delta at the Kilia, or northern mouths, in spite of the much larger volume of material brought down by the Mississippi. The Mississippi flows through its delta, into the Gulf of Mexico, by four principal channels, or passes as they are termed, diverging from the main channel about 15 miles from the Gulf. (*See page* 208.) These passes were impeded by shoals at their starting point, and by a bar at their outlets; so that whereas the river, 35 miles above its outlet, has on the average a depth of 120 feet and a width of 2470 feet, it afforded a depth of only 13 feet over the deepest channel across the lowest of the bars, at the mouth of the South-West Pass, which was with difficulty increased temporarily by dredging to 18 feet.

The South Pass, discharging only about one-tenth of the volume of the river flow, was selected as the channel to be improved, as, owing to its smaller size, the jetty works required were less costly than at the South-West Pass, which possessed a wider channel and a better depth over the bar at its outlet. The yearly advance, moreover, of the delta in front of the South Pass was less than in front of the other three passes, as its discharge, and consequently the material brought down it, is less. Before the commencement of the works, the South Pass was impeded by a shoal at its upper end, with a depth of only 15 feet of water over it, and by a bar in front of its outlet, with a depth of only 8 feet over it.

The method of improvement adopted at the mouth of the South Pass was similar to the works previously carried out with success at the Sulina mouth of the Danube, namely, scouring a deeper channel over the bar by the concentration of the river current between parallel jetties across the bar. The South Pass jetties, commenced in 1875, form artificial prolongations of the banks of the channel seawards for a distance of $2\frac{1}{4}$ miles, placed 1000 feet apart. The jetties are composed of tiers of mattresses of interwoven osiers, weighted with stones along the inner portions, and with large concrete blocks along the outer portions, the blocks at the outer ends reaching over 260 tons in weight, to secure the mattresses against disturbance by the waves. (*See section, page* 208.) The east jetty is $2\frac{1}{4}$ miles long, and the west jetty $1\frac{1}{2}$ miles, extending to the same distance out, in a depth of 30 feet of water; and they were completed in 1879. In 1877 the channel over the bar had been deepened from 8 feet to 20 feet, which increased to 28 feet in 1879, and eventually to 30 feet, with a width of 70 feet, by the action of the natural scour of the river, directed and concentrated by the jetties.

The shoal at the upper end of the South Pass was also deepened by the scour resulting from a contraction of its entrance by willow mattresses; but as this contraction tended to divert a portion of the discharge of the South Pass into the other channels, it became necessary to reduce the sections of the entrance channels to the other passes by sinking willow mattresses across them, so that the South Pass might continue, in spite of its contracted entrance, to receive its due proportion of the discharge of the river. In this manner the channel over the shoal at the upper end of the South Pass has attained a depth of from 30 to 35 feet of water for a width of 275 feet; so that there is a regular navigable channel throughout the South Pass, having a minimum depth of 30 feet, where, fifteen years ago, it was impeded by a shoal at the upper end, with a maximum depth of 15 feet over it, and by a bar at the lower end, with a depth over it of only 8 feet. The contraction of the outlet of the South Pass, from a width of 2 miles to 1000 feet, besides lowering the bar by the resulting scour, has carried the material in suspension, formerly deposited on the bar, into deeper water, and within the influence of the westerly littoral current in front of the pass. Accordingly, the material brought down by the river has been partially carried away by the westerly current; and the remainder has been deposited in a sufficient depth to prevent the accumulations reaching for some years a height impeding navigation. As soon as the continued accumulations of deposit encroach upon the 30 feet depth, it will be necessary to prolong the jetties seawards, so as to scour away the fresh deposits to the requisite depth, and to drive the material into depths where its accumulations will not interfere with the navigable depth at the outlet for another series of years.

The above examples show what remarkable results can be accomplished by dredging and training works in tidal rivers and estuaries, and by parallel jetties at the mouths of tideless rivers, in deepening the outer channels for sea-going vessels; and they also afford evidence of the great advances made in the development of the navigable capacities of rivers within recent years.

CHAPTER XII.

THE WEIRS OF POSES ON THE SEINE, AND OF CHARLOTTENBURG ON THE SPREE; AND THE HYDRAULIC CANAL LIFT OF LA LOUVIÈRE.

THE improvement of the Lower Seine, between the termination of the tidal portion at St Aubin and Paris, has been already alluded to in the preceding chapter. It has been effected by the ordinary method adopted upon all other canalised rivers, namely, by raising the water level of the river by means of barriers, termed weirs, put across the channel at certain places, and thus increasing the depth of water; whilst the passage of vessels at these weirs is provided for by locks placed at the side of the weir, or in a small subsidiary channel. The river is thereby divided into a number of reaches, with different water levels; and the vessels accomplish the change of level at each weir by being raised or lowered, on entering the lock, by the filling or emptying of the lock chamber, which is closed at each end by gates. The discharge of the river has to pass over or through the weirs; and as the water level is raised by the weir, it is important to provide an ample passage for the river in flood time, so that the improvements effected for navigation may not lead to increased inundation of the riparian lands. This consideration has led to the construction of moveable weirs, which keep up the level of the water in dry weather, when the water would otherwise flow away leaving an insufficient depth in places for navigation, but can be removed from the channel in flood time, when an abundance of water renders these barriers unnecessary for navigation, and only an impediment to the passage of the flood waters. Various types of these moveable weirs have been erected across rivers for improving their navigable depth, especially in France, within the last fifty years; for only three such weirs, of the simplest modern type, were erected previous to 1840, whilst now numerous moveable weirs of improved construction may be seen in France, Belgium, Germany, and Russia, and some large examples of similar weirs in the United States.

MOVEABLE WEIRS.

The simplest form of moveable weir consists of a series of small square wooden spars, placed side by side, and resting nearly vertically against a sill in the bed of the river, and against a footbridge supported on a row of wrought-iron frames which, being hinged at the bottom, can be laid flat on the bed of the river in flood time. These spars, sloping slightly upstream towards the bottom, form a continuous barrier across the river in dry weather, and can be removed, one by one, by a man on the footbridge, as the discharge of the river increases; and eventually, when all the spars or needles are removed, the footbridge taken up, and the frames lowered, the channel is left quite unobstructed. These needle weirs have been extensively adopted on the French rivers; and fine examples of them may be seen on the Meuse in Belgium, and on the Main between Frankfort and the Rhine.

Shutter weirs were for the first time introduced, in 1852, on the Upper Seine above Paris. They consist of a series of panels, each revolving upon a central horizontal axis, supported on a moveable iron trestle at the back of the panel. These shutters form a continuous weir across the river; and the discharge of the river over them can be increased by turning them slightly on their axis; or they can be lowered completely on to the bed of the river, by releasing a prop supporting the trestle of each panel or shutter. This type of weir has been used on the Upper Seine, the Rhine, and the Meuse; it has been introduced into Russia, and has also found a home in the United States, on the Ohio and Great Kanawha rivers.

The most novel type of weir is to be found in the recently completed weirs of Poses and Port-Mort, erected for improving the navigable condition of the Lower Seine. Another very ingenious and remarkably easily regulated form of weir, known as the drum weir, was for a long time confined to the River Marne, where it was first introduced in 1857. This type of weir has, however, been adopted for closing the timber passes at the weirs erected for canalising the Main below Frankfort, in 1883-86; and a drum weir, on a still larger scale, was erected about the same time across the navigable pass of the River Spree at Charlottenburg.

Poses Weir.—The canalisation of the Seine below Paris was only commenced in 1838; and the works then begun, and completed in 1866, were merely designed to secure a navigable depth of $5\frac{1}{4}$ feet, by the erection of seven needle weirs, with adjoining locks for the passage of vessels. On the termination of these works, fresh works were deemed expedient to increase the depth from $5\frac{1}{4}$ to $6\frac{1}{2}$ feet, which was accomplished by an additional weir, and by raising three of the existing weirs. In 1878 it was decided to increase the depth of the Seine between Rouen and Paris to $10\frac{1}{2}$ feet, so as to enable vessels of 800 to 1000 tons, and of nearly 10 feet draught, to reach Paris. This involved the rebuilding of all the locks, the reconstruction of some of the weirs, and the modification of the others. The increased height of the weirs, to raise the water level and thus augment the depth, was in some cases too great to enable the old system of closing the weir with spars, or needles, to be retained. In two instances, at Suresnes near Paris, and Port Villez near Vernon, the old frame system, on an enlarged scale, was employed; but the closing is effected in the one case by a series of sliding panels between each pair of frames, and in the other case by hinged curtains rolling up from the bottom.[1] At Poses, however, the weir was entirely remodelled, and a new type of weir was adopted. The principle of the frame weir, with hinged curtains resting against the frames, has

---

[1] This curtain consists of a series of horizontal laths of wood hinged together, increasing in thickness towards the bottom so as to sustain the water pressure which increases with the depth. The curtains, which resemble somewhat in principle the flexible iron shutters for closing shop windows, are rolled up from the bottom by a pair of endless chains, encircling each curtain, wound up by a special winch at the top.

been retained; but the frames, instead of being hinged to a stone floor in the bed of the river, and lowered sideways, are hinged at the top to an overhead girder bridge, and are raised in pairs upstream (with a curtain rolled up upon them), to a horizontal position under the bridge, when the weir has to be removed. By this means all the moveable parts of the weir are lifted entirely out of the river during the winter months, instead of being entirely submerged as in the case of the shutter weirs, or leaving the frames in the bed of the river as in the needle weirs and other similar frame weirs. This new arrangement, however, though avoiding liability to injury, and making the raising and lowering of the frames much easier, involves the somewhat costly adjuncts of a wide overhead bridge, and high piers at the sides of the navigable passes. The bridge is necessary as a support from which the frames can be hung; and it has to be wide, to enable the frames to be raised by chains attached to each frame at some little distance from the hinge.

On the Seine, as on other continental rivers, the locks are submerged during floods, so that vessels in flood time pass over the sites of the moveable weirs at places where the foundations of the weir are specially low. As these navigable passes in the weirs have to be available for navigation at all times when the weir is open, except in extreme floods when the navigation is stopped, it is necessary that any fixed bridge over these passes should afford an ample headway for the masts of such vessels as navigate the river. Accordingly, a clear height of $17\frac{1}{4}$ feet had to be provided at Poses Weir, across the navigable passes, between the highest navigable level and the under side of the frames when raised under the overhead bridge. The bridge, therefore, had to be raised to a sufficient height over the two navigable passes at Poses Weir to secure this headway; whilst the bridge over the rest of the weir has only been placed high enough to ensure that, with the frames raised underneath, there may be ample clearance in the highest possible flood.

The weir at Poses stretches across a wide branch of the river, only separated from the narrower channel in which the locks are situated by the narrow end of an island. The weir has seven openings separated by masonry piers, 13 feet wide, upon which the girders carrying the bridge across these openings rest. Five of the openings have a width of 99 feet; and the two navigable passes are each $106\frac{1}{2}$ feet wide. The head of water retained by this weir, or the difference in level between the upper and lower reaches, is 13 feet at the ordinary water level. The wrought-iron frames, composed of four vertical pieces braced together, are 38 feet long; and the overhead bridge has a similar total width. The curtain resting against each frame is $7\frac{1}{2}$ feet wide (*see note, page 227*); and it is rolled up from the bottom by two chains wound up by a winch travelling on a little footbridge formed by a series of iron flaps hinged to the back of each frame. One of the deep passes of the weir can be entirely opened in five hours, by rolling up the fourteen curtains and raising the frames.

The navigation at Poses is provided for, in ordinary states of the river, by three locks of different sizes, placed side by side, the largest lock having a length of 524 feet, and a width of $55\frac{3}{4}$ feet.

The weir at Poses, which was put into operation in 1885, is the largest work of the kind hitherto constructed. Moreover, the portion of the weir at present visible does not give an adequate conception of the magnitude of the work; for, besides the part submerged in the water, the foundations had to be carried $27\frac{3}{4}$ feet below the floor of the weir; so that the total height of the weir, extending across a width of river of about 800 feet, is 77 feet from the bottom of the foundations to the top of the girders across the navigable passes. These works, together with similar works at Port-Mort, the next weir higher up, and other works of considerably less magnitude, have raised the Seine, for a length of 135 miles, from being a river impeded by numerous shoals, and difficult to navigate by small vessels in dry seasons, into a river possessing a permanent navigable channel of $10\frac{1}{2}$ feet, giving access for large river craft right up to Paris.

Charlottenburg Weir.—The works for canalising the river Spree at Charlottenburg consist of a weir across the main channel, and two locks in a side channel separated from the main channel by an island. The weir is divided into five openings by piers in the river. Four of these openings, having each a width of $34\frac{1}{2}$ feet, are closed by a series of vertical wooden panels, about 9 feet high and 7 feet wide, which can be raised and removed in flood time from a low footbridge crossing these openings. The fifth opening has a width of 34 feet, and is closed by a moveable drum weir, the largest of this type hitherto erected. The footbridge traversing the weir has been raised over this opening, so as to afford a clear headway of not less than 11 feet above the highest flood level, and a greater headway in the centre. As this weir can be very

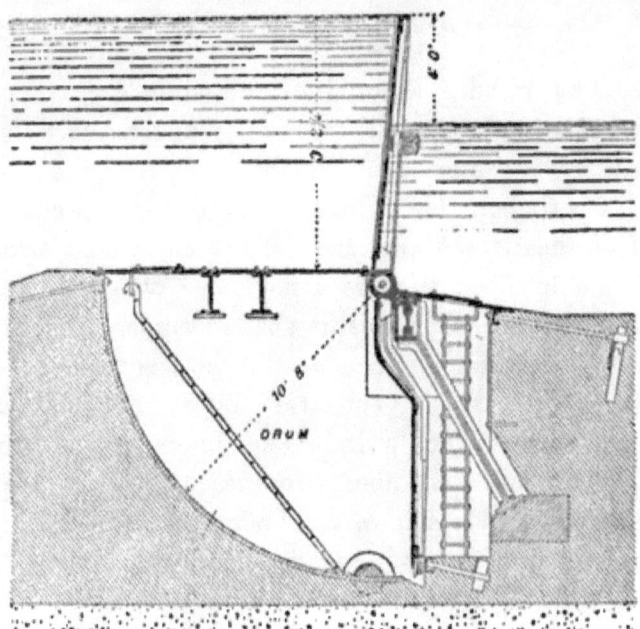

DRUM WEIR ON THE SPREE AT CHARLOTTENBURG.

easily and rapidly lowered or raised, it can be used for regulating the discharge of the river, and thus adjusting its water level, or for the passage of large rafts of timber, for which purpose these weirs are used on the river Main; and the opening would also be available in flood time as a navigable pass for barges. This form of weir consists of an upper and lower paddle revolving upon a central horizontal axis (*see section, page* 232); and the upper paddle, when vertical, forms the weir. The lower paddle turns in a segmental chamber (from the shape of which, resembling a quadrant of a cylinder, the name of drum, given to the weir, was derived), placed below the actual sill of the weir; and this lower paddle controls the motion of the upper paddle for opening or closing the weir. By a special arrangement of sluice gates in the abutment, the communications between the drum and the upper and lower pools, on each side of the weir, can be alternately opened or closed more or less, thus adjusting the water pressure on either side of the lower paddle to any desired extent, and enabling any inclination to be given to the upper paddle, between its almost vertical position when the weir is closed and its horizontal position downstream when the weir is entirely open. The weir is, accordingly, under perfect control, being worked by the water pressure due to the head of water retained by the weir; and the upper paddle can not only be lowered to any position in the quadrant of the circle in which it revolves, but it can also be raised from the horizontal position up to its full height against the rush of the current through the opening. This form of weir, therefore, is perfectly adjustable, and only requires a few turns of a handle, for the opening or closing of the sluice gates, to work it; and the opening or closing of the weir occupies only a very few minutes, and necessitates no footbridge or other accessories. The foundations, however, for the drum have to be carried rather further below the bed of the river than the weir is raised above it, and the weir is therefore costly; but, on the other hand, the cost of maintenance and labour in working are very slight. The upper paddle in the Charlottenburg drum weir is $32\frac{3}{4}$ feet wide, and $9\frac{2}{3}$ feet high; whereas the upper paddles of the drum weirs on the Main are $39\frac{1}{3}$ feet wide, and $5\frac{1}{2}$ feet high.

CANAL LIFT OF LA LOUVIÈRE.

There is never any great difference of level in adjacent reaches of canalised rivers, and therefore a single lock can always be given a sufficient rise to connect the two water levels; though the locks have generally to be put closer together in the upper part of a navigable river, owing to the greater inclination of the river bed in the higher portions of its valley. Canals, on the contrary, have sometimes to cross the summit ridge of a valley dividing two river basins, and to traverse rugged districts; and consequently the difference in level between two adjacent reaches is occasionally considerable. This difference is generally surmounted by a series of locks, placed closed together in steps; but the passage of a flight of locks occupies a considerable time, and expends a good deal of water. Inclines have, accordingly, been used, on which vessels are drawn up or let down in cradles or tanks, to transfer them from one reach to another, where the difference of level is large and water scarce. Another plan, however, of accomplishing the same object, with a saving of time and space as well as of water, consists in raising or lowering a vessel vertically, in a trough, by means of hydraulic power. This method, adopted for the first time at Anderton, in Cheshire, in 1875, to connect the river Weaver with the Trent and Mersey Canal, has since been applied, on a larger scale, to supplement a flight of five locks on the Neuffossé Canal at Fontinettes near St Omer in France, and has also been resorted to at La Louvière in Belgium, on the canal in course of construction for connecting Mons with Liége.

The hydraulic lift at La Louvière is the largest lift that has as yet been erected; and it was completed in 1888, about a year after the completion of the slightly smaller lift at Fontinettes. This lift, like the two previous ones, consists of two parallel wrought-iron troughs, each resting upon a central hydraulic ram, raised by water pressure in a press situated below the bottom of the lift. (*See illustration.*) When the presses are in communication, the troughs exactly counterbalance one another, so that when one trough is at the top on a level with the upper reach, the other trough is at the bottom of the lift and level with the lower reach; and the water in the troughs is level with the water in the canal. The ends of each trough, and the corresponding extremities of the approach channels to each trough, in the upper and lower reaches, are closed by lifting gates with watertight joints; and the adjacent gates are lifted by hydraulic power when a communication has to be made between a trough and the canal. The difference of level between the two canal reaches at La Louvière is 50½ feet. Each trough is 141 feet long, 19 feet wide, and contains about 8 feet depth of water; it is supported by a hollow cast-iron ram, 6 feet in diameter, 3½ inches thick, and 63¾ feet long; and the weight lifted, including trough, water, and ram, is 1037 tons. The lift is effected, after the gates have been all lowered, by putting an additional 10 inches of water in the trough at the top, thereby overweighting it with 62 tons, which causes it to descend, and raises the lower trough; whilst any requisite additional assistance in lifting is furnished by introducing water under pressure into the press under the lower trough. The whole lift of 50½ feet is accomplished in two and a half minutes; and a barge can be admitted to each trough, the lift effected, and the barges taken out of the troughs again, in fifteen minutes; and as barges of 400 tons can enter the lift, 800 tons can be passed from one reach to the other in that period. The water pressure is obtained by two turbines worked by the fall of water from the upper reach, and is stored up by an accumulator; and this power is used for lifting the gates, turning the capstans, and working pumps to keep the lift pit dry, as well as for lifting the rams when required. The troughs are guided in their movement by light wrought-iron lattice towers in the centre and at each end; and a man in a lookout cabin above the lift can control its working. This lift is the first one of four lifts which are required for enabling the traffic on the canal to surmount a difference of level, of 217 feet in the short distance of only 5 miles, with a very small expenditure of water.

HYDRAULIC CANAL LIFT AT LA LOUVIERE, BELGIUM.

The Louvière Lift constitutes a remarkable advance on the original Anderton Lift; for, though the actual height of lift is the same at both places, the length of the troughs and diameter of the rams at La Louvière are double those at Anderton; and this lift can accommodate vessels of four times the tonnage of the largest barges using the Anderton Lift. The raising of the vessel floating in the trough is accomplished with wonderful ease, regularity, and rapidity, with an expenditure of only about 2220 cubic feet of water; and this system, besides expediting the traffic on a canal where the change of level is considerable, enables water communication to be provided across a country whose ruggedness would otherwise appear to preclude the construction of a canal.

CHAPTER XIII.

THE AMSTERDAM SHIP CANAL; AND THE MANCHESTER SHIP CANAL.

THE advantages possessed by towns situated within easy access of the sea have been so fully realised of late years, that several towns not bordering tidal rivers, and at some distance from the sea-coast, have aimed at gaining the same facilities for trade, by artificial means, which towns more favourably situated possess naturally, or have obtained by the improvement of their rivers. Thus a scheme has been proposed for converting Paris into a seaport, by forming a deep, straight channel along the Seine valley, so as to bring the tide nearly up to Paris. The inhabitants of Bruges have for some time been urging upon the Belgian Government the construction of a ship canal to connect Bruges with the sea, in the hope of its restoring the lost commercial importance of the town. A design is also under consideration for converting Brussels into a seaport, by a canal giving it access to the sea. Birmingham, Sheffield, and other inland towns, are also endeavouring to secure an improved communication by water with seaports, so as to enable them to compete on more equal terms with their more favoured rivals.

The commercial importance of towns situated at the upper limit of large navigations, such as Mannheim on the Rhine, and the rapid development of the river traffic up to Frankfort since the canalisation of the Main, in spite of railway facilities on both banks of the river, sufficiently attest the value to inland towns of good communication by water with the sea. The ports of Newcastle, Glasgow, and Middlesborough owe their present prosperous condition to the large works carried out on their rivers. In these cases, however, the channels existed, though in a very defective condition, and were capable of gradual development as the trade of the ports increased. Inland towns, on the contrary, at a distance from any tidal river, can only be converted into seaports by purely artificial canal works, carried out on a large scale and at a great cost, which bring in no return on the capital expended till after the final completion of the works. Such works, accordingly, must be much more limited than improvement works carried out gradually for deepening the channel of tidal rivers. An important work of this description is the ship canal which has provided the shipping trade of Amsterdam with direct access to the North Sea. The Manchester Ship Canal, also, in course of construction, which ere long will convert Manchester into a seaport, is a work of great interest, both as the largest and most important canal work carried out in Great Britain, and also as marking the revival in England of the development of inland navigation, the results of which will be watched with great attention.

AMSTERDAM SHIP CANAL.

In olden times Amsterdam was a port of great importance, and one of the commercial centres of Europe. When, however, the draught of vessels increased, the shallow depth of the Zuider Zee became inadequate; and Amsterdam was forced, early in the present century, to seek an improved outlet for its sea-going trade. The shortest route, however, to the North Sea, across Holland, to the west of Amsterdam, was considered quite impracticable in those days; and a northern, somewhat winding route was chosen for the North Holland Canal, which was constructed in 1819-25, and connected Amsterdam with the Texel Roads by a waterway, 52 miles long, and affording a depth of $18\frac{1}{2}$ feet. The continually increasing draught of vessels, however, and the superior facilities afforded for reaching Antwerp and Rotterdam, again tended to divert the shipping trade from Amsterdam, and obliged Amsterdam to seek a deeper and more direct channel to the sea. The distance from Amsterdam to the North Sea, in a westerly direction, is only $15\frac{1}{2}$ miles, the greater portion of which consisted of shallow lakes, separated from the North Sea by a strip of land, 3 miles wide, connecting North and South Holland. This route, therefore, which was selected for the Amsterdam Ship Canal, was favourable for the purpose, as well as being the shortest way between Amsterdam and the open sea. It involved, however, two difficult problems, which had been considered insuperable when the North Holland Canal route was selected in preference, namely,

Q

SHIP CANALS.
CROSS SECTIONS.

SUEZ CANAL

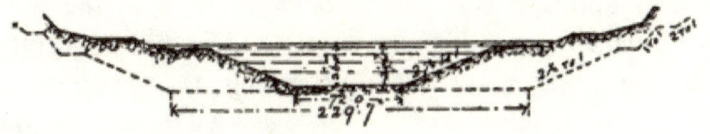

PANAMA CANAL.

SECTION IN EARTH.   SECTION IN ROCK.

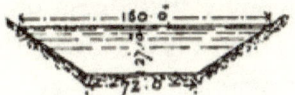 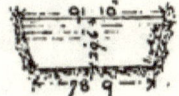

AMSTERDAM CANAL

CORINTH CANAL.   MANCHESTER CANAL.

 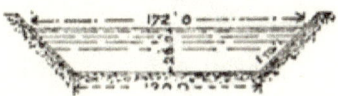

SCALE $\frac{1}{1500}$

the maintenance of a deep entrance across the flat sandy beach of the North Sea, and the preservation of the drainage and water communication of the low-lying lands bordering the lakes. The first difficulty has been surmounted by sheltering the entrance to the canal by two converging piers, built out on the shore of the North Sea, under the shelter of which the entrance channel to the canal is maintained by dredging. The second difficulty has been overcome by shutting off direct communication with the sea at each end of the canal, keeping the canal at a lower level than the sea, and forming branch canals connecting the villages, which formerly bordered on the lake, with the ship canal.

The works consist of two piers, forming a harbour on the shore of the North Sea; an entrance channel, leading from the harbour to the North Sea locks; a canal excavated through the land, and dredged through the lakes (*see cross section*); and a dam, to the east of Amsterdam, shutting off the Zuider Zee from the canal, in which a second set of locks and pumping machinery are situated.

The piers were constructed of a wall of concrete blocks, resting upon a small mound of stone, capped at the top by concrete-in-mass, and protected on the sea side by a mound of large concrete blocks along the outer half of the piers. These piers, each about a mile in length, converge from a width apart of nearly 4000 feet at the shore to 800 feet at the entrance, enclosing an area of about 250 acres, through which a central channel, 740 feet wide, has been dredged.

The North Sea locks consist of a large lock in

the centre, a small lock on one side, and a sluiceway on the other for letting water out of the canal at low tide. The large lock is 390 feet long and 60 feet wide, and the small lock, 227 feet by 40 feet; and both these locks and the sluiceway are provided with gates pointing both ways, so that the water level in the canal can be kept at a uniform level of 14 inches above low-water in the North Sea, the rise of tide being $5\frac{2}{3}$ feet, to ensure the drainage of the low-lying lands.

The canal has been given a bottom width of $88\frac{1}{2}$ feet, nearly three times the bottom width of the North Holland Canal, a depth of 23 feet of water, and side slopes of 2 to 1. (*See cross section, page* 242.) The material dredged out for the canal, through the lakes, was deposited at the sides, forming a continuous bank, behind which the land was reclaimed to the extent of 13,142 acres, and eventually sold at about £70 an acre. These reclaimed lands, and other low-lying lands formerly draining into the lakes, are drained by pumping the surface water into the canal.

The dam across Lake Y, two miles east of Amsterdam, separating the canal from the Zuider Zee, is 4460 feet long, and consists of an embankment of clay and sand, deposited on a series of willow mattresses to reduce the settlement in the silty bed of the lake. The Zuider Zee locks, built in Lake Y in the line of the dam, under the protection of a temporary circular cofferdam, 525 feet in diameter, are three in number, the central one being 315 feet long and 60 feet wide, and the two side ones each 238 feet by 47 feet. These locks, and also four adjacent sluiceways, through which the drainage water is discharged from the canal, are all provided with gates pointing both ways, for the same purpose as at the North Sea locks, of rendering the water level in the canal independent of the tidal oscillations. As the drainage water from the adjacent lands is pumped into the canal, it is necessary to remove this water in order to maintain the canal at a permanent level, which is effected, partly by letting out the water through the sluice at each end during low tide, and partly by pumping machinery erected close to the Zuider Zee locks, at the northern end of the dam.

The canal works were commenced in 1865, and completed in 1876, at a total cost, after deducting the amount realised by the sale of the reclaimed lands, of about £2,000,000. There is a large and gradually increasing traffic along the canal; and the work has been an immense benefit to the trade of Amsterdam, and also an advantage to Holland in general, which now possesses two very accessible seaports at Amsterdam and Rotterdam, having direct railway communication with all parts of the Continent.

MANCHESTER SHIP CANAL.

The ship canal, in course of construction, between Manchester and Eastham, on the Cheshire shore of the Mersey estuary, has been designed with the object of enabling large sea-going vessels to come right up to docks at Manchester, instead of being obliged to discharge their cargoes in the Liverpool Docks on to the quays, from whence they are carted to the railway, and then forwarded by train to Manchester.

As the land rises about 70 feet from the shore of the Mersey estuary up to Manchester, the canal has had to be constructed in sections, forming level reaches at different levels, separated by locks through which the change of level will be accomplished. The total length of the canal, from its commencement at Eastham up to its termination at the Manchester and Salford Docks, is $35\frac{1}{2}$ miles, divided into five reaches of very different lengths. The first reach is tidal, and, skirting the Cheshire shore of the estuary from Eastham up to a little beyond Runcorn (*see illustration*), it passes somewhat inland, and proceeds in a straight course to Latchford, a little past Warrington, where this reach terminates at a set of locks, its length being 21 miles. The level of the canal is then raised $16\frac{1}{2}$ feet for the next reach, which extends along the valley of the Mersey, from Latchford locks to Irlam locks, for a distance of $7\frac{1}{2}$ miles. The level of the canal is again raised, at the Irlam locks, a height of 16 feet for the third reach, which follows the valley of the Irwell, and terminates at the Barton locks, with a length of only 2 miles. The fourth reach is raised 15 feet; and, following approximately the course of the Irwell, and skirting Salford, it ends at the Mode Wheel locks, after traversing $3\frac{1}{4}$ miles. The final reach, above the Mode Wheel locks, $1\frac{3}{4}$ miles long, and raised 13 feet higher than the previous reach, gives access to the docks which are being constructed in the outskirts of Manchester, with a total water area of 114 acres. Vessels will, accordingly, rise $60\frac{1}{2}$ feet in passing through the four locks, from the tidal reach below Latchford to the docks at Manchester. The water level in the tidal reach will be retained by tidal locks at Eastham, at a height of $9\frac{1}{2}$ feet above

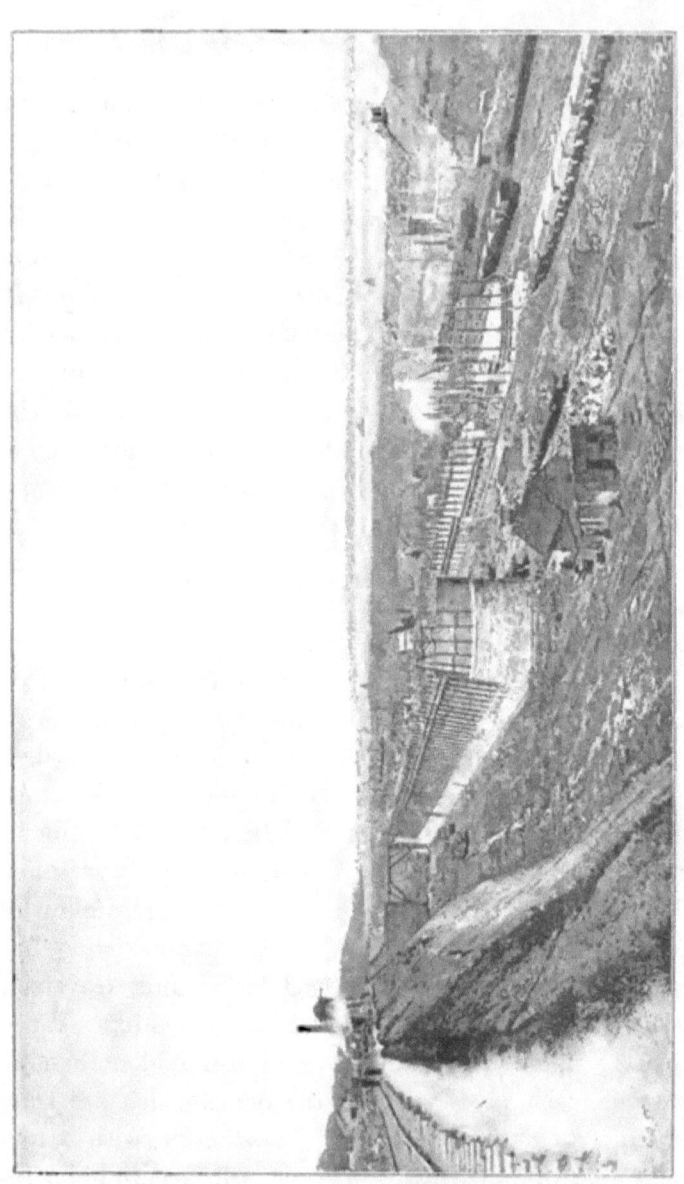

mean tide level in the estuary at that point, or 14½ feet above the Old Dock Sill datum at Liverpool.[1] When the tide, during spring tides, rises above the ordinary water level in the tidal reach of the canal, which is about mean high-water level, it will flow in through the locks, and through certain tidal openings to be left in the embankments, which separate the canal from the estuary, where the canal crosses small enbayments in the shore of the estuary. At the turn of the tide, the lock gates at Eastham will close, and the surplus water above the normal level will flow out again through the tidal openings; and, if desirable, the efflux can be aided by deep sluices at the Weaver, and at Old Randles higher up. Equinoctial spring tides rise about 7 feet higher than the normal water level of the tidal reach of the canal. The canal is to have a minimum depth of water throughout of 26 feet; and the sills of the locks are being placed 2 feet lower, so that the depth can be increased when required to 28 feet. The canal is being constructed with a minimum bottom width of 120 feet (*see section, page* 242), and an average width of 172 feet at the water surface. Above Barton, up to Manchester, the bottom width is increased to 170 feet, and the width at the water level to 230 feet; and the width has also been increased near the locks to facilitate the passage of vessels. Runcorn Bridge, built several years ago, for carrying the North-Western Railway across the Mersey at Runcorn Gap, affords a clear headway of 75 feet above the normal water level adopted for the tidal

---

[1] The Old Dock has been demolished in the course of extensions of the docks; but the level of its sill has been transferred to a tide-guage near one of the dock entrances, and this level is 5 feet below mean tide level at Liverpool.

portion of the canal which passes under it; and the same headway is being given under the other fixed bridges which are being built over the canal.

The approach channel to Eastham locks, from deep water in the Sloyne, is to be dredged to a depth of about 40 feet below high-water spring tides; and the outer sills of the locks have been laid 3 feet lower than the bottom of this channel, to allow for a future increase in depth. There are three locks at Eastham, side by side, 600 feet long by 80 feet wide, 350 feet by 50 feet, and 150 feet by 30 feet; and there are two sluiceways on the land side of the locks, each 20 feet in width, and closed by counterbalanced sluice gates, moving vertically on free rollers, whereby friction is reduced to a minimum, so that they are very easily raised against a head of water. The locks have been arranged to accommodate various classes of vessels without excessive waste of water; and the sluiceways can serve either to assist in filling the canal on a rising tide, or in sluicing the entrance channel at low tide. (*See illustration.*)

As the line of the canal passes across the mouth of the river Weaver where it flows into the Mersey estuary, the embankment of the canal is being carried across the Weaver outlet; and as it will be necessary to provide for the influx of the tidal water into the Weaver, and for the efflux of the tidal and fresh waters of the river at this place, ten large sluice gates, of 30 feet span, with deep sills, have been erected in the embankment in front of the Weaver. These sluice gates, being counterbalanced and moving on free rollers, like those at Eastham and the other locks, will serve to regulate with perfect precision the flow of water at the mouth of the Weaver. Locks are also being constructed at

Weston Point and Runcorn, across the embankment of the canal, to allow the barges of existing navigations and docks to have the same access to the estuary as previously. Two sluice gates, of 30 feet span, have also been erected, by the side of the Mersey, at Old Randles, to regulate the flow into or out of the canal. The groups of locks at Latchford, Irlam, Barton, and Mode Wheel, each consist of a large lock, 600 feet long and 65 feet wide, and a smaller lock of 350 feet by 45 feet; and sluice-ways are provided at each set of locks for discharging any excess of water coming down the Mersey and Irwell, which rivers will practically be absorbed by the canal above Latchford, to supply it with water for locking.

There are four high-level railway bridges constructed over the canal, which have involved considerable deviations of the lines to attain the increased elevation required to afford a headway of 75 feet above the water level of the canal. Two high-level bridges, and five low opening bridges, will carry the roads across the canal; and all the bridges will leave a minimum width of 120 feet for the canal. Owing to the angles at which the railways cross the canal, the actual spans of the bridges are greater than the clear width of 120 feet left for the canal; and in one case the span amounts to 266 feet.

Where the Bridgewater Canal crosses over the ship canal at Barton, at too low a level to provide the requisite headway for masted vessels passing along the ship canal, a swing aqueduct is provided, turning on a central pier, and leaving an opening on each side of 90 feet across the ship canal. This aqueduct, containing the same depth of water as the Bridgewater Canal, will enable the barges on this canal to cross over the ship canal. A pair of lifting gates at each end of the aqueduct will enable the ends of the trough, forming the aqueduct, and the adjoining ends of the canal to be closed, when the aqueduct has to be swung round a quarter of a circle to leave the passages on each side of the central pier quite clear for masted vessels passing along the ship canal. Hydraulic lifts, similar in principle to the lift described in the last chapter, will provide communication for barges at Barton between the Bridgewater Canal and the ship canal.

In addition to the docks of 114 acres at Manchester, there will be a dock at Warrington in connection with the canal, having an area of 23 acres. The canal is being made wider at Partington, just above the Irlam locks, so that steamers will be able to lie there at anchor; and arrangements are being made for the shipment of coal. The normal width of the canal is sufficient for vessels to pass at any point; and by giving the canal an additional width at any places where it is desired to establish quays, vessels will be able to lie alongside without impeding navigation, and thus facilities for trade can be extended along the banks of the canal. Vessels will be able to traverse the whole length of the canal in ten hours; and by the employment of the electric light, it will be possible to navigate the canal by night as well as by day. The canal is being excavated through silt, sand, gravel, clay, marl, and red sandstone, by the aid of nearly one hundred excavators, or steam navvies, of various types; and out of the 46 million cubic yards of excavation required for the canal and docks, about 10 millions are in sandstone. Some of this stone is being used for protecting the slopes of the canal, and the river slopes of the embankments. The excavations generally are being used for the embankments along the sides of the canal, for filling up hollows, and for raising low-lying land bordering the canal. The side slopes of the canal vary, according to the strata traversed, from slopes of 2 to 1 in soft material to nearly vertical sides in rock. One cutting near Runcorn has a depth of 66 feet; and another cutting at Latchford has an average depth of 55 feet for a mile and a half.

The Manchester Ship Canal was authorised in 1885; the works were commenced in 1887; and it is anticipated that the works will be completed in 1892 or 1893. The cost of the works has been estimated at £5,330,000; but a committee has recently reported that the total expenditure on the whole undertaking, including the purchase of the Bridgewater Canal, will amount to nearly £13,000,000. The lower portion of the canal is to be opened for traffic in 1891. This canal will afford a navigable waterway, from the sea to Manchester, for large sea-going vessels, wider and deeper than the Amsterdam Ship Canal, and of the same depth as the Suez Canal before the enlargement works were commenced, and a bottom width 48 feet greater. (*See cross sections, page* 242.) Accordingly, Manchester will soon possess a waterway for its trade superior to the one provided for the capital of Holland by the Dutch Government, and more convenient than the waterway hitherto provided for the shipping of the world through the Isthmus of Suez. If the financial results of the traffic on the canal should realise the anticipations of its promoters, a great stimulus will be afforded to the prosecution of other schemes of a similar nature; and, accordingly, the traffic returns and receipts of this canal after its opening will be followed with great interest by the general public, as well as by those more directly concerned. Manchester will undoubtedly derive great indirect advantages from the canal in any case; but the actual financial results will be the test by which this great navigation undertaking will be gauged. The success of the work, from an engineering point of view, is assured; and though larger works have been carried out, none of equal magnitude have been attempted by a private company for affording a single district an access to the sea.

CHAPTER XIV.

THE SUEZ, PANAMA, NICARAGUA, AND CORINTH CANALS.

THE canals described in the last chapter have been constructed for the sea-going trade of single cities and districts; but there are localities where the cutting of a waterway across an isthmus shortens the navigable distance between remote ports, and thereby affords very important facilities to the shipping of the world. The cutting of a channel through the Isthmus of Suez, by connecting the Mediterranean and Red seas, has considerably shortened the routes to India, Australia, and various eastern ports, and has enabled vessels to avoid the circuitous and stormy voyage round the Cape of Good Hope. The Isthmus of Panama presents a natural barrier to communication between the Atlantic and Pacific oceans, forcing vessels to make an enormous detour to the south, round Cape Horn, a passage noted for storms; and the piercing of this barrier would be almost as great a benefit to the trade of the world as the Suez Canal. Another smaller and less important obstacle is the Isthmus of Corinth, which is being cut through for the benefit of the local trade of the Mediterranean and Black Sea. Another canal is in course of construction across Holstein, to form a shorter connection between the Baltic and the North Sea, for the benefit of German trade; and canals have been proposed to be made across the peninsula of Florida, across the Isthmus of Perekop which connects the Crimea with Russia, and through the shoals between Ceylon and India, with the object of providing more direct routes. In some of these undertakings, however, the truth of the old proverb, that 'there is nothing new under the sun,' is curiously borne out; for traces of an old canal were found in the Isthmus of Suez, which is believed to have been used for the passage of small vessels many centuries back. A canal, also, across the Isthmus of Corinth was commenced in the time of Nero; and a suggestion was made for cutting through the Isthmus of Panama more than three centuries ago. It has been, however, reserved for the present generation to witness the successful completion of one of these undertakings on a large scale; the approaching completion of another which the Romans failed to carry out; the partial execution of a third, of the greatest magnitude and difficulty; and the commencement of a fourth, across the same Isthmus of Panama, which its promoters intend should supersede the earlier undertaking.

SUEZ CANAL.

The advantages of a communication between the Mediterranean and the Red Sea were so obvious, even within the limited world known to the ancients, that

Route of Canal across Isthmus of Suez. 255

Herodotus mentions a proposal for cutting a channel through the Isthmus; and the work appears to have been actually accomplished, on a very small scale, about twenty-five centuries ago, but eventually allowed to fall into decay. When Napoleon took possession of Egypt, at the close of the last century, he conceived the idea of reopening this channel; but, beyond some surveys, nothing was done till, in 1847, a series of levellings established the fact of the identity of the levels of the seas on both sides at low-water, which had previously been supposed to be different. Soon after proposals were made for the construction of a canal, at a uniform level without locks, across the Isthmus, for large vessels, following the shortest route along the natural depressions of lakes Menzaleh, Ballah, and Timsah, and the Bitter Lakes; and this work was at last commenced in 1860. (*See illustration.*)

The canal starts at Port Said, on the Mediterranean, and runs nearly due south to Suez, on the Red Sea, with only a slight deviation to make it traverse the Bitter Lakes in its course. It has a length of about 100 miles; and it was formed with a bottom width of 72 feet, and a width at the water level of 196 to 328 feet, according to the material traversed, and a depth of 26 feet. (*See cross section, page* 242.) The bottom width, however, is now being increased to an average of $229\frac{1}{2}$ feet, and the depth to 28 feet, which will eventually be carried to $29\frac{1}{2}$ feet throughout, to provide for vessels passing at any part, and not merely at specially widened passing places, and also for the increased draught of vessels. (*See dotted line on cross section, page* 242.) The great increase of traffic has necessitated these widening works; and the original depth, when reduced by deposit from erosion of the banks, has caused delays and inconveniences in the transit.

The excavation for the first 45 miles very little exceeded the 26 feet of depth required for the canal, as the surface of the ground across lakes Menzaleh and Ballah was at about the low-water level of the canal. (*See illustration.*) The deepest cutting was 85 feet to the bottom of the canal; whilst some parts of the depression of the Bitter Lakes, which was filled with water by the construction of the canal, were at, or a little below the level of the bottom of the canal. The material excavated was mainly sand and clay; but south of the Bitter Lakes, some rock was traversed, especially at the Chalouf cutting, where rock-cutting rams have been employed for removing the rock under water for the recent widening of the canal. (*See page* 161.) Sixty dredgers were employed for widening and deepening the canal during its construction; and long shoots were used for removing the dredged material to form the banks at the sides in the low parts, the material being carried along the shoot by a current of water pumped into it. The shoot, 230 feet long, was attached to the dredger at a considerable height above the water, and was also supported by a floating pontoon nearer the side; and it delivered the material direct on to the bank. (*See illustration.*) The total amount of excavation was about 98 million cubic yards. A freshwater canal, from the Nile at Cairo to Timsah, and then going nearly parallel to the canal to Suez, formed one of the principal auxiliary works, required for the supply of fresh water and the conveyance of materials. A harbour was constructed at Port Said to protect the entrance to

THE SUEZ CANAL

the canal, so as to enable a channel to be dredged from deep water in the Mediterranean, and to divert the silt-bearing current issuing from the Nile delta, which flows from the west along the coast. The harbour is sheltered by two converging piers, starting from the coast on each side of the canal entrance, the eastern pier being 6233 feet long, and the western pier 9800 feet long, and projecting considerably in advance of the other to keep the Nile current further from the entrance. The piers consist of mounds of concrete blocks, 20 tons in weight, composed of sand and cement, as stone could not be procured nearer than Alexandria. A deep channel has been dredged under the shelter of the west pier, and is being maintained to deep water without difficulty by dredging, in spite of the deposits produced by storms and the alluvial current in front of the western pier. Basins for accommodating vessels have been formed at the entrance to the canal. The outlet of the canal into the Gulf of Suez, at the head of the Red Sea, has been merely protected by an embankment on one side, and by a mole, 2900 feet long, on the other. The canal was opened in 1869; and its total cost was about £20,500,000.

The Suez Canal has been a great success, both as a gigantic engineering work, and also from a financial point of view; and though the credit of the work is due to French engineers, British shipping mainly uses the canal. The canal has, indeed, at times proved inadequate for the traffic seeking to pass; the wash of the steamers in the narrow channel erodes the soft banks; and when a ship runs aground the whole traffic is blocked. These inconveniences will, however, be in a great measure removed when the widening works are completed. The congestion of traffic in the canal, within twenty years of its opening, has been to some extent mitigated by the introduction of the electric light, both on shore and on the vessels navigating the canal, and by the use of luminous buoys, so that the navigation can now be conducted safely during the night. The capacity of the canal for traffic has been thereby nearly doubled; and the delays involved in the passage of the canal have been greatly reduced, so that vessels are now able to accomplish the transit in $22\frac{1}{2}$ hours on the average.

PANAMA CANAL.

The commencement of an undertaking for connecting the Atlantic and Pacific oceans, through the Isthmus of Panama, was a natural result of the success achieved by the Suez Canal. Various sites have been proposed from time to time for the construction of a canal across the Isthmus, the most northern being the Tehuantepec route, at a comparatively broad part of the Isthmus, and the most southern the Atrato route, following for some distance the course of the Atrato River. The site eventually selected, in 1879, for the construction of a canal was at the narrowest part of the Isthmus, and where the central ridge is the lowest, known as the Panama route, nearly following the course of the Panama Railway. It was the only scheme that did not necessarily involve a tunnel or locks. The length of the route between Colon on the

Atlantic, and Panama on the Pacific, is 46 miles, not quite half the length of the Suez Canal; but a tide-level canal involved a cutting across the Cordilleras, at the Culebra Pass, nearly 300 feet deep, mainly through rock. The section of the canal was designed on the lines of the Suez Canal, with a bottom width of 72 feet, and a depth of water of 27 feet, except in the central rock cutting, where the width was to be increased to $78\frac{3}{4}$ feet on account of the nearly vertical sides, and the depth to $29\frac{1}{2}$ feet. (*See cross sections, page* 242.)

The work was commenced in 1882, and was carried on with dredgers at each extremity, and with numerous excavators in the other portions. The difficulties and expenses, however, of the undertaking had been greatly under-estimated. The climate proved exceptionally unhealthy, especially when the soil began to be turned up by the excavations. The actual cost of the excavation was much greater than originally estimated; and the total amount of excavation required to form a level canal, which had originally been estimated at 100 million cubic yards, was subsequently computed, on more exact data, at $176\frac{1}{2}$ million cubic yards. The preliminary works were also very extensive and costly; and difficulties were experienced, after a time, in raising the funds for carrying on the works, even when shares were offered at a very great discount. Eventually, in 1887, the capital at the disposal of the company had nearly come to an end; whilst only a little more than one-fifth of the excavation had been completed. The greatest progress had naturally been made at the two end sections of the canal: the canal had been opened up to the tenth mile from Colon, and there only remained about two-fifths of the excavation to be accomplished in this first section of $16\frac{1}{3}$ miles towards the end of 1887; and one-third of the excavation had been done in the last section at the Panama end, $10\frac{3}{8}$ miles long. In the remaining 19 miles however, a very small proportion of the excavation had been carried out, especially in the deep cutting at Culebra, where constant slips occurred owing to the treacherous nature of the material overlying the rock, under the influence of tropical rains. Some idea of the work that was being carried out in 1887 may be gathered from the fact that seventy-two excavators, twenty-four dredgers, and a number of locomotives, waggons, and other appliances, were in operation. At that period it was determined to expedite the work, and reduce the cost of completing the canal, by introducing locks, and thus diminish the remaining amount of excavation by 85 million cubic yards; though the estimated cost, even with this modification, had increased from £33,500,000 to £65,500,000. It was arranged to place four locks on each slope, with from $26\frac{1}{4}$ to $36\frac{3}{4}$ feet differences in the level of adjoining reaches; and the summit level was to be 125 feet above sea level in the Atlantic. The financial embarrassments, however, of the company have prevented the carrying out of this scheme for completing the canal; and the works are at present at a standstill, in a very unfinished state. It will be unfortunate if all the executed work, and the money expended, should turn out to have been absolutely fruitless. If the Panama route was the only route deemed practicable for connecting the two oceans, it is fairly certain that the unfinished enterprise would be eventually purchased, at a low price, by some company or syndicate capable of bringing the works to a satisfactory termination. The Americans, however, who are the nation that would most profit by the proposed waterway, have always stood aloof from the Panama scheme, and have in the end given the preference to the Nicaragua route over other alternative schemes.

NICARAGUA CANAL.

Numerous explorations of the Isthmus of Panama have been made by American engineers, with the view of discovering the most feasible route for a canal, which would be of such inestimable value to the United States in providing communication by water between their eastern and western coasts. The result of a series of surveys, instituted by the Government between 1870 and 1876, was a report to the President in favour of the Nicaragua route as the most practicable and convenient site for a canal. A concession was granted by the Nicaraguan Government to an American company for the construction of a canal some years ago; and another concession was granted in 1885 to a second company, who have endeavoured to establish their claims to the sole right of constructing the canal by actually commencing works on the Atlantic side, at Greytown, in 1889. Careful surveys of the site have been made since 1876, so as to locate exactly the line of the canal. The site is nearer the United States than the other possible routes, with the sole exception of the Tehuantepec route in Mexico, which, like the Nicaragua route, would have to traverse a comparatively broad part of the Isthmus, without the advantage of a lake in its course.

Both the American schemes are similar in general principles, though differing in details. The canal, as designed, is to start from Greytown, or near it, on the Atlantic; then, rising by locks, it is to follow the valley of the San Juan River, which is to be dammed up so as to form a lake navigation. Lake Nicaragua is to be the summit level of the canal, which will, after leaving the lake, descend by locks to Brito, on the Pacific. The length of the canal, according to the design actually commenced, will be $169\frac{1}{2}$ miles, of which $56\frac{1}{2}$ miles is through Lake Nicaragua, with a water level about 110 feet above sea level. The summit level is proposed to be reached by three locks on each side; and the locks are to commence, on the Atlantic side, about $9\frac{1}{4}$ miles from Greytown, being comprised in the next $4\frac{3}{5}$ miles, from which point the canal will mainly pass through basins enclosed by embankments, and formed by the damming up of the San Juan River, till Lake Nicaragua is reached, the total distance between Greytown and Lake Nicaragua being nearly 96 miles. The slope on the Pacific side of the central ridge is much steeper than the other, as at Panama; so that the distance from the western end of the lake portion of the canal to the ocean is only 17 miles, of which $5\frac{3}{5}$ miles are to be carried through a basin formed by an embankment, and the remainder of the distance is to be excavated for the canal. The locks on this slope are to be comprised in the last $2\frac{1}{4}$ miles. Harbours are to be formed at Greytown and Brito, the two extremities of the canal. The breakwater to protect the harbour at Greytown from the accumulations of deposit, to which it is exposed by the action of the waves, has been already commenced. Altogether, out of the $169\frac{1}{2}$ miles of navigation by this route, as designed, $142\frac{2}{3}$ miles will be free navigation by lake, basin, and river, and only $26\frac{5}{6}$ miles in actual canal. A free waterway, besides obviating large excavations, enables vessels to travel at a greater speed than in a restricted canal, and constitutes one of the special advantages of this scheme, especially across so wide a part of the Isthmus. The estimated time of transit by steamer is twenty-eight hours. The estimated cost of the works, exclusive of all other incidental charges and expenses, is £18,000,000. It remains to be seen whether this scheme will be able to avoid the troubles which have overwhelmed its predecessor on the Isthmus; whether the capital required will be forthcoming; and whether this work, unlike other similar gigantic undertakings, will be accomplished at the estimated cost, and within the limited period of seven years from its commencement. It would be impossible to form a reliable opinion as to the prospects of the scheme, without the most ample information and investigations; but whatever fate the future may have in store for this undertaking, which has the advantage of a comparatively small amount of excavation, but the disadvantage of a bad site for a harbour at Greytown, it is fairly certain that, sooner or later, the problem will be solved, and the two oceans united by a waterway piercing the barrier at present offered to navigation by the Isthmus.

CORINTH CANAL.

The vessels which run between the Mediterranean ports of Spain, France, Italy, and Austria, and Greece, Turkey, Asia Minor, the Black Sea, and the Danube, have to make a stormy detour round Cape Matapan, and will obtain a shorter and calmer voyage in traversing the Corinth Canal. The Isthmus of Corinth was a very serious barrier to navigation in early times, when Italy, Greece, and Asia Minor formed the most important part of the civilised world, and vessels were small, and sea voyages slow. Accordingly, proposals to cut a canal across it naturally originated some centuries before the Christian era; but the only work actually commenced appears to have been that undertaken in the reign of Nero, which terminated with his death; and the trial pits and traces of Nero's canal were visible when the surveys were made for the ship canal in course of construction. The canal, in fact, follows the line of cutting commenced by Nero; and the old trial pits were relied on for indicating the nature of the strata to be traversed.

The canal is being made in a straight line across the Isthmus; and its length is about 100 yards short of 4 miles. This short length, combined with easy access, a convenient locality, and a healthy climate, makes the Corinth Canal a much less arduous task than the undertakings previously described in the present chapter. The depth of cutting, however, to the bottom of the canal reaches a maximum of 285 feet, whilst the mean depth, for a length of 2⅜ miles, is 190 feet; so that in this respect it nearly equals the greatest depth of the original design of the Panama Canal, and is more than three times the greatest depth of cutting on the Suez Canal. Nevertheless, the slopes of the rocky portion of the cutting were designed to be 1 in 10, greatly reducing the amount of excavation compared with that which would have been needed in soft soil. The canal is being formed with the same bottom width of 72 feet, and depth of 26 feet of water, as the original Suez Canal (*see cross section, page* 242); but as the slopes in rock are only 1 in 10, the width at the water level and the cross section of the waterway are considerably less, so that the resistance to the passage of vessels will be greater, and the wash along the banks more powerful.

The works were commenced in 1882; but as the cuttings were opened out, it became evident that the nature of the strata had not been accurately ascertained, for numerous faults were discovered, due, doubtless, to volcanic disturbances; so that the sides could not in places stand at the intended slopes, and slips occurred. Eventually it was decided, in 1887, to modify the slopes in certain parts, and to protect the sides of the canal against erosion by masonry, and to pave the slopes in places with stone. This involved an increase in the amount of excavation, from 12,865,000 cubic yards, to 14 or 15 million cubic yards, and an estimated addition to the cost of the works of about £600,000. During 1888 the works were continued upon this new basis, the Société du Comptoir d'Escompte of Paris providing the funds. On the collapse, however, of this company, in 1889, the works were stopped for want of money; and the Canal Company having gone into liquidation, the canal passed into the hands of a new company, who have let the work to a new contractor; and the time of completion, originally fixed for 1888, has been extended to 1894. The excavation remaining to be done at the time of the liquidation, in 1889, was 3,156,500 cubic yards, so that only a comparatively small proportion of the work remained to be accomplished; and the fresh energy imparted by the reconstitution of the company, and the extension of time, ought to suffice to complete the work. As deep water is found only about 200 to 300 yards from each end, a sheltering harbour at each outlet, and a channel formed by dredging, lead the canal into the open sea. Two converging rubble mound breakwaters, 1310, and 1640 feet long respectively, with an entrance between their ends, 262 feet wide, enclose the harbour in the Gulf of Corinth; whilst a single breakwater on the northern side of the canal entrance, in the Gulf of Athens, affords adequate protection at that end. Only one metal bridge, having a span of 262 feet, and a clear height of 141 feet above the water level of the canal, will connect the Morea with the mainland, and serve both for the railway and the road traffic.

Isthmian canals are the most important engineering works that can be carried out; for whilst railways, bridges, and tunnels, afford means of communication between districts, and even countries, these canals modify the navigable highways of the trade of the world, and shorten the distances between remote portions of the globe. The Suez Canal, in realising the dreams of past ages, and by the rapid development of its traffic, gave a great impetus to similar schemes, which the collapse of the Panama Canal, in the middle of its execution, and the financial difficulties of the Corinth Canal, have tended to restrain; though the initiation of the Nicaragua Canal indicates that faith in the financial success of such enterprises, under difficult conditions, has not been abandoned. The difficulties naturally attending such gigantic works are enhanced by the immense sums that have to be raised, without any prospect of a return till after the completion of the works, rendering it necessary to raise portions of the capital on very onerous conditions, after the enthusiasm of the first starting of the concern has subsided, and the funds of sanguine promoters have become exhausted. Moreover, whilst the actual cost of vast works of this nature, extending over some years, cannot be determined with certainty, depending upon somewhat unknown conditions of soil, supply of labour, and climate, neither can the actual trade that a new waterway will attract, under novel conditions, be predicted with precision. Whatever uncertainties, however, may attend the financial prospects of such enterprises, works which shorten and facilitate the routes for navigation confer important benefits on the world at large.

Ship Railways.—It might be supposed that canals across isthmuses were quite secure from the competition of railways, which, both in England and the United States, has proved so very detrimental to the traffic on inland canals. In ancient times, the Greeks used to drag their triremes across the Isthmus of Corinth on inclined ways of polished granite, with the aid of cribs and rollers; and inclines, provided with rails, are used in Great Britain, Germany, and the United States, for enabling vessels to surmount considerable differences of level between adjacent reaches of a canal, effecting an economy of time and water as compared with a flight of locks. An extension of this system of inclines was, however, proposed some years ago, in the form of a ship railway across the Isthmus of Panama, at Tehuantepec, where the width is 144 miles; and the vessels were to be bodily lifted out of the water on one side, and carried on suitable trucks, running on rails and drawn by several locomotives, to the ocean on the other side. This project appears to have been dropped on the death of its designer, Captain Eads, the engineer of the St Louis Bridge and of the Mississippi delta works. The system, however, has been adopted for transporting vessels across a narrow neck of land, 15 miles in width, connecting Nova Scotia with New Brunswick on the mainland of Canada, between Chignecto Bay, an inlet from the Gulf of Fundy, and Bay Verte in the Gulf of St Lawrence. This Chignecto Ship Railway is in course of construction, and approaching completion; and it will carry vessels of from 1000 to 2000 tons, in cradles supported on trucks running on two lines of rails, 18 feet apart, and drawn by locomotives. Hydraulic lifts will raise the vessels from the dock, at each end, on to the railway; and the transit is expected to be effected in two hours. This railway will shorten the voyage between the ports of New England and those of Prince Edward's Island and the St Lawrence by from 500 to 600 miles of stormy sea. This work is intended to accommodate coasting vessels, and has therefore not been made available for the largest class of ships; but it will inaugurate a novel method of shortening the routes for sea-going traffic.

CHAPTER XV.

THE MANCHESTER WATERWORKS; AND THE VYRNWY DAM AND LAKE.

HITHERTO engineering works for facilitating communication and trade have alone been considered; but the labours of the engineer are not confined within even these very comprehensive limits, for the sanitary requirements of cities and towns are entrusted to his care. The most urgent want of masses of people, crowded into large towns, is an ample supply of pure water; for water is not only one of the first necessaries of life, and essential for health and cleanliness, but it is also a very common and insidious vehicle for the spread of disease when in a polluted state. Unfortunately, impurities in water are not generally of such a palpable kind as to be readily detected by the senses; and some waters, which to all appearance are pure from their bright and sparkling qualities, contain most deadly germs of disease; whilst rain water, which is the purest water obtainable, being distilled by the sun, is not very palatable when unaerated, and, from its very purity, readily absorbs any soluble salts or impurities with which it may come in contact. Accordingly, the only method of securing a pure supply

Sources of Water Supply for Towns.

is to gather the water from the purest sources available, and to keep it, as far as possible, free from contamination till it reaches the consumer.

The sources of water supply are tanks, in which the rain water is collected as it falls; springs, which are the outlets of natural underground reservoirs; streams, and rivers; and wells, from which the underground waters are brought to the surface. Tanks are unsuitable for a large and constant supply; springs and wells are often used for moderate supplies, or as supplementary sources of supply for large towns; but rivers and mountain streams are the sources from which the largest supplies are derived. Water from springs and deep wells is generally uncontaminated, having filtered through a large thickness of soil, and being removed from contact with impurities; but it frequently contains considerable quantities of inorganic salts in solution, chiefly of lime and iron, collected in its underground flow, which constitute the hardness of water, and though quite innocuous as regards health, are bad for washing and manufactures. Waters of this kind are supplied to London by the New River Company, from springs issuing from the chalk at Amwell and Chadwell, in Hertfordshire, and by the Kent Waterworks Company from deep wells in the chalk to the east of London. River water is liable to contamination in passing towns and villages, though the impurities thus introduced are to some extent rendered innocuous by contact with the air in the flow of the river. This water, however, is much less liable to be impregnated with salts, except where, as in the case of the Thames, the river is partly fed by springs. Water from the Thames, which supplies a large part of

London, though harder from this cause than many other river waters, is much softer than the water derived wholly from chalk springs and wells; but, on the other hand, it is less satisfactory as regards the presence of other impurities of an organic nature, from which the other waters are wholly free.

The purest water is derived from streams draining mountainous, uninhabited districts, composed solely of rain water flowing rapidly off the steep, rocky, impermeable mountain slopes, subject only occasionally in flood time to a slight discoloration by peat, and turbidity from earthy matters in suspension. These streams, however, have a very variable flow, being almost dried up when evaporation is active in the summer time and there is little rain, and becoming rushing torrents during a rainy winter. As a water supply for towns must be constant throughout the year, and more water is required in the summer, when the streams are liable to be dry, than in the winter, when there is an abundant flow, mountain streams can only be made available for this purpose by impounding a sufficient quantity of the surplus winter flow, to make up for the deficiency in the summer months. This is effected by putting a watertight barrier or dam across a narrow part of a mountain valley, and thus arresting the flow of the stream till it forms a lake above the dam, providing a reservoir of water which can be drawn upon in times of drought. These dams, composed of an earthen embankment, having a considerable width, or a masonry wall of great strength and solidity, constitute the largest works undertaken for water supply, and convert portions of mountain valleys into extensive lakes. Occasionally natural lakes can be utilised as reservoirs for water supply, by merely forming a conduit from the lake to the town to be supplied at a lower level. Thus Glasgow is supplied with an abundance of the purest water from Loch Katrine; and Thirlmere is to afford Manchester an additional water supply; whilst Bala Lake was suggested many years ago as a suitable source for an abundant supply of pure soft water for London; and the Lake of Neuchatel has been recently proposed to be drawn upon for supplying Paris with water.

MANCHESTER WATERWORKS.

Manchester is furnished with a supply of excellent water, collected from a tract of high land, of 19,300 acres, lying between Manchester and Sheffield, drained by the river Etherow and its tributaries, the water being stored in a series of reservoirs formed in the Longdendale Valley, by a series of dams across the valley impounding the flow of the river Etherow. The works were commenced in 1848, and completed in 1877. Altogether seven collecting reservoirs have been constructed, in an almost continuous chain, along the Longdendale Valley, the highest two of which have areas of 135, and 160 acres respectively, and the others have areas varying from 63 to 13 acres. Five of these reservoirs communicate with service reservoirs lower down, by means of conduits and a tunnel, 1¾ miles long, with a fall of 5 feet in a mile, and a diameter of 6 feet, and capable of passing 50 million gallons of water in a day. Before reaching the first service reservoir, the conduit from the impounding reservoirs has to traverse a valley, which is accomplished by means of cast-iron inverted syphon pipes, a method always adopted now for crossing valleys, in place of the aqueducts by which the Romans, in ancient times, maintained their channels for water supply at a uniform slope in passing over low-lying lands. The tunnel had to be carried through the ridge separating the valleys of the Etherow and the Tame; it was driven by the aid of five shafts, a considerable quantity of water being encountered in its execution; and the work was completed in 1850. The Denton reservoirs, near Manchester, are lined with brickwork; and the water is there passed through copper wire gauze to intercept any floating matter. The water is then distributed by gravity from the service reservoirs to Manchester, having descended from the high ground by gravity alone.

The reservoirs in the Longdendale Valley were formed by erecting dams of earthwork, 70 to 100 feet high, deposited in thin layers, and formed with very flat slopes, protected on the upper side, facing the water, with a layer of stones, and having a clay puddle trench[1] in the centre, carried up from a solid watertight stratum, below the rest of the embankment, to the top. The dam for forming the Woodhead Reservoir, the highest up the valley, was commenced in 1848; but it was injured by a flood overtopping it in 1849, when in progress; and eventually, owing to the defective nature of the strata upon which it was founded, resulting in continued leakage, a new dam was formed a little lower down, where the continuity of the rock had been ascertained by boring; and the lower

---

[1] When clay is worked or kneaded up with water, it becomes more impervious to water than in its ordinary condition, and is termed 'clay puddle,' or puddled clay; and this material is used to form the central watertight core, wall, or trench as it is technically called, of an earthen reservoir dam.

part of the central trench, carried down to a depth of about 90 feet below the main portion of the embankment, was filled with concrete instead of clay puddle. Accordingly, the Woodhead Reservoir, though one of the first works commenced, was also one of the last of the works finally completed. Discharge pipes were laid at first under the embankments; but subsequently, owing to dislocations from settlement of the superincumbent mass, the pipes were carried round the side, and in one case in a syphon over the embankment, the flow through them being controlled by valves. The water can thus be discharged into the next lower reservoir, or into a side conduit leading it towards Manchester. Waste weirs have been also provided, over which the surplus water flows in flood time, and is discharged along a flood watercourse into the river Etherow below the lowest reservoir. Weirs across the main streams, above the reservoirs, arrest the heavier sedimentary matter brought down in flood time, and thus keep it out of the reservoirs. The two impounding reservoirs at the lower end of the valley are at too low a level to supply Manchester through the conduit; and they are used for supplying compensation water to the river Etherow, so that, in spite of the large volume of its flow impounded for the requirements of Manchester, its discharge may never be less than a definite volume in the twenty-four hours, a condition imposed upon the promoters of such schemes of water supply to guard the interests of riparian proprietors lower down.

The mountain streams to the north of the reservoirs are intercepted by the supply conduit before reaching the reservoirs; and in ordinary weather the whole of their flow is conveyed direct to Manchester. These streams, however, are made to flow over special separating weirs, so that, when their flow is moderate, the water drops quietly over the weir, and through an opening at its foot, into the conduit. When they become turbid in flood time, and unsuitable for water supply, their volume and velocity being increased, they leap over the opening, and pass into subsiding reservoirs, whence the water can be passed away for compensation water, or into the main reservoirs after becoming clear.

The total storage capacity of the whole of the reservoirs is about 4590 million gallons; and the total available supply for the district is about 24 million gallons a day. Considering that the consumption of water in Manchester, for all purposes, rose from 8 million gallons per day in 1855 to 18 million gallons per day in 1881, it is evident that the scheme of 1848, ample as it originally appeared to be, is becoming insufficient for the increasing requirements of Manchester. In 1879, accordingly, authority was obtained for procuring an additional supply from Thirlmere, the works for which are in progress. The total cost of the existing Manchester Waterworks has amounted to about £3,070,000.

Thirlmere Water Supply.—In seeking for an additional water supply for Manchester, it was decided to go to the lake district to the north; and from the three lakes at a sufficient elevation to supply Manchester with water by gravitation, namely, Haweswater, Ulleswater, and Thirlmere, the latter was finally selected as the most suitable. Though Thirlmere is considerably smaller than Ulleswater, its level can be raised without injury to property; it is at a higher level than

Ullswater; it necessitates a considerably less length of tunnel, at a much less depth below the surface, for leading the water from it; and it is situated in the middle of the most rainy district in England. The scheme now in progress provides for raising the level of the lake 50 feet, by a dam across its natural outlet at the end furthest off from Manchester, in order to increase the storage capacity of the lake, which has an area of only 350 acres, so that the water level may not be unduly lowered in dry seasons. The eventual maximum daily supply of 50 million gallons will be conveyed to Manchester by an aqueduct, or conduit, about 100 miles long, starting from the upper end of the lake, in a tunnel 3 miles long under Dunmail Raise. The aqueduct will be formed partly in tunnel, and will be chiefly constructed in open cutting in the solid rock, subsequently covered over by an arch; and it will pass to the east of Windermere, Kendal, Lancaster, and Preston, and by Chorley to near Bolton, whence the water will be conveyed in iron pipes to the service reservoirs near Manchester. Inverted iron syphon pipes will carry the supply across the valleys of the Kent, the Lune, the Ribble, and other rivers. The water will descend from the lake wholly by gravitation, as the lake is 533 feet above mean sea level. The principal works are being carried out to their full extent, the aqueduct as far as Bolton being made large enough to pass the whole future supply, though at first provision will only be made near Manchester for furnishing a supply of 10 million gallons a day. The necessary additions will be made in the future, at the Manchester end, to admit the further supply in increments of 10 million gallons, as required for the wants of the city. The estimate for the first portion of the supply, involving the construction of the aqueduct and dam, is £1,740,000; and the total ultimate cost of the works, for the whole supply of 50 million gallons a day, is estimated at £3,500,000. These works will, accordingly, eventually furnish more than double the existing water supply of Manchester; and therefore the total supply of water provided for will be three times the present supply. The cost, also, of the new supply appears very moderate, in spite of the great distance it has to be conveyed, when compared with the expenditure involved in furnishing the present supply of about half the volume from a much nearer district. Moreover, though the initial cost of procuring the first instalment of 10 million gallons a day, only a fifth of the whole, is comparatively large, it is a great advantage for Manchester to have secured a gathering ground which might later on have been appropriated by others, and which will amply supply the city for a long period.

VYRNWY DAM AND LAKE.

Liverpool has for many years been supplied with water from wells in the red sandstone, and from reservoirs in the Rivington district, near the headwaters of the river Yarrow. Though Liverpool is not a manufacturing town like Manchester, it has a much larger population; and the existing supply of water has become inadequate for its requirements. Liverpool, accordingly, has been obliged to search at a distance for a gathering ground for an additional supply; and the site selected is the upper valley of the Vyrnwy River, a tributary of the Severn near its source. The Vyrnwy River, rising in a mountainous part of Montgomeryshire, has been arrested by a masonry dam stretching across a gorge of the valley; and the water thus impounded, rising to the level of the top of the dam, has flooded the lower portions of the valley above the dam, thus forming an artificial lake, 1121 acres in extent. (*See illustration.*) This portion of the valley had a little village, with its church, situated below the level of the proposed reservoir; and therefore a new church had to be built, on a suitable neighbouring site, before the valley could be submerged.

The foundations for the masonry dam had to be carried down to a considerable depth below the surface, through porous material, to reach the solid rock; so that, in the deepest place, the bottom of the dam is 132 feet below the level of the lake, though the deepest part of the lake is only 84 feet. The dam rests upon the rock throughout, a condition necessary for masonry dams, to secure them against settlement, or against the percolation of water under their foundations leading to settlement, and consequent dislocation, and on account of the weight on the foundations, due to the weight of the masonry combined with the water pressure on the dam when the reservoir is full. The dam has been built of solid masonry throughout, from the foundations to the water level of the lake, with the exception of two tunnels, 15 feet in diameter, just above the surface of the ground towards each end of the dam, which served to discharge the flow of the river during the construction of the dam, but which are now closed with only discharge pipes encased in them. The dam has a nearly vertical face on its upper side, facing the lake; but it has a curved face on its lower side, so that it increases in width from about 22 feet near the top to 120 feet at the deepest part of the base, a form necessitated by the increase of the water pressure against the dam with the depth; and it contains between six and seven hundred thousand tons of masonry. A road is carried on arches over the top of the dam; and the surplus water flows over the dam under the arches, so that these openings serve as a waste weir to discharge the excess of water into the stream below. The length of the dam along the top is 1172 feet; its height from the lowest part of the foundations to the parapet of the roadway is 161 feet; and the width of the roadway along the top is about 20 feet. The pipes placed in the old discharge tunnels are reached from the top, through a valve chamber and a valve pit above each tunnel. The pipe in the north-eastern tunnel, $3\frac{1}{4}$ feet in diameter, and controlled by two valves from the valve chamber below the roadway, is intended to regulate the water level of the lake. The two pipes placed in the south-western tunnel are similarly controlled; and one of them, 18 inches in diameter, provides for the discharge of the daily compensation water to the stream below of not less than 10 million gallons; whilst the other, 30 inches in diameter, discharges the monthly compensation water of four times the above volume, for the Severn Commissioners, on thirty-two days between March and October. The works were authorised in 1880; and in November 1888, the dam was sufficiently near completion to enable the valves in the dam to be closed; and the filling of the reservoir was accomplished in the course of 1889.

The Vyrnwy Lake, formed by means of the dam, has an area of 1121 acres, a length of $4\frac{3}{4}$ miles, a

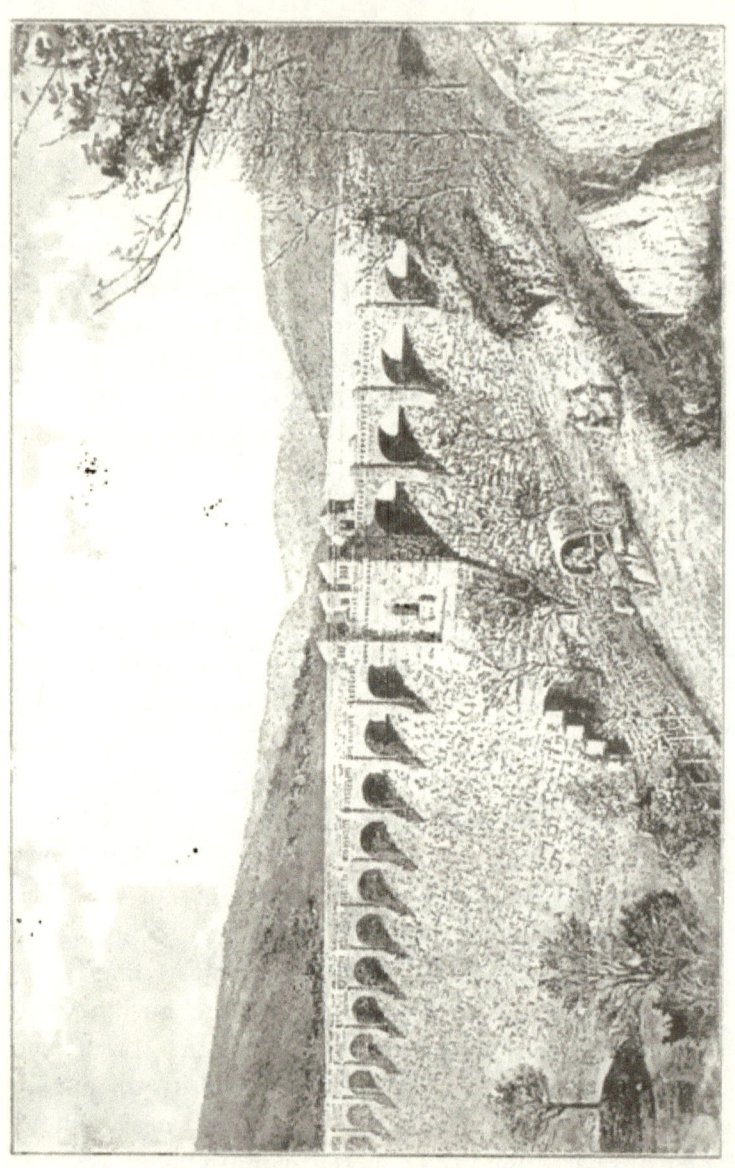

width of from ¼ to ⅜ of a mile, and a maximum depth of 84 feet. The storage capacity of the lake, down to the level to which water may be drawn off for Liverpool at the rate of 40 million gallons per day, amounts to 12,130 million gallons. The lake, with its surroundings, is very picturesque; and, out of sight of the dam, it is difficult to realise that it is artificial, except where an old road abruptly terminates at the lake, and at a few points where trees and hedges are only partially submerged. A road constructed round the lake enables it to be viewed from every point; and the wildest part of the district is at the head of the lake which has added a fresh beauty to the valley; whilst the dam, being formed of dark stone, presents no unsightly appearance of newness, and offers a striking contrast to the cascade falling over it when the lake overflows. (*See illustration.*)

The Vyrnwy tower, a picturesque structure with a conical roof, has been built down the slope of the valley; so that it now stands in deep water near the side of the lake, and is reached from the road by a stone bridge. Adjoining this tower are the cylindrical inlet valves, by which the water can be drawn off from various levels, according to the level of the lake; so that the purest and most bleached surface water may be delivered into the tower, by lifting one or more lengths of iron pipes placed vertically over the circular inlet. The water thus delivered into the tower will pass through cylinders of very fine copper wire gauze (which will arrest all but the finest particles in suspension in the water), before reaching the conduit which will convey it to Liverpool. A concrete culvert in the bed of the lake leads from the Vyrnwy tower to the Hirnant Tunnel, 2¼ miles long, which will convey the supply from the lake, through a ridge, into another valley, the nearest point of the conduit being over 3 furlongs distant from the dam. The length of the aqueduct between Lake Vyrnwy and the Prescot service reservoirs, near Liverpool, is over 68 miles; and in this distance it has to pierce through three ridges in tunnel, to cross several streams and canals; and it has to pass, in steel tubes, both under the river Weaver, and through a subway under the Manchester Ship Canal, and also in steel tubes through a tunnel under the river Mersey above Runcorn, carried out, like the Thames subways, with a series of segmental cast-iron rings. (*See page* 106.) The main portion of the aqueduct will consist of three lines of cast-iron pipes, laid not less than 3 feet below the surface, and following the general contour of the country which it traverses. One line of pipes only, 42½ inches in diameter, has hitherto been laid, which will be capable of discharging over 13 million gallons a day, or a third of the available supply of 40 million gallons a day that can be drawn from the lake by laying the other two lines of pipes as the requirements of Liverpool increase. The lake, at its lowest available water level, is 496 feet higher than the top water level of the Prescot reservoirs; so that the average fall from the Vyrnwy lake to Prescot is nearly 7¼ feet per mile. The discharge will accordingly be readily effected by gravitation, though the fall has not been made uniform throughout, in order to reduce the length of tunnelling, and the pressure at certain places on the pipes passing across valleys. With the object of diminishing the head,[1] and consequently the pressure of water on the pipes, which, with a closed conduit throughout, would have reached 496 feet vertical water pressure at Prescot when the flow was stopped there, and 848 feet in the tunnel under the Mersey, the aqueduct has been divided into six sections, between each of which a reservoir has been formed, in which the water can rise and overflow; so that the water pressure is reduced to the difference of the level between the highest and the lowest points of each section. In four out of the five reservoirs constructed for this purpose, advantage has been taken of places where the ground level rises to the line of the hydraulic gradient, or the average fall, or gradient, from the lake to the Prescot reservoirs. The fifth reservoir has had to be constructed on the top of a tower, 113 feet high and 90 feet in diameter, built on the summit of Norton Hill, as none of the ground in the vicinity along the line traversed attained the height of the hydraulic gradient.[2] The basin-shaped reservoir, placed on the top of this tower, formed of steel plates, will contain 651,000 gallons of water.

[1] A head of water is the difference of the water level at the two extremities of a closed conduit, or on the two sides of a reservoir dam, or any barrier such as a weir in a river. The water pressure increases in proportion to the head, being equal, for any given area, to the weight of a volume of water having the cubical contents of this area multiplied by the head.

[2] A conduit, or aqueduct, through which the water from a reservoir is conveyed by gravity, follows the undulations of the surface where the surface is not higher than the hydraulic gradient, or line of average fall between the two extremities. Though, however, the conduit may be laid below the level of this mean gradient, which merely causes a water pressure in the conduit proportionate to the vertical distance of the conduit at any point below the mean gradient line, the conduit must never be raised above this line, otherwise the water would cease to flow at this part; and in such cases tunnelling or deep cutting has to be resorted to, in order to place the conduit at the level of the hydraulic gradient.

The reservoir near Oswestry, situated at the outlet of the Llanforda tunnel, leads to filter beds a little lower down, where the water will be purified from any fine matters in suspension which may have passed the strainers in the tower on the lake.

The total estimated cost of these works, for providing the first instalment of about $13\frac{1}{3}$ million gallons of water a day for Liverpool, is £1,991,200, or in round numbers about £2,000,000. Two other instalments, however, can be provided when required, bringing up the total supply to 40 million gallons a day, at the cost of laying two more lines of pipes; for the dam, lake, tunnels, and some other portions of the work, have had to be constructed to the full extent needed for the whole of the proposed supply. Liverpool, accordingly, like Manchester, is providing itself with a water supply of excellent quality, which is capable of gradual extension, and will suffice for the requirements of the city for a long period.

London possesses the natural advantage over Liverpool and Manchester of the river Thames, from which it has continually to draw larger supplies of water. The water, however, supplied from the Thames and other sources is distinctly inferior in quality to the water which the Liverpool and Manchester corporations have provided, at considerable expense, but with great care and foresight, for their respective cities. In London the supply is furnished by several independent water companies, at a considerable profit to themselves; but the service is not, for the most part, constant as at Liverpool and Manchester, being only delivered into cisterns once or twice in the day, instead of being drawn straight and fresh from the mains. London and its suburbs are increasing at a very rapid rate; and already the whole of the dry weather flow of the river Lee, and more than one-third of the summer discharge of the river Thames at Teddington, are abstracted for water supply. As the metropolitan water supply has been quadrupled within the last forty years, and the average yearly increase has exceeded $3\frac{1}{2}$ million gallons a day, it is evident that the Thames will have to be still more largely drawn upon year by year, and eventually its whole summer flow abstracted, or fresh sources of supply sought for. It is therefore clearly expedient, under existing circumstances, that the whole water supply of the metropolis should be brought under the control of a single public body, for the general welfare of its inhabitants, and that no less care and forethought should be used to secure a pure and ample supply in the future for the vast and rapidly increasing population of London than has been exercised by the local authorities for the smaller communities of Liverpool and Manchester.

CHAPTER XVI.

THE EDDYSTONE LIGHTHOUSE; AND THE EIFFEL TOWER.

LIGHTHOUSES are of the utmost service to navigation, in both indicating to vessels their proximity to land, and the particular locality by a special arrangement of flashes of light, and in warning them from running on to rocks at some distance from the land. The most powerful lights are exhibited from lighthouses on the coast, as, for instance, on important headlands like St Catherine's, the southernmost point of the Isle of Wight, where the lighthouse emits the strongest ray of electric light in the world; but the lighthouses possessing the greatest interest are those which, erected on rocks barely emerging from the waves far out at sea, stand as solitary outposts to warn passing vessels to keep clear of the reef which they mark. Not only does their desolate position, far off from any sheltering land, on a rocky bed almost continually lashed with surf, form a remarkable contrast to their beneficent object, but their very situation renders it marvellous that any structure can be made to stand on such an exposed site, subjected to the constant attacks of the waves. It is, in fact, a work of great difficulty and danger, requiring the utmost skill and perseverance, to found a lighthouse on a very limited ledge of rock, frequently submerged, and only approachable in the calmest weather and at low-water. The only advantages possessed by these lighthouses are that the rocks on which they are built are of the hardest and firmest character, having for ages withstood the perpetual action of the sea; and that the structures themselves, unlike breakwaters, offer little surface to the waves. In spite, however, of the difficulties attending their erection, many lighthouses have been established on outlying rocks round the British and foreign coasts, of which the Bell Rock, Bishop Rock, Wolf Rock, Skerryvore, Ar-men, and Minot's Ledge are notable instances. The most remarkable, however, of these lighthouses, on account of the important and exposed nature of its position, the interest of its history, and the size of the structure, is the celebrated Eddystone Lighthouse, the rebuilding of which, on a grander scale, has been accomplished within the last thirteen years.

EDDYSTONE LIGHTHOUSE.

The Eddystone rocks, upon which four lighthouses have been successively built, are a group of gneiss rocks situated in the English Channel, about 9 miles from the nearest coast of Cornwall, and 14 miles from the Plymouth breakwater, which are mostly below high-water. As these rocks stand out from the coast, nearly in the track of vessels going up or down the Channel, they were the scene of frequent wrecks before their position was marked by the erection of a lighthouse. The first lighthouse erected on these rocks, nearly two hundred years ago, was constructed of wood resting upon a stone base, having a total height of 100 feet. It was commenced in 1696, and completed in 1700, the light having been first exhibited at the end of 1698, and the structure subsequently strengthened. This lighthouse was polygonal, with numerous projections, and somewhat resembling a Chinese pagoda, having an open gallery about half way up, through which the waves were liable to dash in a storm, as the site is open to the Atlantic. Altogether, the building was very unsuited for its purpose, in such an exposed situation; and in November 1703, when the builder, Mr Winstanley, was superintending some repairs in it, a violent storm swept the lighthouse away. The second lighthouse was also built of wood, in 1706-9, but of a conical form; it was connected to the rock by iron bolts, and its weight was increased by introducing courses of stone at intervals. This lighthouse successfully withstood the storms for nearly fifty years, but was destroyed by fire in 1755. Smeaton was then entrusted with the construction of a new lighthouse, which he built of stones dovetailed together, in 1756-59, conical in form, but spreading out more at the base. This lighthouse was 85 feet high; and being a model of solidity and strength, it withstood the fury of the waves on the reef for over a hundred years, though the water at times dashed over the lantern. Though, however, the lighthouse remained intact, the sea, in striking the lighthouse, began to undermine the rock upon which it stood; so that at length it was decided to take it down, after erecting another lighthouse in its place on an adjacent rock.

The new Eddystone Lighthouse was commenced in

1878, on a rock 120 feet south-south-east of Smeaton's lighthouse. The great difficulties in lighthouse construction on isolated rocks are, the levelling of the rock to receive the foundation courses of the lighthouse tower; the boring of the holes for fastening the masonry to the rock; and the laying of the first few courses, owing to the few days on which a landing can be effected, and the short period during which it is possible to work upon a rock, little raised sometimes above low-water level, and exposed to the wash of waves except in the calmest weather. In this respect the site of the new lighthouse was less favourable than the original site; for whereas the base for the new large tower is 44 feet in diameter, as compared with 26 feet in the old tower, and therefore the area of the foundation and the work in the first few courses was much greater, the surface of the rock was altogether lower, and a large portion below low-water level at the new site, instead of being entirely above low-water and partly above high-water as in the original site. The work, however, of preparing the rock and laying the foundation courses at this low level was greatly facilitated by building a temporary dam of brickwork, laid in quick-setting cement, round the site, 7 feet in height, out of which enclosure the water was pumped by steam power from the attendant steamer as soon as the tide fell below the top of the dam, which enabled the men on calm days to commence work much earlier, to work at the portion below low-water level which was thus laid dry, and to continue working till the tide rose again to the top of the dam. A platform, also, was erected over the site, 10 feet above low-water, on which the men could land with their tools, so as to be in readiness to start work the moment the enclosure round the foundations was dry. The stones, moreover, were rapidly landed by steam power, from the steamer in attendance, on to the site as required. In this way no available time was lost after the commencement of the works in July 1878. An iron mast, 25 feet long, with two jibs acting as cranes, was erected in the centre of the foundations, and was at first sunk 5 feet in the rock, and subsequently lifted up higher as the work proceeded. One of the jibs was used for assisting in the landing of stones from the steamer, and the other for setting the stones in the tower.

By June 1879 the preparation of the foundations and the preliminary work were sufficiently completed to enable the laying of the stones to be commenced. All the stones are dovetailed, both horizontally and vertically, so that they are firmly fixed to the adjacent stones in the same course, and also to the courses below and above. The stones of the foundation courses are each sunk at least 1 foot into the rock, and secured to the rock by two Muntz metal bolts, $1\frac{1}{2}$ inches in diameter. The base of the lighthouse has been made cylindrical for a height of 22 feet; and this portion was completed in July 1880, two years after the commencement of the work, 518 hours of work having been accomplished in 1879, during 131 landings on the site. The actual tower commences from the top of this base, with a somewhat curved slope on the face, so that, like all lighthouse towers, it is reduced in diameter as it ascends, the reduction being greatest near the bottom. (*See illustration.*) The cylindrical base was adopted in order to prevent the waves running up the tower as they did up the old lighthouse, rising sometimes above the top,

THE EDDYSTONE LIGHTHOUSE, 1882, WITH BASE OF SMEATON'S LIGHTHOUSE.

descending with some force on the lantern, and hiding the light for about half a minute. The cylindrical base, rising 2½ feet above high-water spring tides, diverts the waves, and also forms a convenient landing place. The tower was built of solid granite up to 23 feet above the base, with the exception of the central cylindrical hollow left for the water tank. Above this the entrance to the lighthouse was constructed, which is reached by a gun-metal ladder from the base of the tower; and two similar ladders give access on two sides up the cylindrical base. The tower contains nine rooms, including the entrance room at the bottom, just above the solid portion, and the service room at the top below the lantern; the intermediate rooms consisting of two oil rooms, a store room, a crane room from which a crane hoists stores, the living room, the low light room from which a white fixed light is exhibited to mark a shoal $3\frac{1}{4}$ miles distant, and the bedroom just below the service room. The seven upper rooms are 14 feet in diameter, and 10 feet high; and a winding staircase inside leads from the entrance room to the lantern, giving access to each room. The tower was raised nearly to the top of the first oil room in November 1880, completing the season's work, which had been commenced in March, 657 hours of work having been accomplished during 110 landings in that period. As the tower had been raised above the reach of the waves, work could be commenced again as soon as a landing could be effected, about the middle of January 1881; the last stone was laid in June 1881; and the lantern was erected before the end of the year. A temporary light was exhibited from the new lighthouse in February 1882, and the light in the old tower was discontinued; and in May 1882 the permanent lamps were lit in the new lighthouse, within four years of the commencement of the work. The lantern and four rooms of the old tower were taken down, and the staircase well and entrance below this level were filled up with masonry; so that the base of the old tower forms a distinguishing mark by day alongside the new lighthouse. (*See illustration.*) The portion taken down has been erected on a new granite base on Plymouth Hoe, to form a landmark out at sea, and to serve as a memorial of Smeaton's lighthouse.

The light originally exhibited from Smeaton's lighthouse consisted of twenty-four tallow candles, which, unassisted by any lenses, emitted a light which has been estimated as equivalent to an illuminating power of 67 standard candles, such as are used at the present day for measuring the intensity of gas flames. Latterly the fixed colza oil light exhibited from this lighthouse, aided by lenses, had an intensity equal to one hundred times the original light. The new lighthouse is provided with two superposed seven-wick burners, placed in the foci of two superposed tiers of lenses; and each burner emits a light having an intensity of 950 candles, which is raised by the lenses, in the direction of the ray of illumination, to 79,800 candles. On clear nights, when the light of the lighthouse on Plymouth breakwater, 10 miles off, is distinctly seen, the lower burner alone is lighted at its lowest power of 450 candles; but whenever any mist obscures the light on the breakwater, the full power of 1900 candles is exhibited, with an intensity through the lenses of 159,600 candles. This maximum intensity is more than twenty-three times the power of the light previously exhibited from the old lighthouse, and nearly two thousand four hundred times the power of the original light, and is the strongest light hitherto produced by oil in a lighthouse. Colza oil is always used in isolated lighthouses, on account of its greater safety against fire; whereas in lighthouses on the coast, mineral oil is employed, as cheaper and equally efficient. In order to distinguish the Eddystone light from other lights, the light is made to exhibit a double flash at intervals of half a minute, by causing the optical apparatus to revolve and obscure the light at intervals. Each flash lasts three and a half seconds, with an interval of darkness of three seconds between the first and the second flash, which latter is followed by an eclipse of the light for twenty seconds. By modifying these arrangements of flashes in every case, each lighthouse exhibits a distinctive feature in its light; so that the mariner not only sees the light, but also is informed from what lighthouse it proceeds, and therefore by sighting a light knows also what position he has reached. Many wrecks have occurred from sailors mistaking one light for another, an error which these flashing arrangements are intended to obviate.

Two bells suspended on each side of the lighthouse, under the gallery round outside the lantern, serve to give warning in foggy weather, the clappers being moved by the same machinery which turns the optical apparatus. The windward bell is always sounded during a fog; and two strokes, given close together every half minute, afford the same distinguishing feature in the fog signal which the flashes do with the light.

The new Eddystone Lighthouse cost £59,255, a smaller sum than many other isolated lighthouses, such as, for instance, Skerryvore, Dhu Heartach, Wolf Rock, Great Basses, Minot's Ledge, and Spectacle Reef. As, however, it is larger than any previous rock lighthouse, the real cheapness of its construction, compared with other similar structures, can only be appreciated by a comparison of cost per cubic foot. Judged by this standard, the new Eddystone is the cheapest isolated lighthouse hitherto erected, its cost being a little less per cubic foot than the Longship's and Bishop Rock, less than half the proportionate cost of the Bell Rock, and less than one-third that of the old Eddystone Lighthouse. The focal plane of the old lighthouse was 72 feet above high-water; whereas the focal plane of the upper light of the new lighthouse is 133 feet above the same level, and its range over the sea is $17\frac{1}{2}$ miles.

THE EIFFEL TOWER.

The gigantic tower which formed the prominent feature of the Paris Exhibition of 1889, dwarfing by its unprecedented height all the other buildings of the exhibition, has the shape of a lighthouse tower above its second stage, and, moreover, exhibited from its summit during the exhibition a flashing tricolour electric light, which could be seen for many miles round Paris. In other respects, however, it differs entirely from the lighthouse tower just described; though its foundations necessitated much more extensive underground operations, in the alluvial bank of the Seine, than would be imagined by a casual visitor passing under its widespread arches supporting the first stage. Some high lighthouse towers have, indeed, been built of iron, as, for instance, the Roches-Douvres Lighthouse, on a reef to the west of the island of Jersey, 167 feet high up to the lantern gallery; but the great height of the Eiffel Tower necessitated an openwork structure to reduce the weight, and to offer less surface to the wind.

High structures have always been objects of fascination to mankind from the very earliest times, as exemplified by the first recorded instance of a large work being the building of the Tower of Babel. The Colossus of Rhodes, a bronze statue, 105 feet high, erected 2170 years ago, occupied twelve years in construction, and was regarded as one of the seven wonders of the world. The pyramids, however, of much greater antiquity, though apparently built more with a view to great massiveness and durability than elevation, have a much greater height. The pyramid of Cheops, with a height of 484 feet, exceeded in height all other buildings, with the single exception of the spire of old St Paul's[1] from about 1240 to 1561, till the completion of Cologne Cathedral, in 1880, and the erection of the obelisk of Washington, with heights respectively of 528 and 541 feet, displaced it from the foremost position, which it had held for the greater part of the thirty centuries of its existence. The idea of a tower of 300 metres (984 feet), nearly double the height of any previous edifice, appears not to have been quite novel when proposed by Mr Eiffel, in 1886,

---

[1] Old St Paul's Cathedral in London, completed about 1240, and destroyed in the great fire, had a spire reaching a height of 520 feet; but this spire was destroyed by lightning in 1561.

as an object of special attraction for the Paris Exhibition of 1889. Mr Trevithick, in 1833, proposed the erection of a cast-iron column, 1000 feet high, in commemoration of the Reform Bill of 1832; it was to have a diameter of 100 feet at the base, and 12 feet at the top; but the death of its designer the same year put an end to the project. The Americans, also, at the time of the centenary of the independence of the United States, conceived the idea of commemorating it by a tower 1000 feet high; but eventually they contented themselves with the Washington Obelisk, which, till the erection of the Eiffel Tower, was the highest structure in the world.

The tower, weighing 6500 tons, and resting at the base on four trellis-work piers, required very solid and secure foundations; and as a great leverage is exerted by the wind in blowing against the upper portion, it was essential to connect the tower very firmly at its base with its foundations. The foundations were commenced at the beginning of 1887. The foundations of the two piers furthest from the Seine could be excavated and built up in the open air, as a thick layer of gravel was met with $16\frac{1}{2}$ feet below the surface, at the level of the ordinary water level of the Seine; but the foundations of the two piers nearest the river had to be carried down double this depth to reach the gravel, and therefore $16\frac{1}{2}$ feet below the ordinary level of the Seine. These two foundations were, accordingly, excavated and laid by the aid of compressed air, four wrought-iron caissons, 49 feet long and 13 feet wide, being sunk for each pier down to a depth of 33 feet. The masonry foundations rest upon beds of concrete; and the four ribs of each of the four pedestals, converging in pyramid form towards the first platform, are each fastened to the masonry foundations by two anchorage bolts, 25½ feet long and 4 inches in diameter, fixed at their lower ends to a large anchorage plate embedded in the masonry. These bolts, besides fastening the pedestals supporting the tower firmly to their foundations, which, moreover, is mainly accomplished by the great weight of the structure, were also very serviceable in supporting the slanting pedestals during their erection. The four pedestals were further supported in their overhanging position by temporary props, till they could be connected and mutually supported and strengthened by the girders spanning the intervals between them, and supporting the first platform.

The tower has been built of a series of main ribs, formed of riveted angle-irons and plates, braced and connected together by a trellis-work of angle-irons, connecting plates, and bars. (*See illustration.*) The pieces, though large, appear light in comparison with the size of the whole structure, and form a graceful network, adding beauty to the tower which, in its general outline above the second platform, has an artistic appearance. The only heavy-looking part of the edifice is the high screen surrounding the first platform, necessitated by this part being used as a restaurant. The second platform, of much smaller dimensions than the first, is borne on four pedestals, resting on the lower pedestals, but with a smaller amount of convergence, and is supported by straight girders across the much smaller intervals between the pedestals, without the embellishment of arches, which, placed under the lower platform as a structural adornment, add nothing to the strength. The actual tower starts from the second platform, and is surmounted, above the third platform and balcony, by a campanile, and a lantern at the summit. The work involved the employment of $2\frac{1}{2}$ million rivets, of which 600,000 had to be riveted in place, to connect the several parts together. The whole of the parts were, as far as possible, completed at the workshops; so that when lifted into place by special cranes, the junctions only had to be completed, every piece having been so carefully fitted beforehand as to require no further adjustment. Most large buildings require a considerable period for their erection; but, owing in great measure to the care exhibited in every detail, the tower was completed from the foundations to the top in about two and one-third years. The cost of the tower was about £200,000.

In order to regulate, if necessary, the respective heights of the four lower pedestals supporting the structure, a hydraulic press was inserted under each of the four cast-iron bed-plates on which the pedestals rest, capable of exerting a pressure of 800 tons. These presses, however, were little used in the course of construction, owing to the accuracy with which the parts were erected. The verticality of the tower was tested by angular measurements when the tower had reached a height of 720 feet, and was found to be exact. Cast-iron pipes, connected with the metal pedestals at the base of the tower, have been carried down to the water-bearing strata underneath, so as to ensure the ready escape of the electric fluid which may reach the tower. In this manner the tower forms an enormous lightning

THE EIFFEL TOWER.

1. Cologne Cathedral. 2. Strasburg Cathedral. 3. Salisbury Cathedral. 4. Victoria Tower, Houses of Parliament. 5. St. Paul's Cathedral, London. 6. St. Peter's, Rome. 7. The Great Pyramid. 8. The Pantheon, Paris. 9. The Duomo, Florence. 10. The Invalides, Paris.

conductor, ensuring a large neighbouring area against danger from lightning.

The width across the base of the tower is 410 feet; and the width of the openings between the bottom pedestals is 243 feet. The first platform is 189 feet above the ground, only 27 feet lower than the top of the towers of the cathedral of Notre Dame in Paris. The second platform is situated at an elevation of 380 feet, which is 14 feet higher than St Paul's Cathedral in London. The height of the actual tower, rising from the second platform, and supporting the third platform, with an intermediate floor half way up, is 526 feet; so the third platform is at a height of 906 feet from the ground, more than double the height of all but about half-a-dozen of the highest buildings in the world, and within a few feet of the height which would be attained by Cologne Cathedral if perched on the summit of the Great Pyramid. The projecting balcony of this platform is the greatest height to which the general public are admitted. The campanile, however, with the lantern above, increases the elevation of the tower to its full height of 984 feet above the ground, or 1094 feet above sea level. The total height of the tower is therefore more than double the height of all existing buildings, with three exceptions, namely, the Washington Obelisk and Cologne Cathedral, already mentioned, and Ulm Cathedral, which was completed in 1890, having a total height of 530 feet. There is, accordingly, at the present time no building in the world which reaches within 440 feet of the Eiffel Tower.

The summit of the tower can be reached by staircases, with a total number of 1793 steps; but the ascent as far as the balcony below the campanile can be made, by hydraulic lifts, in four stages. Three systems of lifts have been adopted for this purpose, two of them being designed so as to follow the inclination of the pedestals in their journey, and one of these two systems being adapted for changing the inclination in ascending to the second platform; and the third system is arranged as a vertical counterbalanced lift, in two equal sections, to provide communication between the second and third platforms. Four lifts lead from the ground to the first platform; and two of these continue the ascent to the second platform. The ascent to the third platform from the second is effected in two stages, by means of two counterbalancing lifts performing half the journey, and a change of carriage is effected at the midway floor. The two lifts leading only to the first platform have carriages, $16\frac{1}{2}$ feet high, divided into two floors, running on wheels inside the pedestals, and holding 100 persons; and they can ascend at a speed of $3\frac{1}{4}$ feet per second. The two other lifts, going up to the second platform, only hold 50 passengers each, but travel at double the speed of the others. Like the previous lifts, they are partially counterbalanced to diminish the force needed to drag them up, the haulage being effected by six steel wire cables. In each case the lifts can descend empty by their slight excess of weight over the counterpoise; and self-acting safety brakes arrest a too rapid descent. In the ascent from the second to the third platform, which is accomplished by two equal stages of 263 feet of vertical ascent, the two lifts, each performing half the ascent alternately, work in unison, one ascending as the other goes down, being connected by four chains passing over pulleys at the top. One of the lifts is moved up and down by two hydraulic presses at the sides, and controls the motion of the other; and both of the lifts travel along vertical guides forming part of the framework of the tower. Each lift can hold about 63 passengers; and the journey, including the change of lift midway, can be effected in about five minutes.

The campanile at the top is reserved for meteorological and other scientific observations; and the lantern contains an electric lamp with optical apparatus of the first order. The oscillation at the top of the tower in a gale has been estimated at a maximum of about 6 inches.

The tower has admirably answered the object for which it was designed, of greatly surpassing all other erections in height, and thus attracting sightseers, and imparting novelty to the Paris Exhibition of 1889. Its construction was also effected at a comparatively moderate cost, and in a short space of time, and has combined simplicity with a moderate degree of gracefulness. The tower has, moreover, achieved a world-celebrity for its designer, which the Douro and Garabit viaducts did not accomplish, though these structures unite the simplicity and boldness of the tower with far greater utility, and a distinctly greater elegance. The tower is in fact the result of the experience gained in these earlier designs; and no portion of the construction of the tower equalled in difficulty the erection of arches of 525, and 541 feet span, across the valleys of the Douro at Oporto and the Truyère at Garabit, without any scaffolding or intermediate supports. The renown of the tower is due to its absolutely unrivalled height, the occasion of its erection, and its position in the most popular capital of the world; but it is unquestionable that the Garabit Viaduct, the Antwerp quays, the Danube and Mississippi delta works, the Alpine, Rocky Mountain, and Transandine railways, the Severn Tunnel, the Brooklyn and Forth bridges, and several other works, are far greater engineering triumphs.

Concluding Remarks.—Enough has been said in the preceding pages to indicate the great influence the works of engineers exercise over the destinies of mankind, and how much they conduce to the progress, comfort, and well-being of nations. The works, however, described are merely a few remarkable instances chosen out of a great number of very important works which engineers have carried out in almost every part of the world. Moreover, it is impossible, within a limited space, to refer to various other branches of engineering science in which the skill of the engineer has conferred inestimable benefits on the human race. It has been shown how all the various works for facilitating locomotion on land, and affording access from the sea to ports, and by waterways to the interior of a country, are due to the labours of engineers, and how the indispensable water supplies for large towns are secured by their aid. Engineers, however, also provide for the drainage of large towns and districts, the mitigation of inundations on low-lying lands, the reclamation of lands from the sea, and the irrigation of large tracts of land in warm countries, by which crops are preserved and famine averted; and they carry out the works for the illumination of streets and houses with gas and electricity. The improvements, also, of marine engines have increased the speed of vessels, and notably shortened the time of transit across the Atlantic, and to different parts of the world; whilst improvements in telegraphy and the laying of submarine cables enable communications to be rapidly exchanged between distant quarters of the globe. Moreover, the development of most of these advantages, like the works described, have been achieved within the last fifty years; and if engineers in the future continue, as in the last half century, increasing and extending the benefits resulting from their works, they will justly be regarded as ranking amongst the greatest benefactors of mankind.

INDEX

A.

ABT RACK RAILWAYS, 66-69; various, 67; Transandine, 68; advantages, 68-69.

AIR-LOCK at Hudson River Tunnel, 90; description, 90; in compressed air diving-bell, 161; for caissons at Antwerp quays, 183.

ALEXANDRIA HARBOUR, 194-195; description, 194; section of breakwater, 192, 194; method of construction of breakwater, 195; rapid construction of breakwater, 195.

ALPINE RAILWAYS, 26-38, 59-61, 62-66; descriptions of principal, 26-38; sections, 30; compared with Rocky Mountain railways, 38-39; along Mont Cenis road, 59-61; up mountains, 62-66; considerations affecting, 71-73; fresh routes proposed, 82-84.

ALPINE TUNNELS, 70-84; descriptions of principal 70-81; contrasted with ordinary tunnels, 71; proposed, 82-84. *See* MONT CENIS, ST GOTHARD, etc.

AMSTERDAM SHIP CANAL, 240-245; object and route, 240; section, 242; difficult problems involved, 243; description of works, 243-245; land reclaimed and drained, 244, 245; duration and cost of works, 245.

ANDES, sections of railways over, 30; descriptions of railways across, 46-50, 68.

ANTWERP, Port of, 182-184; early condition, 182; development, 182-183; Kattendyk Dock, 182; Africa and America docks, 183; construction of river quays, 183-184; increase of trade, 184.

AQUEDUCT, swing, across Manchester Ship Canal, 249; for Manchester Waterworks, 273-274; from Thirlmere to Manchester, 277; from Vyrnwy to Liverpool, 281-284.

ARCHED BRIDGES, materials and spans of various, 113, 118-119; Douro, and Garabit, 119; St Louis, and Harlem, 121; principles of, 127; limits of span, 128; bowstring type, 128; illustrations, 134; descriptions of, 136-141.

ARLBERG RAILWAY, 37-38; object, 37; description, 37-38; elevation attained, 38; Trisana Viaduct on, 118.

ARLBERG TUNNEL, 80-81; rapid driving of headings, 80; machinery, strata, and construction, 81; temperature during construction, 81; cost, 81.

ATLANTIC AND PACIFIC RAILWAY, 40-41; route, 40; incomplete state of, 40-41.

B.

BERLIN METROPOLITAN RAILWAY, route, and description, 16.

BLASTING OPERATIONS AT HELL GATE, 162-171; description of improvement works, 162-171. *See* HELL GATE, HALLETT'S POINT, MIDDLE REEF.

BLOCK SYSTEM, principle of, 14; adopted on Inner Circle Railway, 14.

BOGIE CARS, on American railways, 43.

BOGIE ENGINES, New York Elevated Railway, 19; Fairlie duplex, 56-58.

BOULOGNE HARBOUR, 195-197; importance of, 195; enlargement of, 196; works carried out, 196-197; form of breakwater, 192, 197; estimated cost of, 197.

BOWSTRING GIRDER BRIDGES, form of arched bridges, 128; instances of, 116-117, 128.

BRAKES, continuous, on Inner Circle, 15; on Rigi and Pilatus railways, 64, 65-66

BREAKWATER, Alexandria, 192, 194-195; Boulogne, 192, 196-197; Colombo, 192, 198-199; Dover, 192, 200-201; Marseilles, 185-186; Newhaven, 202-203; Table Bay, 192, 193-194.

BREAKWATERS, 189-205; protecting Marseilles basins, 185-186; various, 189-190; improved construction of, 189, 204-205; arrangements of, for sheltering harbours, 190; sections, 192; different types, 193, 204-205; descriptions of various, 193-203; difficulties, and experience needed in construction, 203-204.

BRENNER RAILWAY, 28-32; object, 28; section, 30; description, 31-32; elevation attained, 31.

BRIDGE, Britannia Tubular, 114-116, 134; Brooklyn, 120, 127, 132, 143-146, 153; Channel (proposed), 156-158; Clifton Suspension, 114; Conway Tubular, 115; Crumlin, 118; Forth, 121, 132, 146-153; Garabit, 119, 132, 134, 139-141; Harlem River, 121; Hawkesbury, 132, 134, 135-136; Hooghly, 132, 134, 141-143; Hudson River (proposed), 120, 127, 146; Kentucky and Indiana, 130, 143; Kentucky River, 118, 128-129; Kieff Suspension, 114; Montreal Tubular, 115; Niagara Cantilever, 129-130, 134; Niagara Suspension, 119-120, 127; Portage, 118; Poughkeepsie, 130-131, 143; St Louis, 121, 132, 134, 136-139; Saltash, 116-117, 128; Sukkur, 131, 153; Tay, 118; Tower, 132, 135, 153-156; Trisana, 118. *See also* SPANS OF BRIDGES.

U

BRIDGES, 112-158; progress of construction, 112-121; materials and spans, 112-114, 120-121; arched, 113, 118-119, 121, 127-128, 134; suspension, 113-114, 119-120, 125-127; tubular, 114-116, 134; girder, 114-119, 123-125, 134; cantilever, 121, 128-131, 134; principles of construction, 121-131; influence of increased spans, 122; descriptions of long span, 132-158.
BRIDGEWATER CANAL swing aqueduct on, 249-250; lifts connecting it with Manchester Ship Canal, 250.
BRITANNIA TUBULAR BRIDGE, 114-115; cast-iron arch proposed, 114; tubular system adopted, 114-115; spans and headway, 115, 134; erection, 115.
BROOKLYN BRIDGE, 143-146; largest suspension bridge, 120; dip of cables, 127, 144; span compared with other bridges, 134; object, 143; length, spans, piers, and headway, 144; suspension cables, 144; erection, accommodation, and cost, 145; compared with Forth Bridge, 153.

C.

CALAIS HARBOUR, 195-196; importance, 195; improvement works, 195-196; results achieved, 196.
CANADIAN PACIFIC RAILWAY, 44-46; section, 30; description, 44-46; elevation attained, 44, 45.
CANAL, Amsterdam, 240-245; Bridgewater, 249-250; Corinth, 242, 253, 264-267; Manchester, 242, 245-252; Nicaragua, 261-264; Panama, 253, 258-261; Suez, 162, 253, 254-258.
CANAL LIFT, 234-237; object, 234-235; employed at Anderton and Fontinettes, 235; description of La Louvière, 235-237; for connecting Bridgewater and Manchester canals, 250.
CANALS, 238-267; lifts on, 235-237; advantages for trade, 238-239; descriptions of ship canals, 240-267; sections, 242; ship railways as substitutes, 267-269; importance and difficulties of, across isthmuses, 266-267.
CANTILEVER BRIDGES, definition, 128-129; principle of, 129; Niagara and Fraser, 129-130; advantages for building out, 130; Kentucky and Indiana, and Poughkeepsie, 130-131; Sukkur, and Forth, 131; illustration, 134; descriptions of, 141-143, 146-153.
CAPITAL IN BRITISH RAILWAYS, 23.
CENTRAL PACIFIC RAILWAY, 39-42, 43. *See* UNION PACIFIC RAILWAY.
CHANNEL BRIDGE (proposed), 156-158; proposed instead of tunnel, 156-157; length, piers, spans, and headway, 157; estimated weight and cost, 157; height of structure compared with high buildings, 157; compared with Channel Tunnel, 157-158.
CHANNEL TUNNEL (proposed), 109-111; preliminary investigations, 109-110; route and length proposed, 110; gradients and drainage headings, 111; prospects, 111.
CHARLOTTENBURG WEIR, 230-234; description, 230; portion closed with drum weir, 230; section of drum weir, 232; description of drum weir, 233; perfect control of drum weir, 233-234; compared with weirs on River Main, 234.
CHICAGO RIVER TUNNELS, 86-87.
CHIGNECTO SHIP RAILWAY, 268-269; object, and route, 268; description, 268; advantages, 268-269.
COLOMBO HARBOUR, 197-199; exposure of site, 197-198; breakwater, and shelter afforded, 198; form, and construction of breakwater, 192, 198-199; cost and revenue, 199; northern breakwater proposed, 199.
COMPRESSED AIR, used for constructing Hudson River Tunnel, 90-94; in driving Thames Subway, 109; for sinking caissons of St Louis Bridge piers, 137; in founding Brooklyn Bridge piers, 144; for piers of Forth Bridge, 150; for foundations of Eiffel Tower, 296.
COMPRESSED AIR DIVING-BELL, 160-161; for removing submarine rocks, 160; description, 160-161; method of working, 161.
CORINTH CANAL, 264-267; section, 242; object, and ancient commencement, 264; length, and depth of cutting, 264-265; width, and slopes, 265; progress, and difficulties of works, 265-266; prospects, 266; harbour works at entrances, and bridge over, 266.
CURVES, on following railways: Arlberg, 38; Brenner, 31; Canadian Pacific, 45; Denver, 43-44; early main lines, 25; Elevated, 19; Fell, 60, 61, 62; Festiniog, 55; Metropolitan, 8; Mexican, 46; Mont Cenis, 32; Mountain, 63, 65, 67; Peruvian, 48; St Gothard, 35-36; Semmering, 27; Southern Pacific, 43; Union, or Central Pacific, 42.

D.

DAM, across Lake Y for Amsterdam Ship Canal, 244; Woodhead, and others in Longdendale Valley, 274-275; masonry, in Vyrnwy Valley, 279-280.
DANUBE, River, 216-219; size of basin, 216-217; shallow outlets owing to delta, 217; possible methods of improvement, 217-218; improvement works at Sulina mouth, 218; influence of works on bar channel, 218-219; blasting reefs at Iron Gates, 219.
DELTA, plan of Mississippi, 208; instances of, 209; length and advance of Danube, 217; area, and advance of Mississippi, 220.
DENVER AND RIO GRANDE RAILWAY, 43-44; remarkable features, 43-44; narrow gauge, 54-55.
DETROIT RIVER TUNNEL, 88-89; object, 88 method of construction, 88-89; progress, difficulties, and abandonment, 89.
DOCKS, description of, along Thames, 173-177; hydraulic machinery for, 177; difficulties in construction, 177-178; area of, in Port of London, 178; description of, in Port of Liverpool, 178-180; area of, in Port of Liverpool, 179; extension of, at Antwerp, 182-183; description of, at Marseilles, 184-186; quays and jetties at New York, 186-188; for the Manchester Ship Canal, 246-250.
DOVER HARBOUR, 199-201; original scheme, 200; portion completed, 200; form and construction of breakwater, 192, 200-201; cost of

western breakwater, 201; instance of upright wall breakwater, 201.

DREDGING, for removing shattered rock at Hell Gate, 166-167, 170; in Calais Harbour, 196; in River Tyne, 208, 210, 211-212; amount removed by, from Tyne, 211-212; importance of, for trade, 213; in River Maas, 216; for construction of Suez Canal, 256; at entrance to Suez Canal, 257.

DRUM WEIR, introduced on River Marne, 226; across timber passes on River Main, 235, 234; at Charlottenburg, 230-234; section, 232.

E.

EARTH-WAVE, caused by explosion at Hell Gate, rate of transmission, 170.

EASTHAM LOCKS, at entrance to Manchester Ship Canal, 248.

EAST RIVER, Brooklyn Bridge across, 143-146, obstructions in, 162; quays along, 187-188.

EDDYSTONE LIGHTHOUSE, 287-294; site, 287; history of successive structures, 287-288; description of new, 288-294; rapid construction, 289-292; accommodation, 291; removal of Smeaton's, and re-erection on Hoe, 292; old and new lights exhibited, 292-293; distinctive character of light, 293; fog bells, 293; cost compared with other lighthouses, 294; height of focal plane, and range of light, 294.

EIFFEL TOWER, 294-302; resemblance to lighthouse tower, 294; high towers proposed previously, 295-296; foundations, 296-297; description, 297-298; rapid erection, 298; cost, 298; provisions against divergence and lightning, 298; dimensions, 299; compared with high buildings, 299; ascent by steps and lifts, 299-301; oscillation, 301; remarks on, 301-302.

ELECTRIC LIGHT, used at Hudson River Tunnel works, 91; in compressed air diving-bell, 161; in working chamber at Antwerp Quay works, 183; to light Manchester Ship Canal at night, 250; for navigation of Suez Canal at night, 258; exhibited at St Catherine's Lighthouse, 286; on top of Eiffel Tower, 294, 301.

ELEVATED RAILWAY, NEW YORK, 16-22. See NEW YORK ELEVATED RAILWAY.

EXPLOSION, at Hallett's Point, 166; at Middle Reef, 170; of basin wall at Albert Dock, London, 176.

F.

FELL RAILWAYS, 59-62; Mont Cenis, 60-61; Cantagallo, Brazil, 61-62; New Zealand, 62.

FESTINIOG RAILWAY, 55-56; description, 55-56; locomotive, 56-58; passengers, 56.

FORTH BRIDGE, 146-153; instance of large span steel bridge, 121; span compared with other bridges, 134; schemes proposed, and site, 146; favourable situation for high level bridge, 147; description, 147-149; length, headway, and span, 149; sinking caissons for piers, 150-151; erection of superstructure, 151; weight of steel, and cost, 151; appearance, 151-152; compared with other structures, 152; compared with Brooklyn Bridge, 153.

G.

GARABIT VIADUCT, 139-141; example of large arch, 119; instance of erection by building out, 132, 140; illustration, 134; length, height, and spans, 139; size of arch, 140; method of erection, 140; height compared with high edifices, 140.

GIRDER BRIDGES, instances of, and spans, 114-119; principles of, 123-124; continuous, 124-125; illustrations, 134; descriptions of, 115, 135-136.

GRADIENTS, on following railways: Arlberg, 38; Brenner, 31; Canadian Pacific, 44; Denver, 43-44; early main lines, 25; Elevated, 19; Fell, 60, 61, 62; Festiniog, 55; Metropolitan, 7-8; Mexican, 46; Mont Cenis, 32; Northern and Southern Pacific, 42, 43; Peruvian, 47-50; Rack, 63-68; St Gothard, 35-36; Semmering, 27; Simplon, 82; Union, or Central Pacific, 42.

GREAT ST BERNARD RAILWAY (proposed), 83-84.

H.

HALLETT'S POINT, 162-167; plans and section, 164; galleries driven under, 165; arrangements for explosion, 166; method of simultaneous explosion, 166; removal of shattered rock, 166-167; period of works, and cost, 167.

HARBOUR, Alexandria, 194-195; Boulogne, 195-197; Calais, 195-196; Colombo, 197-199; Dover, 199-201; Marseilles, 184-186; Newhaven, 201-203; Table Bay, 193-194.

HARBOURS, 189-202; early works, 189; various recent, 190; size and form dependent on site, 190; methods of sheltering, 190; descriptions of, 193-202.

HAWKESBURY BRIDGE, 135-136; instance of deep foundations, 132; illustration, 134; sinking caissons for piers, 135; floating out girders, 136; accommodation, length, and cost, 136.

HEIGHT OF BUILDINGS: Brooklyn Bridge towers, 144; Cologne Cathedral, 295; Colossus of Rhodes, 295; Eiffel Tower, 295; Forth Bridge cantilevers, 152; Garabit Viaduct, 140; Old St Paul's Cathedral, 295; Pyramid of Cheops, 295; Ulm Cathedral, 299; Washington Obelisk, 295.

HELL GATE, NEW YORK, 162-171; blasting operations for improving channel, 162-171; reason of name, 162; earlier works, 162; illustrations, 164; removal of Hallett's Point, 165-167; removal of Middle Reef, 167-171.

HOOGHLY BRIDGE, 141-143; peculiar form, 132, 134, 143; unequal spans adopted, 141; sinking caissons for piers, 141; erection of superstructure, 142; cost, 143.

HOOSAC TUNNEL, 73-74.

Index.

HUDSON RIVER BRIDGE (proposed), proposed span, and object, 120; height proposed for towers, 127; compared with Brooklyn Bridge, 146.
HUDSON RIVER TUNNEL, 89-94; object, 89; method of approach, 90; use of compressed air, 90, 92; method of construction, and progress, 91, 93; inrush of water, 91-92, 93; sinking caisson, 92, 93; employment of pilot tube, 92; shield for protecting face, 93, 94; stoppage, and resumption of work, 94.

I.

INNER CIRCLE RAILWAY, 3-15. *See* METROPOLITAN RAILWAY.
INLAND NAVIGATION, schemes for extending, 238; advantages, 239; revival in England, 239.

J.

JETTIES, at Port of New York, 187; at new outlet of River Maas, 216; at Sulina mouth of Danube, 217-218; at South Pass of Mississippi, 221.

K.

KENTUCKY RIVER BRIDGE, continuous girders, but called cantilevers, 118, 128-129; spans, 118.
KENTUCKY AND INDIANA BRIDGE, form, and spans, 130; central cantilever, like Hooghly Bridge, 143.

L.

LA LOUVIÈRE CANAL LIFT, 234-237; object of hydraulic lifts, 234-235; description and working, 235-236; compared with Anderton Lift, 237; advantages, 237.
LAKES MICHIGAN AND ERIE TUNNELS, for water supply of Chicago, 87; for water supply of Cleveland, 87-88.
LANDING STAGE, floating, at Liverpool, 181.
LIGHTHOUSES, 286-294; importance of, 286; difficulties of construction on reefs, 286-287; instances of, 287; description of Eddystone, 287-294.
LIVERPOOL, Port of, 178-182; early condition, 178-179; great extension of docks, 179; description of docks, 179; areas of principal docks, 179; access and entrances to docks, 180; sluicing arrangements, 180-181; floating landing stage, 181; importance of, 181-182.
LOCKS, Amsterdam Ship Canal, 244; Liverpool Docks, 180; Manchester Ship Canal, 246-249; Millwall Docks, 174; Nicaragua Canal (contemplated), 262-263; Panama (proposed), 260; Poses, on Lower Seine, 229; Tilbury Docks, 176, 177; Victoria and Albert Docks, 174, 175.
LOCOMOTIVE, smokeless, proposed for Metropolitan, 9; bogie, on Elevated Railway, 19-20; tractive force of, on Semmering, 27-28;

Fairlie, 46, 56-58, 59; gripping central rail, 60-62; Baldwin, on Cantagallo Railway, 61; Rigi Railway, 63-64; Pilatus Railway, 65-66; Abt system, 67-69; compressed air, for St Gothard Tunnel, 80.
LONDON, Port of, 173-178; early dock extensions, 173; Victoria Dock, 173-174; Millwall Docks, 174-175; South West India Dock, 174-175; Albert Dock, 175-176; Tilbury Docks, 176-177; area of docks, and extent, 178; importance of, 181-182.
LONDON WATER SUPPLY, from springs and wells, 271; unsatisfactory condition, 284; increasing demand, 285; need of control, 285.

M.

MAAS, River, 215-216; peculiarities of outlet, 215-216; shoaling of outlet channels, 216; new cut, training, and jetties, 216; improved depth, and trade, 216.
MANCHESTER SHIP CANAL, 245-252; object, 245; description, 246-248; accessory works, 248-250; accommodation for trade, 250; strata traversed, plant, and extent of works, 250-251; facilities for navigation, 250-251; advantages, and interest of undertaking, 251-252.
MANCHESTER WATERWORKS, 273-278; reservoirs in Longdendale Valley, 273-276; conveyance of water to Manchester, 274; description of works, 274-275; compensation water, 275; separating weirs, 276; volume, and cost of supply, 276; supplemental supply from Thirlmere, 276-278.
MARSEILLES, Port of, 184-186; early condition, 184; sheltered by breakwaters, 185; development, 185-186.
MERSEY TUNNEL, 94-100; site, and object, 94-97; section, 96; preliminary works, and shafts, 97; driving of drainage tunnel, 97-98; construction of tunnel, 98; stations, 98-99; ventilation, 99; length, and cost, 99.
METROPOLITAN RAILWAY, 3-16; commencement, 3; extensions, 3, 11, 12; description, 5-9; connections, 12-13; safety appliances, 14-15; cost, 21; for Paris, proposed, 15-16; in Berlin, 16.
MEXICAN RAILWAY, 46; section, 30; description, 46; Fairlie engine used on, 46.
MIDDLE REEF, East River, N.Y., 167-171; plans and sections, 164; site, and area, 167; driving of galleries under, 167; preparations for explosion, 167-169; rackarock for charges, 168; arrangements for sympathetic detonation, 168-169; firing of charges, 169-170; rate of transmission of shock, 170; removal of shattered rock, 171; cost, 170; advantages of work, 170-171.
MILLWALL DOCKS, area, and size of lock, 174; concrete in dock walls, 175.
MISSISSIPPI RIVER, 219-223; plan of delta, 208; length, and basin, 219-220; delta, and material brought down, 220; passes, and shoals, 220; jetty works at South Pass, 221; improvement in bar channel, 221; deepening at head of pass, 222.
MOLLENDO AND PUNO RAILWAY, 47; section, 30; length, elevation, and route, 47.

Index. 309

Mont Blanc Tunnel (proposed), 83-84.
Mont Cenis Railway, 32-33; description, 32-33; advantages of, 33; temporary Fell, 60-61.
Mont Cenis Tunnel, 73-77; method of construction, 74; progress and enlargement, 75; completion, 76; ventilation, 76; temperature during construction, 77; cost, 80.
Monte Generoso Railway, 66.
Mount Washington Rack Railway, 62-63.
Moveable Weirs, 225-234. *See* Weirs, Poses Weir, Charlottenburg Weir.

N.

Narrow Gauge Railways, 54-59; Denver and Rio Grande, 54-55; Festiniog, 55-56; various, 58-59; Fell, 59-62.
Newhaven Harbour, 201-203; site, and prior condition, 201-202; improvement works, 202; line, length, and cost of breakwater, 202; method of constructing breakwater, 202-203.
New York, Port of, 186-188; advantageous position, 186; quay walls and jetties for vessels, 187; extensions of quays and jetties, 187-188; large trade of, 188.
New York Elevated Railway, 16-22; object, 17; description, 17-21; cost, 21; success of, and passenger traffic on, 22.
Niagara Cantilever Bridge, 129-130; description, 129-130; elevation of, 134.
Niagara Suspension Bridge, 119-120; description, 119; reconstruction, 119; used for railway, 119, 120.
Nicaragua Canal, 261-264; selection of route, 261; commencement of works, 261, 263; description of scheme, 262-263; estimated cost, 263.
Northern Pacific Railway, 42-43; route, 40; description, 42-43.

O.

Oroya Railway, 47-50; section, 30; description, 47-50; switchbacks introduced, 48; difficulties encountered in works, 49; elevation attained, 50; cost, 54.

P.

Pacific Railways, 38-53; North American, 39-46; Mexican, 46; Peruvian, 46-50; Transandine, 68.
Panama Canal, 258-261; section 242; various routes proposed, 258; length, depth of cutting, and dimensions, 259; progress of works, and difficulties, 259-260; plant employed on works, 260; estimated cost, 260; proposed introduction of locks, 260; stoppage of works, 260; preference given to Nicaragua route, 261.
Paris Metropolitan Railway (proposed), 15-16.
Passenger Traffic, on Elevated Railway, 22; British Railways, 23-24; United States Railways, 52; Festiniog Railway, 56.
Peruvian Railways, 46-50; sections, 30; Arequipa to Puno, 47; Callao to Oroya, 47-50; cost, 54.
Pilatus Railway, 65-66; route, 65; construction, 65; brakes, and speed, 65-66; self-propelling carriage, 66.
Port, Antwerp, 182-184; Liverpool, 178-182; London, 173-178; Marseilles, 184-186; New York, 186-188.
Ports, 172-188; importance of, for foreign trade, 172; recent development of various, 172; history of some principal, 173-188.
Poses Weir, 227-230; new type, 226, 227-228; advantages, 228; requirements, 228-229; position and description, 229; magnitude, 229-230.
Poughkeepsie Bridge, form and spans, 130-131; central cantilever, like Hooghly Bridge, 143.
Progress of Railways, 51-53.

Q.

Quays, construction of, at Antwerp, 183; built on breakwaters at Marseilles, 185; along river frontages at New York, 187; extension of, at New York, 187-188.

R.

Rackarock, explosive used at Hell Gate, 168; composition, and advantages, 168; economy effected by using, 170.
Rack Railways, 62-69. *See* Rigi, Pilatus, etc.
Railway, Abt Rack, 66-69; Arlberg, 37-38; Berlin Metropolitan, 16; Brenner, 28-32; Canadian Pacific, 44-46; Chignecto Ship, 267-269; Fell, 59-62; Festiniog, 55-58; London Metropolitan, 3-15; Mersey, 94-100; Mexican, 46; Mont Cenis, 32-33; Narrow Gauge, 54-59; New York Elevated, 16-22; Paris Metropolitan (proposed), 15-16; Peruvian, 46-50; Pilatus, 65-66; Rigi, 62-65; St Gothard, 33-36; Semmering, 26-28; Simplon (proposed), 37, 82-83; Transandine, 68; United States Western, 39-44.
Railway Extensions, in London, 2-3; of Metropolitan, 11, 12; in United Kingdom, 22-23; in the world, 51-53.
Railway Statistics, 22-23, 51-53; for the United Kingdom, 22-23; progress of railways in countries of the world, 51-53.
Reservoirs, made for water supply by damming up streams, 272; in Longdendale Valley, 273-275; Thirlmere, for Manchester water supply, 276-278; Vyrnwy Lake, for Liverpool water supply, 279-281.
Rigi Railways, 62-65; description of first line, 63-64; accommodation, and speed, 64; second, and third lines, 64-65.
River, Danube, 216-219; Maas, 215-216; Mississippi, 219-223; Tyne, 210-213; Seine, 213-215.
Rivers, 206-223; contrast between tidal and tideless rivers, 206-209; plans and sections of, 208; object of improvement works, 209-210; descriptions of improvement of tidal, 210-216;

improvement of tideless, 216-223; weirs on, 224-234; sources of water supply, 271-272, 284-285.
ROCK-BREAKING RAMS, 161-162; for excavating rock under water, 161, 256; method of working, 161-162; rate of working, at Suez Canal, 162.
ROCKY MOUNTAINS, railways across, 38-46.

S.

ST GOTHARD RAILWAY, 33-37; section, 30; description, 34-36; loops and spirals, 35; influence on traffic, 36-37; schemes in competition with, 36-37, 82-84.
ST GOTHARD TUNNEL, 77-80; commencement, 77; method of construction, 77-78; rate of progress, 78; accuracy of driving, 79; temperature of rock near centre, 79; ventilation, 80; cost, 80.
ST LOUIS BRIDGE, 136-139; first instance of steel bridge, 121; example of building out, 132; illustration, 134; object, and site, 136; foundations, 137; construction of arches and erection, 137-138; accommodation, and cost, 138.
SALTASH BRIDGE, 116-117; site, and form, 116; spans, headway, and length, 117; example of bowstring girder, 128.
SARNIA TUNNEL, 109; site, and object, 109; description, and mode of construction, 109.
SEINE, River, 213-215; plan and section, 208; contrast to River Tyne, 213; canalisation to Paris and above, 213, 224; area of basin, 213; improvement by training walls, 213-214; training works and dredging compared, 214-215; weirs on, 224, 226-230.
SEMMERING RAILWAY, 26-28; description, 26-27; cost, 27; traction on, 28.
SEVERN TUNNEL, 100-106; section, 96, 101; object, and site, 100; shafts, and headings, 101; flooding of works by spring, 101-102, 104; stopping influx of water, 101-103; modification of works, 103; influx of river, 103-105; shutting off spring, 105; pumping, and ventilation, 105; length of tunnel, and time of traversing, 105-106.
SHIP CANALS, 238-267. *See* CANAL, AMSTERDAM SHIP CANAL, etc.
SHIP RAILWAYS, 267-269; ancient inclines for vessels, 267-268; proposed across Isthmus of Panama, 268; Chignecto, described, 268-269.
SIMPLON RAILWAY (proposed), to compete with St Gothard, 37, 83; route proposed, 82; prospects, 83; compared with other schemes, 83-84.
SIMPLON TUNNEL (proposed), 82-83; description of scheme, 82; estimated cost, 82-83; possible objections, 83.
SLUICE GATES, on free rollers at Eastham Locks, 248; for discharge of Weaver waters, 248; for regulating flow in Manchester Ship Canal, 249.
SOUTHERN PACIFIC RAILWAY, 42-43; route, 40; description, 42-43.
SOUTH WEST INDIA DOCK, 174-175; area, site, and locks, 174; use of basin, 174-175; concrete in walls, 175.
SPANS OF BRIDGES, Alma, 112-113; Britannia, 115, 134; Brooklyn, 120, 144; Budapest, 114; Channel, 157; Cincinnati, 117, 118; Cincinnati Suspension, 120; Clifton, 114; Coalbrookdale, 113; Coblentz, 119; Connecticut, 113; Conway, 115; Crumlin, 118; Dirschau, 117; Douro, 119; Forth, 121, 149; Fraser River, 130; Freiburg, 114; Garabit, 119, 134, 139; Grosvenor (Chester), 113; Harlem River, 121; Hawkesbury, 134, 138; Henderson, 117; Hoogly, 134, 141; Hudson, (proposed), 120; Kentucky and Indiana, 130; Kentucky River, 118; Kieff, 114; Kuilenberg, 117; London, 113; Louisville, 117; Mainz, 117; Menai, 113; Monongahela, 120; Montreal, 115; Moerdyk, 117; Niagara Cantilever, 129, 134; Niagara Suspension, 119; Passau, 117; Portage, 118; Poughkeepsie, 130-131; St Louis, 121, 134, 137; Saltash, 117; Schaffhausen, 113; Southwark, 113; Sukkur, 131; Sunderland, 113; Tay, 118; Tower, 154; Trezzo, 113; Trisana, 118; Victoria, Pimlico, 119; Wittengen, 113.
SUBAQUEOUS TUNNELS, 85-111. *See* TUNNEL.
SUBMARINE MINING AND BLASTING, 159-171; ordinary methods, 159-160; with compressed air diving-bell, 160-161; at Hell Gate, New York, 162-171.
SUEZ CANAL, 254-258; rock-breaking rams for widening, 162, 256; section, 242; advantages of, 253, 254; made in ancient times, 255; route, length, and size, 255; widening, 255-256; description, and cost of work, 256-257; large traffic, 257; improved facilities for navigation, 258.
SUKKUR BRIDGE, site and span, 131; span compared with other bridges, 134; compared with Forth Bridge, 153.
SUSPENSION BRIDGES, instances of, and spans, 113-114; for railway, 119-121; principle of, 125-127; contrasted with arched bridges, 127; description of, 143-146.

T.

TABLE BAY HARBOUR, 193-194; sheltering breakwater, 193-194; section of breakwater, 192; progress of breakwater, 194.
THAMES SUBWAYS, 106-109; description of, at Tower, 106-107; method of construction, 107; compared with Thames Tunnel, 108; for city and South London Railway, 108-109; description, and progress, 108; access to, 109.
THAMES TUNNEL, used by East London Railway, 2-3, 86; description, and cost, 86.
THIRLMERE WATER SUPPLY, 276-278; selected for Manchester, 276; description of scheme, 277; volume available, 277; estimated cost, 277-278.
TILBURY DOCKS, 176-177; object, site, and dimensions, 176; tidal basin, and lock, 176-177; foundations, and walls, 177.
TOWER BRIDGE, 153-156; example of drawbridge, 132, 154-155; crossing Thames below London Bridge, 135, 153-154; river piers, and spans, 154; description, 154-155; foundations for piers, 155-156; length, and estimated cost, 156; peculiar features, and importance, 156.
TRANSANDINE RAILWAY, 68; elevation attained, 68; steep inclines worked by Abt locomotives, 68; variety of gauge, 68.

Index.

TUBULAR BRIDGES, Britannia, 114-115, 134; Conway, and Montreal, 115.
TUNNEL, Arlberg, 80-81; Channel (proposed), 109-111; Chicago River, 86-87; Detroit River, 88-89; Great St Bernard (proposed), 84; Hudson River, 89-94; Mersey, 94-100; Michigan, and Erie Lake, 87; Mont Blanc (proposed), 84; Mont Cenis, 73-77; St Gothard, 77-80; Sarnia, 109; Severn, 100-106; Simplon (proposed), 82-83; Thames, 86; Tower, and another under Thames, 106-109.
TUNNELS, Metropolitan Railway, 5; Semmering Railway, 26-27; spiral, 35, 43; lengths, 26, 70-71, 74, 76, 77, 80, 86, 99, 108, 109, 110; difficulties of construction, 70-71; Alpine, 70-84; subaqueous, 85-111.
TYNE, River, 210-213; plan and section, 208; early works, 210; breakwaters at mouth, 210-211; dredging operations, 211-212; improvements effected, 212.

U.

UNDERGROUND RAILWAY, description, 3-15; proposed for Paris, 16. *See* METROPOLITAN RAILWAY.
UNION OR CENTRAL PACIFIC RAILWAY, 39-42; section, 30; route, 40; description, 41-42; elevation attained, 40.
UNITED STATES WESTERN RAILWAYS, 39-44; Pacific lines, 39-40; Union or Central Pacific, 41-42, 43; Northern Pacific, 42-43; Southern Pacific, 42-43; Denver and Rio Grande, 43-44.
UPRIGHT WALL BREAKWATER, advantages of type, 193; adopted at Dover, 200-201; constructed at Newhaven, 203; improvements in, 204-205.

V.

VENTILATION, Metropolitan Railway, 9-11; Mont Cenis Tunnel, 76; St Gothard Tunnel, 80; Mersey Tunnel, 99; Severn Tunnel, 105.
VIADUCT, Crumlin, 118; Garabit, 119, 134, 139-141; Portage, 118; Trisana, 118.
VICTORIA AND ALBERT DOCKS, LONDON, 174-175, 175-176; site, dimensions, and area, 173, 175; basins and locks, 173-174, 175; peculiar graving docks, 174; connecting new lock with basin, 176.
VYRNWY WATER SUPPLY, 278-284; for Liverpool, 278; origin, 278-279; description of reservoir dam, 279-280; lake forming reservoir, 280-281; supply and straining tower, 281; conveyance to Liverpool, 281-283; balancing reservoirs, and water tower, 283-284; volume, and estimated cost, 284.

W.

WATER SUPPLY, 270-285; importance of, 270; sources, and respective advantages, 271-273; Manchester waterworks, 273-276; from Thirlmere, for Manchester, 276-278; Vyrnwy, for Liverpool, 278-284; London, 284-285.
WEAVER, River, Manchester Ship Canal passing in front of, 248; sluice gates for regulating flow of, 248.
WEIR, Charlottenburg, 230-234; Port Villez, 227; Poses, 227-230; Suresnes, 227.
WEIRS, 224-234; object of, 224-225; moveable, 225-234; needle, 225-226; shutter, 226; hinged frame, 226, 227-230; improvement of Seine by, 230; drum, 226, 230-234.

THE END.

COLSTON AND COMPANY, PRINTERS, EDINBURGH.

EVENTS OF OUR OWN TIME.

A Series of Volumes on the most important Events of the last Half Century, each containing 300 pages or more, in large 8vo, with Plans, Portraits, or other Illustrations, to be issued at intervals, cloth, price 5s.

Large paper copies (250 only) with Proofs of the Plates, Roxburgh, 10s. 6d.

THE WAR IN THE CRIMEA. By General Sir EDWARD HAMLEY, K.C.B. With Five Maps and Plans, and Four Portraits on Copper, namely:—

THE EMPEROR NICHOLAS.   LORD RAGLAN.
GENERAL TODLEBEN.   COUNCIL OF WAR.

"Sir Edward Hamley has exceptional qualifications for the task he has undertaken. His 'War in the Crimea' is a well-knitted, historical narrative, written by a competent critic, and well-informed observer."—*Times.*

"As a history of the Crimean War, from a military standpoint, General Hamley's work is excellent."—*Graphic.*

"General Hamley's account of this memorable war is sure to achieve the popularity it deserves."—*Morning Post.*

THE INDIAN MUTINY OF 1857. By Colonel MALLESON, C.S.I. With Three Plans, and Four Portraits on Copper, namely:—

LORD CLYDE.   SIR HENRY LAWRENCE.
GENERAL HAVELOCK.   SIR JAMES OUTRAM.

"Battles, sieges, and rapid marches are described in a style spirited and concise." *Saturday Review.*

"Colonel Malleson's book is a valuable one, and should be universally read."—*Graphic.*

THE THREE AFGHAN WARS. By ARCHIBALD FORBES. With Portraits on Copper and Plans.

THE LIBERATION OF ITALY. By EDWARD DICEY. With Portraits on Copper.

THE REFOUNDING OF THE GERMAN EMPIRE. With Portraits on Copper.

THE EXPLORATION OF AFRICA. With Portraits on Copper.

THE CIVIL WAR IN AMERICA. With Portraits on Copper.

THE OPENING OF JAPAN. With Illustrations.

Other Volumes will follow.

LONDON: SEELEY & CO., LIMITED, ESSEX STREET, STRAND.

www.ingramcontent.com/pod-product-compliance
Lightning Source LLC
Chambersburg PA
CBHW030317240426
43673CB00040B/1190